Reading for Storyness

Susan Lohafer

Reading for Storyness

Preclosure Theory, Empirical Poetics, and Culture in the Short Story

The Johns Hopkins University Press

Baltimore and London

© 2003 The Johns Hopkins University Press
All rights reserved. Published 2003
Printed in the United States of America on acid-free paper
9 8 7 6 5 4 3 2 1

The Johns Hopkins University Press
2715 North Charles Street
Baltimore, Maryland 21218-4363
www.press.jhu.edu

Library of Congress Cataloging-in-Publication Data

Lohafer, Susan.
   Reading for storyness : preclosure theory, empirical poetics, and culture in the short
story / Susan Lohafer.
       p.   cm.
Includes bibliographical references and index.
   ISBN 0-8018-7398-3 (acid-free paper)
   1. Short story—Technique. 2. Short story. I. Title.
PN3373.L57 2003
808.3'1—dc21
                                                                    2002156773
A catalog record for this book is available from the British Library.

Pages 193–194 are an extension of the copyright page.

For Michael,
and in memory of Walter

Contents

Acknowledgments

My initial debt is to the many cognitive scientists who have inspired me from a distance. In particular, I wish to thank William F. Brewer for giving me more suggestions than he realized. Neither he nor his colleagues are remotely to blame for the liberties I have taken in my lay adaptations of empirical study. To the Department of English at the University of Iowa, I am grateful for a chance to try out early ideas in the Sloan Lecture Series. Others who have generously invited me to speak—and thereby helped me to think—include Miriam Marty Clark, James Schiff, and two long-standing associates: Per Winther, whose lucidity and dedication are a gift to the field, and Michael Trussler, whose words—in fiction, in criticism, and in person—always move and inform me. For ongoing encouragement, I am grateful to the Society for the Study of the Short Story, and especially to the pioneering theorist, Charles E. May. Footnotes cannot measure my debt to John Gerlach, whose closural theories I have absorbed so completely that I have surely failed to catch and to credit every echo of his influence. For research assistance, I thank Anne Peterson, who helped me ferret out scholarship on "Young Goodman Brown," and Elizabeth Clark, who took time from her work to chase errant details through the library stacks. Ann Kuhlmann, Will Kuhlmann, and Elizabeth Blackwell have my love and thanks for their vital support. The editors at the Johns Hopkins University Press have been unfailingly generous, and my deepest gratitude goes to Trevor Lipscombe for taking an interest in the book, and to Julia Ridley Smith for her thoughtful review of the manuscript. Finally and always, my greatest debt is to my husband, Michael, for his patience, wisdom, and shared love of literature.

Reading for Storyness

Introduction

Who studies the short story? Almost everyone, and almost no one. Is there a student anywhere who hasn't welcomed this genre, thinking "shorter is easier"? Is there a freshman instructor—or, for that matter, a creative writing teacher—who hasn't thought of the short story as the training ground of fiction? There are exceptions, of course, but the bane of the short story is its manageability. You can tuck it into the curriculum, squeeze it into a class period, and use it as a "demo" for the elements of fiction and the issues of the day. So, among English-speaking critics, few have taken the form seriously as a genre. Even fewer have devoted careers to its study. Yet surely all—certainly all Americanists?—have read an article or consulted a footnote on "Young Goodman Brown" or "Hills Like White Elephants."

Many of those who have written about the genre have been storytellers, too, like Edgar Allan Poe, Frank O'Connor, or Elizabeth Bowen. But they are not alone now. There is an emerging field of short fiction studies. If it does not quite yet march, it began making strides in the 1970s. For a time, we were concerned with definitions and taxonomies. What is a short story? What are its markers? Following in Poe's footsteps, we thought the imminence of closure was the signature feature of the short story genre. Papers on "how stories end" are still on the programs of short story conferences.

However, for many people now, structural analysis and genre classification no longer matter. Whatever a story *is*, however it *behaves*, the important thing is what it *reveals*. It's a magnifying glass for examining the techniques of impressionism, say, or the assumptions of postmodernism, or the social data caught in its prism. Famously associated with "submerged populations" and the "lonely voice" of the individual, the short story is the window on marginalized identities.[1] Scholars have crowded round. The story is viewed as a cultural diorama.

Meanwhile, a parallel plot has evolved. Psychology, textual linguistics, and cognitive science have brought short narratives into their laboratories, initially in the most rudimentary form of test sentences. One goal was to determine the smallest unit of story; another was to parse the syntax of narrative. After the vogue of story grammars came other models for storyness, sometimes based on goal-outcome scenarios, sometimes on hardwired constructs in the brain, sometimes on cultural scripts, or variations and combinations of these approaches.[2] Psychologists like William F. Brewer began to study "real," full-length, even "literary" texts.

In the late 1970s, I had not yet looked seriously at this work. Like most critics and writers of the genre, I was concentrating on the kinship between the lyric poem and the short story, which is closer than the tie between story and novel. Trained as a New Critic, I inherited a vocabulary from the analysis of poetry. In *Coming to Terms with the Short Story* (1983), I tried to find a language and a set of reference points more specific to the genre I was studying. I wanted to locate a rhythm of just the right length—longer than the line and shorter than the book.

My inspiration was Charles E. May's groundbreaking collection of historic and modern commentaries on the genre, *Short Story Theories* (1976). In my own work, I turned to reader response theory, the phenomenology of Roman Ingarden, and the rhetorical and stylistic analysis familiar to the formalist. Soon I was beginning to learn about the Amsterdam school of text processing, and I drew upon Teun van Dijk's theories of macrostructure to help me describe the experience of entering, moving through, and exiting from story. That experience, that rhythm, was, I felt, largely determined by the periodicity of an overdetermined, early-signaled closure. So I argued in *Coming to Terms with the Short Story*.

By the late 1980s, two things happened: I realized that the end of a story was only the most obvious of its closural points, and I listened more closely to the scientists. My coedited collection *Short Story Theory at a Crossroads* (1989) was a remapping of the field of short fiction theory as it was emerging from the intuitive and formalist stages into an exploration of the idea of genre itself. Other contributors to that volume shared my interest in the descriptive possibilities of frame theory and textual linguistics, though I focused more on the scientists' own experiments. I had become intrigued and reenergized by the promise of clear, clean access to the substratum of story. I had always believed that "storying," like counting, was one of the elemental cognitive processes that make experience intelligible. To expose it in action became my objective.

Throughout the 1990s, cognitive science offered a detour around the turmoil in my profession. Psychologists were generally unaffected by either the sentimental privileging or the ideological snubbing of the old god, "literariness." Yet they seemed far closer than anyone else to understanding the how and the why of what humanists took on faith—the primacy of narrative as a method of understanding. I came to feel that, as a complete outsider, a scholar without any training in or pretensions to science, I might nevertheless "borrow" from the cognitive scientists a few ideas and procedures. I would use them only as heuristics—often loosely and idiosyncratically—while remaining wholly committed to the short story *as art*. This book is the result.

It carries forward the work begun in *Coming to Terms with the Short Story;* however, its focus is not simply on closure but on the nature and significance of *pre*closure. Each chapter revolves around an experiment in which one or more readers identify sentences within a short story where the text *could* end. In doing so, readers tap a deeply ingrained ability to recognize narrative wholeness, which I call *storyness.*[3]

Before the legends and myths, before the hunting stories and the war stories, before the folk tales and the fairy tales, was the neuroscenario. A hand reaches out, touches a flame, starts back in pain, and registers a meaning. Antiquity's child and tomorrow's infant are similarly equipped. Both have this built-in plot-making talent, although it takes several years before humans can recognize or tell a "story." My notion of "storyness" is based on this neuroscenario, which is infinitely rewritten in simple or complex form, with infinite variety, to produce the world's cache of short stories. However, I am making no formal claim for a transgender, transethnic, or transracial Ur-model. All I am asserting is that preclosure study brings assumptions about storyness to light, no matter how relative they may be to their corner of the world.

The choice of preclosure points is, of course, triggered by the text (where? how?) but is also independent of any one text, drawing upon inherited and learned strategies for recognizing storyness. Each chosen sentence—or "preclosure point"—becomes salient not just in itself but as the "end" of a putative story within the actual one the author wrote. What are these reader-detected stories like? How are they related to each other and to the "real" story? What can they teach us about storyness—in itself, or, perhaps, in a given historical period? Most importantly, what can they add to our critical understanding of the text at hand? Answering these questions will mean looking at the putative stories from a number of perspectives.

Preclosure study yields relatively direct access to readers' story-making and story-recognizing habits, and this information is a rich resource for the scholar seeking to understand a particular story, author, or period, as well as the genre itself. The size of this book's claim and the apparent simplicity of its method are likely to raise eyebrows in a period when "theory" is almost synonymous with arch neologisms and specialized vocabularies. The rich complexity of literary prose is, of course, what this book exists to honor and elucidate; however, when it comes to the critical tools for doing so, there is something to be said, I believe, for the scientist's notion of economy. The simpler the theorem, the broader its application, the deeper its value.

The experiments in this book are directed exercises in "text processing." They yield the raw material from which my arguments are fashioned. However, my aim has always been to travel *through* the data toward a reunion with art. I've picked stories that test limits: Can a story be interpreted to death? Can a plotless fugue still be a story? How minimal is minimalism? Can art survive cultural studies or, in some cases, its own critical aura? Can we draw a line between fiction and creative nonfiction? These theoretical issues dominate the work, but each chapter focuses on a specific story or group of short stories.

Some of these stories are canonical, all are by authors of note, but some are dated or clumsy by contemporary standards. They are included to make a point: preclosure study does not simply enhance the reading of "good" stories; it retrieves value from lesser works of art that may have information we value about a culture, a period, or an author. Studying preclosure can be an efficient and sometimes dramatic way of overcoming obstacles to interpretation. Sometimes dated lexical and social categories are obscured by more current ones, or a "simple" story triggers preemptive ideologies or knee-jerk reactions that can blind a student—or a scholar, for that matter—to an author's vision. Not all of the stories discussed in this book will be among your favorites, but each has a place in the spectrum and history of short fiction in English. Although it is a task for other books and other readers, the methodology explored here could be applied to the written text of any short story in any language, with telling results. The following chapters are only a beginning.

Roughly speaking, the book is divided into three stages: an introduction to preclosure study in nontechnical terms (chapter 1); a number of preclosure experiments, each focusing on one or more stories that illustrate a problem of interpretation (chapters 2, 3, 5–8), with an intervening survey of forty-five canonical American short stories (chapter 4); and—because it offers a test case of growing importance today—a comparative application of preclosure theory to a short story and a narrative essay on the same subject by the same author (chapter 9). Some of the concepts are explained early on, while others, by design, come more slowly into view. All of the chapters have an empirical basis, but some are more technical than others, and a few resemble, in some fashion, a personal essay. The rhetoric of each is slightly different.

My avoidance of, and occasional challenge to, the dominant critical discourses of the day may surprise some readers. Surely the undernourished field of short fiction theory needs more scholars versed in, let us say, feminist or Marxist/materialist or psycholinguistic or other existing theories. I urge such work upon those who are committed to it, but I am not among them. I offer instead a new paradigm, one that is indigenous to the short story and useful to readers of most critical persuasions. In some cases, where an alternative approach makes for an interesting contrast with my own, I've initiated the debate myself, mainly in the second half of the book. My interest, finally, is in adding to a pluralism of ideas about the genre.

I am, indeed, writing for short fiction theorists but also for the aficionado of Hawthorne or Cisneros or any of the authors I discuss. I would like very much to provoke a few scientists and a few humanists to compare notions of storyness, but I am writing, too, for the general reader who is simply curious about the power of short stories, and for the harried teacher who needs help with tomorrow's class. We are all linked by the tale.

Once More into the Forest of "Young Goodman Brown"

I n my office, in my study, on various shelves around the house, I'm likely to run across an extra copy of "Young Goodman Brown." Texts of that story collect over the years, the residue of a career in teaching American literature. For me, when the occasion arises for talking seriously about short fiction, what other story could be closer to hand, or better known to the audience? That is why, nearly twenty years ago, after publishing my first book on short fiction theory, I turned back to this American classic to see where to head next. I intended to work my way through this most familiar of stories in the most disciplined way possible. But I never did reach the final analysis. What I'm about to give you, instead, is the tale of my going back. It begins in 1983, on the occasion of a talk I was asked to give, but it leads up to the present day and to the book you are holding. In the end, it turns out to be several stories rolled into one.

They all begin on a doorstep. There stands a figure well known to most college sophomores. He's got one foot in the door of his home and one foot on the road to his destiny. He's young Goodman Brown. We all know what happens. Parting from his wife, who is "aptly named Faith," this newly married young Puritan heads toward the forest, to meet the Devil by arrangement. The necessity for going overcomes the inertia of staying. The story begins. Yet even as he sets his course for entry into the forest, Brown is already imagining his exit. "After this one night," he thinks to himself, "I'll cling to [Faith's] skirts and follow her to heaven."[1] He begins his adventure as if its end has occurred, a fait accompli. That's a telling presumption, and a mocking one, for he hasn't yet sighted the trees. But soon he'll reach them, and the street will turn into a foot trail. In a brand-new world, he's on an age-old track. Along it, he'll encounter the Devil in human form, resembling both his father and his grandfather.

Several times this latest of the Browns hesitates on his journey, refuses to take one more step in the company of the Evil One. Yet he proceeds. And soon he wonders whether Faith isn't on the same path. Convinced by what he takes to be her ribbons on the trail, sure now that there is no good person remaining in Salem, Goodman Brown holds back no longer but plunges hysterically toward the center of the forest. The movement that began in hesitation turns into a free fall. He lands in a clearing. Humanity has preceded him. There, in the congregation of the Antichrist, he is offered a final knowledge of the evil in all hearts. He sees Faith waiting to be initiated. But he calls on her to resist, and—presto—there he is, alone in the forest, as if waked from a dream.

In a famous equivocation, the narrator gives the reader a choice—was all this a dream? Well, "be it so if you will." But there's no doubt about what follows. Brown returns to the morning light of Salem a changed man. Suspicious, fearful, he lives out his life, and, says the narrator, "his dying hour was gloom." So ends the story. What a difference there is between this somber finish and the outcome Brown expected. It was foolish of him to think he knew the end of his story. But consider the irony, if not the cruelty, of his getting no closure at all, except the common one of death. Remember that he calls upon Faith, he begs her to resist the Devil, and she does—or she doesn't. Any logic of narrative increments, not to mention human curiosity, demands to know which. But Hawthorne moves right along with his story. In effect, he denies Brown any real end to his engagement with the Devil. Brown's still in the woods. He dies in its shade.

But *we're* out, aren't we? We're practiced readers and students of literature. We make our way into and out of stories all the time. And when we leave them feeling confused, or still curious, we enter them again. And again. But suppose a story is at the very core of our literature. We feel obliged to make headway, to look for some guidance. We may not even have a point to prove; we may simply want to know what's there, already, in print. It's our habit, our duty, or is it just our compulsion? And so we enter the forest of criticism.

If you don't already know the Devil we meet there, take a few steps with me. I've read a great many articles and chapters aimed at opening my eyes. I've not read them all, nor have I tracked down every textbook note and pedagogical aid to be found in anthologies. I've maybe missed your favorite article. Still, I've been a traveler in these woods, and I know the main routes. There are, I'd say, four of them: the moral and/or theological (I'll call it the religious), the psychological, the aesthetic, and the historiosocial (I'll call it the cultural). They often overlap. Starting down one, you meet with another.

Before the 1950s, there are scattered discussions of religious themes and symbols, and after the 1960s, there are studies of religion as part of the cultural complex. But the greatest activity occurs between 1952 and 1965. In a brief but influential note, D. M. McKeithan turns Brown into an average Christian. He's a man who has already sinned—*how* doesn't matter—and who thinks he can sin one more time and *then* change his ways. Reading this critic, we find a Brown who is an Everyman of rather weak fiber, whose journey is a figure of speech for moral procrastination.[2]

Seven years later, Joseph McCullen makes Brown a different kind of aberrant Christian. Citing a 1951 *Encyclopedia of Religion and Ethics,* as well as those two other authorities, Augustine and Milton, he defines an error called "presumption" and its penalty, "despair." Asserting a "cause-and-effect relationship" between them, McCullen argues that Brown's fate is a standard one in the Christian repertory.[3] He's a textbook sinner. And indeed there's an approach to the story via classic Christian literature. In 1959 the story is compared with Book I of *The Faerie Queene.* Young Goodman Brown and the Redcross Knight come across as fumbling adventurers, rash young Everymen on quests much too big for them. But Brown's no champion. Reading this critic, we meet a Hawthorne well aware of the Spenserian worldview—and unable to share it.[4]

What's next? We might call it a branching trail or a deepening rut. I'm speaking now of attention to a special kind of Christianity—seventeenth-century New England Puritanism. Hawthorne has been called a Puritan. He's been called an anti-Puritan. We could stop here and debate the contradiction, but keep in mind, if you will, the main character before you—the reader on his way through the forest of criticism. What is it like to turn from a story and face the overwhelming maze of explanation and commentary that is both the effect and, in some sense, the cause of that story's good name? For me it has been like mapping my way toward the many Browns in one.

I was about to go by way of Puritanism. Thomas Connolly, writing in

1956, says that Brown didn't lose his Faith at all. What he lost was the false optimism of the bridegroom, the assurance that, married to Faith, he was one of the elect. What he got was a lesson in Puritan theology. His religion's faith wasn't a hopeful, pink-ribboned sort at all; it was a hopeless kind that Hawthorne deplored.[5] But according to David Levin, the story also recalls, with historical accuracy, the Puritans' battle with Satan. Reading Levin, you feel you're getting somewhere. He's done research in seventeenth-century documents. He explains the debate over "spectral evidence"; he shows you that Hawthorne's Devil is behaving like Cotton Mather's Devil—he's conjuring up specters, the look-alike, sound-alike images of real people who may—or may not—be willing helpers of Satan. Those pink ribbons? Just another bit of ghostly material, like the Devil's own staff, like the Devil himself. Levin shows us a Brown who is unfairly tricked, a Brown to excuse.[6]

By the 1970s, the approach to the story by way of religion seems well cleared, well marked. We've easy access to the paradigms that explain the risk Brown is taking when he enters the forest. He is either a sinner already, or he becomes one; at any rate, he has a "fall" of some kind. He loses something—whether it be an abstract innocence or the human rewards of faith, hope, and charity. Have. Lose. We, of course, as readers of these critics, acquire a kind of knowledge. Yet we lose something, too. In my case, I speak knowingly of beliefs I don't share, turn—as I just now did—qualms of the soul into sets of ideas. It's the "fall" we must take to grow up as critics.

For the reader beginning to make sense of the terrain by following the best guides, it's interesting to notice the shift from predominantly religious interpretations to mostly psychological ones. It happens as early as 1934, when Austin Warren sidesteps the issue of guilt or innocence. In a much-quoted phrase, he says the story illustrates "the devastating effect of moral skepticism."[7] He claims Hawthorne "merely depicts a state of mind." There's a forward-looking challenge in "merely depicts." It turns our attention away from one kind of meaning—encapsulated themes—toward another kind—unresolved tensions. Yet those words "state of mind" echo the older categories, "state of sin," "state of grace." Psychological criticism doesn't really get going until readers stop seeing the entry-exit pattern as an exchange of states, a kind of moral switchboard, and begin seeing it as rhythmic—that is to say, as an experiential unit or phase taking Brown *through* something.

In 1959, Paul Miller reminds us that in seventeenth-century Salem, hypocrisy was a way of life. The one exception is Faith, who admits in her parting speech to her husband that she has fears and self-doubts. Furthermore, her pink ribbons are an open confession of her natural infirmity. But it is this very candor that saves her. It's what lets her survive the night with her life still intact. A thought comes to mind—if Brown were a Christian Everyman, or even a typical Puritan, wouldn't he have compromised, too? Suppose he'd been more like Faith. He'd have sighed and then smiled. But Miller gives us a Brown who differs from the crowd *and* from Faith. He's just the sort of fellow—the psychological type—who *would* fail to see the hypocrisy around him, and who *would* suffer more than anybody else when the facts are revealed. It's something he lives through but doesn't survive. He's the psychological victim of a Puritan society.

Yet the arena is still one man's soul. Almost every critic of this story says that the journey into the forest is a journey into the self. And when we look inside, we see a recent bridegroom, a husband just beginning to suspect his wife's potential for carnality. Questioning himself and her can only lead to similar doubts about the husbands and wives who engendered *him.* Brown's journey is not something that happens to change him but rather is the working out of a psychological process, a phase of experience that begins when he first suspects a discrepancy between the facts of life and the model of purity.[8]

Opening before us now is the broad and well-traveled path of Freudian analysis. As early as 1928, Régis Michaud says Hawthorne is a "prophet heralding the Freudian gospel."[9] In 1957 Roy Male calls the journey "essentially a sexual experience,"[10] and in 1964 Jean Normand writes that Faith may really be Brown's sister. He also argues that the penetration of the forest, the rhythm of sounds, the moment of climax make the story an allegory of sex.[11]

Frederick Crews is rather tame by contrast. Yet his 1966 book, *The Sins of the Fathers,* is still the landmark in Freudian criticism of Hawthorne. From its perspective, Brown's entry into the forest acts out an attraction-repulsion toward adult sexuality, an experience that undermines his respect for parental authority figures. Brown's lurid fantasies make the Devil his forebear. The man who goes into the forest is no innocent lad driven by smug yet naïve curiosity. No, he's a nasty-minded fellow with an Oedipal complex, caught in the acne stage of sexual development.[12]

If you accept Freudian paradigms, you can call this Brown normal. But in the same year as *The Sins of the Fathers* comes Paul J. Hurley's article on "Young Goodman Brown's 'Heart of Darkness,'" in which Brown looks like a would-be subversive. Hurley points out that Brown systematically discredits family, neighbors, and church. The Devil, the embodiment of Brown's own "psychic rationalization," aids in this process.[13] It's what people do who have criminal instincts; in other words, Brown fits the profile of a sociopath. What can I say now that isn't anticlimactic? In the 1970s, three things happen: the Freudian way is directly challenged (most notably in favor of R. D. Laing's existentialist psychology);[14] it is broadened into something more Jungian (the journey as "quest,"[15] the forest as collective Puritan unconscious[16]); or it is blended with other approaches.

And so to Brown the presumer, hypocrite, blasphemer, and possible adulterer, we've added Brown the neurotic, the lurid fantasizer, the possible psychopath. Over the years, we've imputed to Brown the worst of our self-images, whether by God's law or Freud's. And they fit. As critics of American literature, we make them fit. He's our available test case, and he confirms what we're looking for. (Oh—I forgot Brown the incestuous brother. I never looked for that reading, but I'm no longer innocent of it. Nor are you, now.)

The third main avenue is the most familiar to those of us who were schooled in New Criticism. Henry James cleared the way in 1909. He's quite unable to take Calvinism as the point. He can't see Hawthorne as morbid. So he calls the story a gambit of the imagination.[17] Of course, nobody wants to call this story a bagatelle. But it *has* been called a dramatic poem. In 1951, Q. D. Leavis writes an article entitled "Hawthorne as Poet." Her great contribution is an orientation: *Let's look at this prose as if it were poetry.* It's what people say when they want to enhance the status of short stories. But even though Leavis speaks of "the wonderful control of local and total rhythm" in the story, she doesn't go far with her analysis of technique.[18] She just makes it logical for others—New Critics, image hunters, structure builders, style enthusiasts—to do so. Instead of wondering, *What kind of man is this Brown?* people start asking, *What kind of prose is he made of?*

We've stumbled right onto the work of Richard Harter Fogle. Revised in 1964, his 1952 book, *Hawthorne's Fiction: The Light and the Dark,* lays out the patterns we all teach our students. Light and dark, town and forest, red and black, flame and damp. These dichotomies do not simplify meaning; rather, they build a world of disturbing and irreducible con-trasts.[19] Eventually, Fogle will move from the study of images to the be-ginnings of stylistic and rhetorical analysis.[20] He'll find not would-be po-etry but exquisite prose.

I won't even try to account for the many articles on imagery and sym-bolism, on tensions and unities. For me, the most telling of the symbol studies are those that do something more than pin another tail on the story. They imply theories of creativity, and ultimately they say something about the short story as an art form. Take Darrel Abel, who talks about those pink ribbons as a "metonymic symbol."[21] Yes, they rivet the struc-ture together, and yes, they bear up the theme, but what they really do—I think he means—is teach semiotics. As signs, they're established in one context, only to pop up in another—"wrong"—context. In other words, they strain the code they're inscribed in.[22] Could you argue that such anomalies are what galvanize story?

In a different way, Edward Clay tries to get at the spring of creation for Hawthorne in particular. He claims that Hawthorne's fiction succeeds when, and only when, he begins with a unified symbol drawn from the New England past.[23] In 1969, Taylor Stoehr says, too, that Hawthorne's stories evolve from a single image or emblem or pun—as do jokes or dreams.[24] Reading this critic, we get close to another important way of thinking about stories. Rather than being the most polished of forms, they may be the most raw—psychic spasms writ large.

Either way, though, the aesthetic approach leads toward an interest in writing *as* writing. What is the story *really* about? A Puritan engaging in sinful thoughts? No, a Hawthorne engaging in fiction. Is there a differ-ence? Isn't writing, for Hawthorne, a suspect endeavor? Well, "be it so if you will." In 1981 James Williamson says the story is about the activity of writing. Referring to Hawthorne's "Devil in Manuscript," he says the narrator resembles the Devil, that Arch Storyteller, because both take a sly pleasure in burlesquing the sentimental fictions by which live the Browns of the world—and Hawthorne's nineteenth-century competitors.[25]

There's less interest nowadays in the doctrine of guilt, less novelty in psychoanalysis, few images left untagged. We've lost our fascination (and in some cases our vocabulary) for stylistic and rhetorical analysis of the kind beloved by formalists. So what does a critic do, who wants to avoid the impressionism, the elitism, or the triviality of the aesthetic approach? He or she enters, in many cases, the fourth avenue I named. It's the approach that integrates many kinds of learning outside the conventional domain of literary studies. It's the turn toward cultural studies.

In 1971, Michael Davitt Bell finds Hawthorne more focused on history than on sin (or, let's add, "neurosis" and "artful writing").[26] Ten years later, Daniel Hoffman discusses the witchcraft in the story as an historically valid expression of the popular mind. There's a coming together of pulpit doctrine and superstition, the high and low culture of the time.[27] For Barbara Rogers in 1978, the story deals with the same conflict Tocqueville saw in Jacksonian democracy—the tension between individual freedom and social order.[28] Her way of drawing upon history, politics, economics, anthropology, other arts such as painting, and even a bit of cognitive theory may well stand as a good example of cultural criticism.

On this journey through the forest of criticism, we've reached 1980. The paths change now, retracing themselves in more intricate ways. The same four trails are apparent: the religious, psychological, aesthetic, and cultural. More often now, the religious is joined with other tracks: the post-Freudian psychosexual, the neoformalist (vide deconstruction), and the New Historical.

Let's begin with new skepticism about the uses of Freud. In 1993, John K. Hale cautions that sometimes a "serpentine staff" is a crooked piece of wood; it is better explained by Spenser or the Bible than by psychoanalysis.[29] As early as 1986, Michael Tritt questions the watered-down uses of Freudian terminology. Brown, we tend to say, escapes his own guilt by projecting it on others. Technically speaking, however, if Brown is "projecting," he is not so much escaping his anxieties as disclaiming them altogether.[30] Welcome to denial.

The most pointed updating of the Freudian model may come even earlier, in 1982, with Elizabeth Wright's article, "The New Psychoanalysis and Literary Criticism." She challenges the canonical work of Fredrick Crews, who found a stable meaning through the Oedipal paradigm. Drawing upon Lacan and Derrida, she argues that *de*stabilization is in the nature of language. Brown's motivation is two things at once: a prelingual desire for the Faith/mother and a protolingual fear of the Devil/father.[31] Deconstruction 101.

Bringing feminism into the mix, another critic points to Hawthorne's own habit of division. In his letters, he often split his fiancée, Sophia Peabody, into a compliant "Dove" and the future "Sophie Hawthorne." Equivocating about Faith, Brown echoes his creator's "ambivalence toward female eroticism" and women's independence.[32] Twelve years later, James C. Keil carries this point further, reasoning that women's place was a more troublesome issue in the nineteenth century than it was in the seventeenth. In Hawthorne's day, the problem was imperfectly managed by the "two spheres" theory of gender roles. That doctrine assigned the woman to the home. But surely there were times, Keil encourages us to think, when Sophie, the domestic "angel," thrust her Peabody head disconcertingly across the threshold.[33]

Along with its psychosexual emphasis, Keil's work is an example of the New Historicism that looms ahead. We can ask how gender was constructed, but we may also wonder how conversion was documented in Brown's time. Invoking Calvin's *Institutes* and the Halfway Covenant of 1662, Jane Eberwein notes the convert's fallacy of believing he has joined the "visible saints." Post-conversion, how shocking to discover that sin still beckons, that faith is in doubt![34] Two critics reread John Cotton's *Milk for Babes,* the catechism Goody Cloyse would have taught young Brown as a boy. One concludes that Hawthorne's story is an attack on the Puritan doctrine of universal depravity.[35] The other, looking more closely at the series of questions and answers, sees a different message: man *is* corrupt, but salvation *is* possible. Despair, the failure of hope, is a breach of the catechism.[36] Had he been paying attention, this is the lesson Brown would have learned. He appears to have been a tragically poor student.

Yet, of course, this is not a story of attention deficit but of driven behavior. Like the paradigms of the Christian "fall" and the Freudian "complex," the patterns of folklore encode these compulsions. In certain Scottish tales known to Hawthorne, "Goodman" was a term for the Devil, strengthening the assumption that the evil Brown meets is already inside him.[37] A much more extensive treatment of folkloric sources places the story as a "Type 400" and "Type 306" fairy tale, in which a husband fails to save his wife from a demon lover or incubus. Barbara Fass Leavy reminds us that Sir Walter Scott is a likely source for interrelated ideas about fairies, demons, and mythological characters. She quotes his observation that, in the American wilderness, where "partially improved spots were embosomed in inaccessible forests," it's not surprising that "the colonists should have . . . [had] fears of the devil."[38] Not just biblical tempter, he's Old World sorcerer and underworld king. "Young Goodman Brown" may be a cautionary reworking of the Orpheus and Eurydice myth reincarnated in the medieval poem, *Sir Ofeo.* There, a wife dreams of a threat from the King of Faeries and confides her alarm to her husband. Orfeo heeds; Brown does not. Both husbands fail to recover their wives. Their loss is as old as Greece.

Brown's fall, however, takes place in New England. Two well-researched essays link his particular "errand" with the Puritan (American) "Errand into the Wilderness"[39] and with the prototypical American psychodrama of the individual's alienation from, and return to, his or her community. That theme is found in other iconic stories like Washington Irving's "Rip Van Winkle" and Henry James's "The Jolly Corner."[40] Brown is Uncle Sam before he learned to point his finger.

Finally, there continue to be "close reading" studies of images—the incidence of tears[41] or laughter,[42] for instance—and of narrative point of view. The more technical analyses bring to bear, for example, Hugh Blair's *Lectures on Rhetoric and Belles Lettres,* which Hawthorne studied at Bowdoin;[43] or the ways in which modal auxiliary verbs locate the position of the speaker (thereby indexing perspective);[44] or the deliberately faulty syllogisms in the "Faith is gone" speech.[45] Christopher D. Morris's "Deconstructing 'Young Goodman Brown'" insinuates itself between word and referent, claiming that the story is about a "departure from *faith in naming.*" Unreliable narrators have given way to unreliable signifiers. There are any number of "undecidables," luring the reader into misinterpretation.[46] Upon this text, no clarity may be carved. Like Poe's "The Purloined Letter," Hawthorne's story seems made to order for a classical exercise in deconstruction. Brown couldn't believe what he was seeing—and yet, to his detriment, he trusted his mind's eye. We cannot believe what our eyes read—and yet we must choose to interpret, failing, by every choice, to find the whole truth.

Here, then, is as far as I've come in the forest of criticism. Straddling many paths at once, I've arrived at the clearing. It's a crowded place. I've mentioned about fifty critics, a mere fraction of those we could name. Getting acquainted with the routes they've followed is the usual way of initiating yourself into their company. Mapping where they've been makes you think you've arrived. Take but one step . . . and you'll believe in them. You'll find in each a little truth about "Young Goodman Brown." Perhaps you'll be tempted to add to it, most likely following some path in the neighborhood of the four I've described. But hang back from that step . . . and where are you? In a kind of limbo, I suppose. After the crowd is lined up, each member looks familiar—like somebody you know, or could easily become. Take any path, and the Devil you meet is yourself in disguise. Are you then more sophisticated or more naïve than before?

I imagine I am both, and I think I've three options: to remain a cynic where criticism is concerned, to make a working choice among pathways, or to pretend to start fresh—not with the critics but with the story. It's a pose, but there's some truth in saying I've nowhere to go except back to page one. What could be more basic than the story's way of taking me in, moving me through, and letting me out—if only to tempt me back in? So I am done with processing the text. Let it now process me.

In *Coming to Terms with the Short Story,* I talked about this experience as a rhythm of entry, passage, and exit. Word by word, clause by clause, the prose of a story is experienced, I said, both as a route to closure—of the sentence, of the story—and as an obstacle to closure. If the syntax is complicated, the experience has one kind of density; if it's simple, the experience may be as rich, but in a different way. If the diction calls attention to itself, the experience is again affected—perhaps deepened, perhaps derailed. Acknowledging Poe, I argued that the whole experience is impelled and conditioned by the imminence of the end, the backwash of closure.

Its force impinges on the very first sentence. At sunset. Into the street. At Salem village. With Fogle on our minds, we find the sunset a transition between day and night, light and dark. There's a sense, too, in which we begin receiving what *isn't* there. Part of reading "came forth into the street" is having the absence of, say, "stepped out into Main Street." The information that's present is more rudimentary, but it's uncharacterized except by its direction—and the fact that it positions us on the outside, rather than the inside, of the house. And as for "Salem village," well, there's no better synecdoche for Puritan New England. It puts us in mind of the witch trials of 1692, and of Hawthorne's ambivalence toward his ancestors. For the kind of reader we become, there is indeed, as William Gass argues, a world in a word.

And we're only thirteen words into story. A clause has ended, but not yet the sentence. When we've passed the semicolon, we find "but put his head back, after crossing the threshold, to exchange a parting kiss with his young wife" (65). Came forth. Put back. It's a rhythm we feel from the start. Later, he'll near the corner but look over his shoulder, walk with the Devil then stand on his virtue, meet with the witches then call on his faith. In short, penetrate the forest, then try to get home.

If I were to go on with this story sentence by sentence, I'd try to make you feel that rhythm not just as a pattern of *this* narrative but as a normal feature of reading. Syntax moves us forward, whether we're speaking technically about strings of words or loosely about narrative sequence. Yet the impetus to read *on* is checked by the need to read *in*, to absorb, to connect, to make sense. Theorists have described this cognitive or, if you will, hermeneutic cycle, and perhaps it is the model for my simple metaphor of entry, passage, and exit. But I've a commitment to the story-size dimensions of that experience. I want you to see it on a scale commensurate with the fiction as a whole, and that's why, in the past, I've stressed the nature of beginnings, with their density of information, their power to engage the reader, and the nature of endings, with their signals of closure, their power to discharge the reader.

Yet I'm intrigued this time by the stop-and-go rhythm itself, for it recurs, on a larger scale, within the story as a whole. There are many places where Brown—and the reader—are caught up short, are prepared to say "the end." One of these is the much-discussed moment when Brown decides his wife is *un*Faith*ful*. The fall of a ribbon signs the fall of a woman.

A distraught Brown has made a next-to-last gesture of resistance, has said, "With Heaven above and Faith below, I will yet stand firm against the Devil!" (70). But a cloud rushes up, blotting out the heavens and almost—if we do not read carefully—obscuring these words: "The blue sky was still visible *except directly overhead*" (70, emphasis mine). Brown is focusing on the cloud, he thinks he hears Faith, and so, when the sky is clear again, a token of the cloud remains. "Something fluttered lightly down through the air and caught on the branch of a tree. The young man seized it, and he beheld a pink ribbon" (71).

He thinks he has tangible evidence that Faith is a fraud. What do *we* have? A diction that is overwhelmingly concrete: "fluttered," "caught," "seized," "beheld"; "branch," "tree," "ribbon." The authority of these verbs and nouns carries over to pronouns that are themselves indefinite. Brown seized "something," and when he looked at "it," he saw a pink ribbon. As critics have noted, "it" could be anything—a twig, a leaf. A bedeviled mind, a beclouded eye, will see what it must.

The grammar takes us into Brown's psyche and shows us its bent. Yet if we don't register the hint quickly, we're swept into Brown's rant at the Devil: "there is no good on earth . . . to thee is this world given" (71). These declarations are so positive, so absolute in their simplicity, that they seem all-embracing. We're given pause only if we remember that, for Hawthorne, "this world" "on earth" is only half of man's story. I imagine only the most cautious—or most experienced—reader can resist the imminent "and," which pulls us right over the paragraph break, as though to compound the hasty conclusion with the precipitous action.

> ". . . [T]o thee is this world given."
>
> And, maddened with despair, so that he laughed loud and long, did Goodman Brown grasp his staff and set forth again, at such a rate that he seemed to fly along the forest path rather than to walk or run. (71)

And so the story *doesn't* end just yet.

At the critical moment, as Brown teeters on the brink of commitment to the Devil, he is joined by a woman and recognizes his wife. He can still be appalled, can still feel the horror of a world without Faith. *In extremis* as a man, a Christian, and a husband, he begs her to "resist." As I said before, we never know her response. Nor does Brown. Suddenly, he finds himself alone in the clearing. On his cheek is "the coldest dew." Had the page gone blank after those words, we'd have had ourselves a story. We'd have seen Brown wake up from a dream. We'd have had the end of the story as *gothic horror show*.

But it isn't over. "The next morning young Goodman Brown came slowly into the street of Salem village" (74). We're positioned on the sidelines again. Brown shrinks from the minister, from everyone, including Faith. End of story? *Some*thing's over. It's the end of the journey away from, and back to, that street in Salem village. It's the end of the dramatized action. Had there been nothing more, we'd have seen the end of the story as *allegorical trip*.

Instead, we get a direct—and disruptive—question from the narrator. Was this all a dream, or wasn't it? Now, finally, we *are* asked to think, to reflect, to evaluate. But without closing the question, the narrator moves on. We're put through a vividly illustrated, a brilliantly condensed biographical summary. It ends, Brown's dead, the story's finished. Really and truly, this time.

When it arrives, this ending is all the more final for having been, in a structural sense, postponed. What sinks in is the full reach of the mortal consequence of a night in the forest: doubt and fear protracted over the whole span of a life as husband, father, and member of the community. The real ending underscores the sense of irreversible doom, of a life wrecked by one gesture of hubris, of a man slowly hounded to death. It gives us, at last, the story as *tragedy*. For as these three endings loom in sequence, there's a procession of genres—gothic, allegorical, tragic. From the last of them, there's no spiritual—or narrative—reprieve.

Through all this talk of entering forests, I've been comparing (1) what happens to a character in a famous short story, with (2) what happens to a reader of the critics of that story, with (3) what happens to that same reader when she tracks her experience of rereading that story. These three—adventures, shall we call them—exist in very different frames of reference, as well as on different ontological levels. Of course, they *do* have something—I've called it a shape, a rhythm—in common. They're all variously staged movements of entry and exit. In all cases, there's a decision to leave home ground and submit to new findings, there's an encounter with the stuff of experience in serial array, and there's a return to the familiar, which has now become strange.

As a story line, it's a favorite. Think (again) of Rip Van Winkle, who leaves his village, meets some unforeseen characters, and returns to a "new" town. In future chapters, I'll talk about this structure not just as an American prototype but as a basic short-story schema. Yet does it really work as a model for a session with the critics? It's convenient. It lets me organize a maze of interpretations. The surprise is that it helps me to see the aggregate readings of "Young Goodman Brown" as a revelation and a trap. We're initiated into it necessarily and beneficially, but ultimately at some risk to our humility, our tolerance for simplicity, our trust in storyness itself as a guide to interpretation.

What I did not realize when I revisited this story was that I'd stumble, experientially, over the notion of preclosure. When I identified places where the story *could* end, I was guided by the emphases of earlier critics. An aggregate authority, they pointed with their staff, and I followed their gaze. But what if they, too, could be made to disappear? What if I could be truly alone in the text? Such innocence is, of course, irretrievable for the scholar—or, to some degree, for any reader—and dubious in value. Yet how tempting it would be to fictionalize here, to say that this is the moment when I realized I had access, as a teacher, to hundreds of naïve readers who might lead me through the story on a virginal path? But no such sentimentalism, no ideal of the "natural" reader, should intrude here.

I've always wanted for my students the most informed and skilled reading that training can provide. No, what I'd glimpsed wasn't innocence. It was a different kind of knowledge.

It depended on a kind of faith, but not, as I'd been schooled to believe, in the text as text, or in the staff of criticism. Instead, it was a faith more apparent in cognitive science and textual linguistics than in literary studies, a faith in our human ability to recognize storyness. More accurately, I should say it was a faith in the empirical evidence of cognitive strategies for story making and story processing—evidence that might explain why, left to my own devices, I could recognize shorter stories within a short story like "Young Goodman Brown."

Why could I do that? Could my students do that, even if they felt lost in the story? What accounted for this ability, shared by children and scholars? Could it offer any leverage on what we "make" of a story in our most sophisticated readings? Scripts, schemas, grammars, macrostructures, affect patterns, reader experiments—I will refer to them all, but with the lightest touch possible. For what I learned in my foray outside of the humanities brought home to me the value of literary analysis. The theory of preclosure explored in this book owes something to cognitive science, discourse analysis, and textual linguistics, yet its practice has to do with the art of prose fiction, the significance of genre, and the relevance of culture.

chapter two

Preclosure Basics in a Kate Chopin Story

After my experience with "Young Goodman Brown," I was confident that I could ask preclosure questions about any short story and learn something new and worthwhile. I could take this approach with any story I might be teaching, or I might generate a list of stories worth interpreting. Both plans survive, to some extent, in this book. However, it became apparent that I would need very specific reasons for choosing stories to discuss.

Kate Chopin's "Aunt Lympy's Interference" seems the unlikeliest of choices. It is a quaint and sentimental tale of love's triumph. From today's vantage point, at the dawn of a second century later, it appears sexist and racist. A young girl gives up her career in order to grace the home and life of a neighbor, a young and handsome aristocrat playing gentleman farmer. A former servant in her household, the black "aunt," engineers this result by "interfering"—with all the rough-edged devotion of the stereotypical mammy.

This is not—and I shall never claim that it is—one of Chopin's better stories. Although it was written in 1896 during the major, late period of her work, it has neither the protofeminist candor of "The Story of an Hour" nor the blithe sensuality of "The Storm" nor the wrenching irony of "Désirée's Baby"—the stories generally known to readers of her most famous work, the feminist/naturalist novel *The Awakening* (1897). On first reading the story, I saw only the deft structure and wry observation she learned from Guy de Maupassant. But where was his cool harshness? The "rose-pink fancy" was there but not, as Elizabeth Bowen found in his work, the "charnel underneath."[1] As it happened, however, I was looking for an obscure and dated story by a writer worth studying.

I wanted to see how a variety of mostly Iowan readers might respond to a story almost certainly none of them had read before, set in a world few of them would know anything about, except in the most stereotypical terms, and dating from an era in the hazy past. For most of these readers, Chopin's story would invoke the "backward South" of a time not just quaintly postbellum but antediluvian. Certainly, in part, I wanted to find out what preclosure could reveal about a story *not* canonized like "Young Goodman Brown." Mostly, however, I wanted to find out how this particular story would be processed by these particular readers, ranging from high school students to college seniors, along with their teachers—including me.

The Story

We read 169 sentences that transported us to Acadian Louisiana, with its caste society and plantation economy. We met a girl of "good" family, on the verge of maturity, drawn to her window on a soft spring day. As in her better-known work, Chopin deftly penetrates the tangle of half-understood feelings, resistances, and yearnings of the feminine psyche in an era when neither sexuality nor independence of mind and pocket was "respectable" for women.

Now that her parents are dead, the young heroine, Melitte, is living with her brother's family in somewhat reduced circumstances. Her social status is further jeopardized by her new occupation as a schoolteacher for the local children. Melitte enjoys the work; it gives her an indefinable sense of worth. Quite the opposite view is taken by Aunt Lympy, whose visit is the precipitating event in the story. She is a woman of color, a former servant in the family (the title "Aunt" is conventional), who sees herself as the guardian of that family's welfare and honor. In her eyes, Melitte's occupation is a degradation, a reproach to the males in the family—especially to the father's brother, who is a wealthy member of New Orleans society.

Aunt Lympy's "interference" is a gesture of meddlesome goodwill. Since Melitte is stubbornly happy in her work, Aunt Lympy goes behind her back to appeal to the girl's uncle, picturing Melitte in "misery." Sentimentally contrite, he writes to Melitte, inviting her to join his family and share in a life of parties, leisure, and money. Melitte seems to have two options: remain a schoolteacher or become a socialite. What gives the story its complication is the existence of another, less clearly defined choice. Although hardly aware of the nature of her feelings, Melitte is attracted to a young Creole neighbor, Victor Annibelle, a childhood play-mate who has recently returned to manage his family's estate. Every day that Melitte walks to school, she passes the Annibelles' house. Every day, Victor is working on the fence that borders her route. They barely speak a word to each other. They are in love, though hampered by shy-ness, by uncertainty about each other's feelings, and by the social con-ventions of the time. Melitte never acknowledges it to herself, but her third option—and the one yearned for by her affectionate nature and budding desire—is marriage to Victor.

What is modern about Chopin's story is her dramatization of the pres-sures bearing upon Melitte as she confronts these three options, these three adult roles: self-supporting worker, perpetual "daughter," and lover/wife/mother. Of course, we might wonder whether teaching is really a role; it might be just a way of staying home, close to Victor. But Chopin calls our attention to Melitte's salary and, specifically, her desire not to "contaminate" it with gift money from her uncle. Having her own money represents to her, fairly consciously, a kind of independence, something earned, not bestowed. She really is being pulled three different ways.

And the pressures increase. Society urges Melitte to accept her uncle's offer; self-esteem keeps her working; nature (she's young; it's springtime) draws her to Victor. Yet it's important to notice that neither Melitte nor Chopin overtly identifies or weighs these alternatives. Instead, the story foregrounds Melitte's chagrin, her pouting sense of hurt because no one begs her to stay where she is. The hurt is half real, half cultivated; she wants to feel needed where her heart is attached. Transparently, yet in-nocently, she's lovesick. When Victor, driven by the fear of losing her, does speak out and declare his need, Melitte responds temperately, even coolly, but with evident relief and deep satisfaction. We know she will marry him.

The story ends, however, with a summary of others' reactions to Melitte's decision. Some sympathize; some don't. The final sentence (actual closure) focuses on Aunt Lympy: "[She] was not altogether dissatisfied; she felt that her interference had not been wholly in vain."[2] The compounding of neg-atives, the hint of wryness, may be taken a number of ways. Aunt Lympy did set in motion a chain of events that will get Melitte out of the schoolroom. Furthermore, in marrying Victor, Melitte will be choosing the kind of fate Aunt Lympy had in mind—a respectable, "womanly" place in the world.

S/55   Scarcely a week after Aunt Lympy's visit Melitte was amazed by receiving a letter from her uncle, Gervaise Leplain, of New Orleans. (513)

Eight percent of the readers thought the story could end at S/54; 4 percent chose S/53.[3] About one-eighth of the readers, then, found preclosure in cluster A. The visit is over; Melitte has held firm.

The B Cluster: Melitte resigns herself to moving to New Orleans
S/105   "Oh, I'll go!

S/106   I will go!" Melitte was saying a little hysterically to herself as she walked [toward school].

S/107   *The familiar road was a brown and green blur, for the tears in her eyes.*

S/108   Victor Annibelle was not mending his fence that morning; but there he was, leaning over it as Melitte came along. (515)

Here, 17 percent of the readers thought the story could end at S/107, and 9 percent chose S/105, for a total of 26 percent. In other words, a full fourth of the readers sensed preclosure just where Melitte gives up on herself—and on Victor.

The C Cluster: Victor begs Melitte to stay
S/137   "Oh, I can't bear to have you go, Melitte!"

S/138   They were so near the school it seemed perfectly natural that she should hurry forward to join the little group that was there waiting for her under a tree.

S/139   He made no effort to follow her.

S/140   *He expected no reply; the expression that had escaped him was so much a part of his unspoken thought, he was hardly conscious of having uttered it.*

S/141   But the few spoken words, trifling as they seemed, possessed a power to warm and brighten [Melitte's day in school.] (516)

Victor makes his confession. In this case, 11 percent of the readers found S/140 a convincing stopping place, and 6 percent identified S/137, for a total of 16 percent of the readers, since the two groups overlapped by one person. In other words, about one-sixth of the readers thought the story could end with Victor's confession of love. He phrases it in the very words Melitte has been longing to hear: if we back up to S/102, we find her wondering, "Why should she stay where no soul had said, 'I can't bear to have you go, Melitte?'" In cluster C, her words, her dreams, are realized.

Clusters A, B, and C represent what I called the "inner shell" of preclosure choices, since they occur within the body of the text. The remaining choices, cluster D, represent the "outer shell." They come right before the actual ending. By now, Victor has waited all day for the children to go home, coming up just as Melitte tries to close the school window. He admits to hoping she will stay if he begs her, taking her hand and asking, "Would you, Melitte—would you?" Each of the italicized sentences was chosen as a preclosure point by someone.

The D Cluster: Melitte tells Victor she will stay

S/162   *"I believe I would, Victor.*

S/163   *Oh—never mind my hand; don't you see I must shut the window?"*

S/164   *So after all Melitte did not go to the city to become a grande dame.*

S/165   *Why?*

S/166   *Simply because Victor Annibelle asked her not to.*

S/167   *The old people when they heard it shrugged their shoulders and tried to remember that they, too, had been young once; which is, sometimes, a very hard thing for old people to remember.*

S/168   *Some of the younger ones thought she was right, and many of them believed she was wrong to sacrifice so brilliant an opportunity to shine and become a woman of fashion.* (517)

Omitting the one-word interrogative of S/165, these are simply the last six sentences before actual closure. Not surprisingly, they provide a high incidence of preclosure choices. In order, excepting S/165, the sentences listed above were chosen by the following percentages of readers: 19, 20, 23, 21, 16, and 24. Because so many people chose more than one of these sentences, there was no point in adding up the percentages. Clearly S/168 was the most favored of all the sentences in the story, with S/164 a close second.

Perhaps it is surprising that no one sentence was chosen by more than 24 percent of the readers. I would have welcomed higher percentages—

and might have gotten them, had I used readers with more in common. But, as we shall see, I had reasons for wanting diversity in age and training. Under the circumstances, it may be remarkable that nearly a fourth of the readers did agree on at least one sentence. In any case, what mattered for this study was *relative* agreement.

Had I devised this study to confirm some notion of "completed storyness," I would have tried to predict the results, especially the location of the "inner-shell" points. Instead, I worked as inductively as possible, letting the readers take their pick and only then asking what these choices could tell me. My own students, of course, had heard the term *preclosure* before. Having been exposed to my way of teaching short fiction, they might have been expected to "give me what I wanted." But I could never have predicted the exact location of the choices they would make.

The Preclosure Signals

What, then, prompted those choices? What markers in the text were responsible for triggering the sense of whole-storyness? In other words, what were the preclosure signals? Later chapters will offer a more detailed anatomy of these signals, especially those that are local to the sentence. Here, I would like to identify some of the more common signals that operate on a higher level. For example, the data show that, for this story at least, preclosure signals included *paragraph breaks, changes of space/time/condition, natural-event terminals,* and *image recursions.*

Five of the highlighted preclosure sentences (54, 107, 140, 163, 167) are followed by a paragraph break. That visual marker gives closural force to the *preceding* sentence. However, there are seventy paragraphs in this very short story, with an average of just over two sentences per paragraph, so paragraph breaks alone would seem mainly to suggest or confirm rather than strongly signal preclosure. More significantly, the preferred preclosure sentences in clusters A and C mark the end of the action at a particular time and place: after Aunt Lympy leaves, the time jumps ahead almost a week; after Victor's first declaration, time shifts to the hours of Melitte's day at work and place shifts to the schoolroom. Because readers can't fully register these changes until they have read on to the next sentence, perhaps we should say that paragraph breaks and changes of space/time/condition are retroactive signals, pointing back to the sentence just left.

However, natural-event terminals do register within the preclosure sentence itself. We usually think of night and day as natural units of time and activity.[4] They have a built-in (if fuzzy or conventional) beginning and end. Roughly speaking, they echo what is perhaps the most fundamental of the "periods" we use to chunk time into meaningful units: the biological life span, especially the human one, with all its temporal signposts and conventional phases and analogues. Why these spans are so deeply ingrained in our consciousness is a question for cognitive psychologists and students of cultural conditioning, and I will touch on these issues later in this book. For now, however, it is sufficient to note that journeys (departure → arrival) and visits (arrival → departure) are among the most familiar analogues of the life span. Think how many of the short stories you know are coterminal with visits or with journeys. Not surprisingly, readers of Chopin's story felt an intimation of closure—a preclosure signal—at the point where Aunt Lympy ends her visit to Melitte.

The departure that follows an arrival sends a change of space/time/condition signal any child can recognize. The reappearance of an image—usually with some variation—also closes a circuit, in this case sending an image-recursion signal. Perhaps most readers with normal cognitive development will register this kind of signal, as they might *recognize* the identity of two shapes on an IQ test. However, as countless hours in the literature classroom will attest, getting readers to fully explore the meaning of such a recurrence is part of the "training" English departments traditionally offered, and still do, to some extent. Will readers with more formal education do a better job of recognizing this type of signal? What about readers with more or less experience in writing fiction themselves?

The Readers

As I noted above, there were 180 readers, including myself. To form this pool, I used my own students at every level from freshman to doctoral candidate, and asked for the help of two high school teachers with students in "developmental reading" and in creative writing.[5] The total sample divided roughly in half between high school and college students. Adding the graduate students and teachers put 90 readers in each group:

Group I: high school sophomores (2), juniors (54), and seniors (34)
Group II: college freshman (3), sophomores (18), juniors (29), seniors (21), and graduate students and teachers (19)

Table 1:   Preclosure Choices of High School and More Advanced Readers

Cluster	Preclosure point	Group I: 90 High school readers (%)	Group II: 90 College-level readers and above (%)
A	S/54	13	3
B	S/107	17	17
C	S/140	10	13
	S/162	11	28
	S/163	10	32
	S/164	23	23
D	S/166	11	30
	S/167	17	15
	S/168	16	33

Sorting the preclosure choices made by readers at *each school level,* I found no clear-cut correlation between level and preferred choices. However, sorting by readers in *each group* did reveal a clear difference. As Table 1 shows, the percentage of agreement is higher among readers with more formal schooling. In Group I, only one preclosure point (S/164) received more than 20 percent agreement; in Group II, as many as five preclosure points received at least 20 percent agreement, and a third of these readers picked S/168.

Furthermore, some preclosure points were more favored by one group than the other. The percentage of readers choosing S/54 is four times greater for high school readers than for those with more education. This is the sentence in which Aunt Lympy departs, full of sorrow and dignity, after her talk with Melitte. Visit ends, story ends? Readers in Group I were more likely to jump to this simple conclusion, moved by that most basic of preclosure signals, a natural-event terminal. Readers with more schooling seemed to realize that the visit by Aunt Lympy had, as yet, effected no change in the status quo of the story world. Not until something disrupts the equilibrium—the arrival of the letter inviting Melitte to New Orleans—is there a conflict of the sort students are taught to discuss. Savvy about the economy of literary stories, the more "trained" readers of Group II may also have noted that Victor, the obvious love interest, isn't part of this scene; hence, the story can't end with the visit.

The more sophisticated readers of Group II were more than three times more likely than readers in Group I to choose S/163, the sentence with the image-recursion signal. Melitte, asking Victor to remove his arm from the sill, "shut[s] the window," thus closing the aperture through which they have been talking. Foregrounding what I will later discuss as a local semantic closural signal ("shut"),[6] this sentence points to a window. At the very beginning of the story, in S/1, Melitte is looking through a window at the fecund fields and at Victor's "imposing white house," which would become her home if she married him. One hundred and sixty-three sentences later, Victor literally has reached through the schoolroom window to take her hand and offer her what those images prefigured. Melitte's shutting *this* window is a gesture of reserve, but also a close to her life as a teacher. College-trained readers could be expected to sense the thematic resonance of the repeated imagery. Certainly, in this experiment, they were more likely to respond to this type of preclosure signal.

Overall, then, the information in Table 1, which compares the choices made by high school students with those made by readers with college-level-or-above schooling, gives some concrete particularity to generalizations about "training." Students with more experience in "academic" reading *were* more likely to pick up on cues embedded in the local linguistic fabric of the text or encoded in classroom talk about unity and conflict. Readers with less experience *were* more likely to be satisfied by cues conveyed by larger, event-related, structural units per se. If there is, as some claim, a "maturation calendar" for kinds of aesthetic perception, we may be seeing some evidence of the role education plays in that growth.

Besides wondering about the effects of schooling, I had been curious to know whether experience with fiction writing might have any impact on preclosure choices. Therefore, I asked all the readers to assign themselves to one of the following categories of experience with fiction writing: (1) "Have never tried to write a story," (2) "Have tried, but no formal training," and (3) "Have had formal training and/or publication." I assumed that more experience in writing fiction would tend to correlate with more advanced schooling in general (though I knew creative writing was taught in one of the high school classes). If the assumption held, we would expect Group 3 in Table 2 to make the more sophisticated choices—to be most alert to S/163, the window sentence, and least inclined toward S/54, the sentence marking the end of Aunt Lympy's visit.

Neither expectation was quite fulfilled, for Group 1 was *least* alert to *both* S/163 and S/54, whereas Group 2 was *most* interested in S/163–S/164, and Group 3 was also very responsive to S/163.[7] However, the find-

Table 2: Preclosure Choices and Writing Experience

Cluster	Preclosure point	Group 1: No experience (%)	Group 2: No formal training (%)	Group 3: Formal training (%)
A	S/54	3	10	7
B	S/107	9	18	22
C	S/140	19	8	11
D	S/162	19	19	22
	S/163	3	25	20
	S/164	28	25	18
	S/166	31	23	11
	S/167	19	17	13
	S/168	38	17	33

ings become more interesting when they are placed next to those in Table 1. It appears that the readers with formal training as writers did not always tend toward the same choices as the readers with the greatest amount of schooling in general. In fact, the trained writers paid more attention to S/107 (near "Oh, I'll go!") and S/162 ("I believe I would, Victor") than they did to S/163 ("I must shut the window"). In other words, they focused slightly more on event-related signals (decision to go; decision to stay) than on the closural function of particular images. We cannot conclude that they were less sensitive to imagery, but perhaps, when it came to preclosure, they were more responsive to blocks of experience.

In the area where the most experienced writers *did* share a preference with the more schooled readers in Table 1, there is a new quirk in the results. The Group 3 writers overwhelmingly preferred S/168, the sentence that "ends" the story with an echo of the choice foregone. ("Some of the younger ones thought she was right, and many of them believed she was wrong to sacrifice so brilliant an opportunity to shine and become a woman of fashion.") But in making this decision, these most experienced writers were suddenly, and by a large margin, aligned with the least experienced writers! To my mind, this is one of the more striking, because least predictable, of the findings so far.

It suggests that when the variable is experience in fiction writing, the responses of practiced fiction writers correlate most highly with the responses of readers with *no* experience in this area at all. If we are trying to predict the overall favorite preclosure point, the people who say they have never tried to write a story turn out to be as reliable a guide as the people who have taken writing courses (and in some cases published their stories)—and both are a better guide than those who have tried to write stories but are schooled only as readers (and critics).

This is not, of course, to say that writers are superior readers. What is intriguing here is the bonding of naïveté and sophistication. Story rhythm, the sense of what closes the "period" of a story, may be among the most primitive of the story conventions we all internalize. Group 1 seemed to "go by the gut." On the other hand, "doing" endings is part of the craft of storytelling; Group 3 knew this consciously and well. Yet, in key instances, Group 3 responded much as Group 1 did. The favoring of S/168 joins innocence and experience, intuition and calculation, artlessness and artfulness. The same has been said of the short story genre.[8]

Clearly, the researcher could divide up the readers in whatever ways suit his or her purposes. For example, those interested in gender studies could look at preclosure choices favored by males as opposed to females, and vice versa.[9]

The Interpretations

Percentages, categories, tables—what have they to do with reading a short story? After all, it is my contention that preclosure study teaches us not only about the way stories are processed but also about the way they are understood and interpreted. It's time to put the preclosure choices back into the text. Doing so is like putting magnetized chips of iron back among the metal filings. New patterns emerge.

The first thing we notice is that all of the inner-shell points share certain features. All offer two of the basic preclosure signals: *paragraph break* (S/54, S/107, S/140), and *change of space/time/condition* (Aunt Lympy moves off in her carriage; Melitte sets out for school; Melitte walks away from Victor and toward the children by the schoolhouse). However, each of these sentences does something else, too. It ends a dialectical thought-struggle. S/53 terminates the implicit debate between Aunt Lympy and Melitte over the suitability of her teaching job; S/107 ends Melitte's debate with herself about whether to go to New Orleans or stay home; S/140, starting with "He expected no reply," shows the apparent stalemate between Victor's plea and Melitte's evasion—an impasse that is, of course, false because he has already won his case. He just doesn't know it yet.

Let's look again. Each of the favored inner-shell preclosure points correlates with a tilt toward one of Melitte's three choices as a woman. S/54 affirms her option of continuing to teach school, to become, in nineteenth-century Louisiana terms, a "career woman." S/107, on the other hand, shows her tearful decision to go to New Orleans, to become a "society woman." Although S/140 takes us into Victor's mind just after he has revealed his feelings for Melitte, we know enough about her own desires to realize—as *she* certainly does—that she now has a third option: to become a "married woman."

Once we have identified the preclosure choices, we can do much more than speculate about the signals that prompted them. We can look, as I've just done, for other ways to characterize both the sentences themselves and the portion of the text they "end." For example, let's see what happens when we restate Melitte's three life options as expressions of power. At cluster A, Melitte is confidently asserting her choices; at B she's conceding to Aunt Lympy's conventionality; at C she's surrendering to Victor's emotion. A tidy ending, indeed, for Victor's neediness coincides with society's norm (marriage) and Melitte's own (nascently sexual) feelings. Musing upon preclosure can show us that this story is not just a sentimental bagatelle, nor is it just a feminist warning of the forces that limit a woman's independence. All three of Melitte's choices entail losses and gains. This supposed puffball of a story takes us through three putative struggles between mind and heart, convention and desire, with each turn a potential end to the series—each with a different outcome for Melitte, a different ironic edge, a different stake for Southern womanhood.

The Genre

With the help of preclosure study, I can say that this story is, if not one of Chopin's best, at least more interesting than it initially appears to be. I can also say that it is normative, in certain very basic ways, as a sample short story. The text rewards its readers for intuiting, or looking for, the impress of will. It confirms the importance of phases of experience shaped by goals and their outcome. We have always known that storyness has this shape, but perhaps we have never had so simple a proof that students perceive it before teachers abstract it.[10] Nor, perhaps, have we humanists had such clear evidence that readers, left to their own devices, "chunk" a story this way.[11]

Surely local signals such as change of place do influence the preclosure choices, but the larger sense of storyness, coincident with the victory of one of Melitte's options—that rounding out of a phase of experience—is harder to talk about. For these options are nowhere spelled out in the discourse itself. I arrived at them through a critical analysis of the story. But many readers involved in the preclosure exercise may not have conceptualized them at all, though apparently confirming them in the choice of preclosure points. This "guess" is not entirely without foundation because I also asked my respondents to give me a short summary of the story in their own words. In no case were these retellings clearly and prominently organized around the three options as such. We can assume, then, that it is not only, and perhaps not primarily, the overt, locally processed features of the discourse that signal preclosure—but rather that the signals are coming from, or through, a more complex part of the reading process.

To take us above the level of the word-by-word text, we can use the concept of macrostructure, defined and applied in various ways by different discourse analysts but prominently advanced in the work of Teun A. van Dijk. Macrostructures are identified by statements that do not necessarily appear in the text but are generated—according to certain processing rules—by the propositions within the text. These rules simulate or stand in place of the cognitive operations we perform as we read, for "macrostructure formation in complex discourse is a necessary property of cognitive information processing."[12] As we read a story, we process it into macropropositions that identify macrostructures. Van Dijk's rules insure a systematic, more or less objective way of replicating this process—moving up the ladder of generalization by dropping out redundancies, subsuming details, and reducing a large number of propositions (impossible to hold in memory) to a smaller number, easier to retain.

Informally identifying a proposition as the minimal unit comprising subject + finite verb + complements, I rewrote the 169 sentences of the story as 387 propositions. So, for example, S/52–S/54 became the following propositions:

P/120   But Aunt Lympy would not eat
P/121   [She would not] drink
P/122   [She would not] unbend
P/123   Nor [would she] lend herself to the subterfuge of small talk
P/124   She said good-by with solemnity
P/125   [She parted] as we part from those in sore affliction

P/126   She mounted into her old ramshackle open buggy
P/127   The old vehicle looked someway like a throne

I then turned to van Dijk's rules of *deletion* (omitting details that do not condition future states or actions), *generalization* (grouping individual details under an umbrella), and *construction* (building a stereotypical configuration), as well as the *zero rule* (importing a microstructure into the macrostructure unchanged). The resulting macroproposition was:

M/x   Aunt Lympy departed in state.

I carried out the application far enough to determine that a macrostructure statement never swallowed up a preclosure point; that is to say, it always netted propositions up to, but not across, the preclosure point. This discovery confirmed the prominent role of preclosure points in the processing of the story text. Since I already knew, however, that these points were associated with gaps in the discursive continuum—authorially signaled by the break between paragraphs—my experiment with macrostructures gave me only a more generalized version of what the sentences had told me. I needed to look "higher."

Van Dijk does identify another level of cognitive organization called the superstructure. It reduces and generalizes the macrostructures even further and is specific to various genres or types of discourse.[13] Thus, in scientific discourse, the superstructure might identify a fundamental relationship between evidence and inference; for narrative, it would involve certain relations between events. By definition, the superstructure of a story is a conventionalized grammar of narrative, usually represented as a causally connected chain of events by which one state of affairs is transformed into another.[14] It might, therefore, be interesting to see whether a superstructure derived from "Aunt Lympy's Interference" shows any correlation with the favored preclosure points.

Van Dijk uses a simple and conservative model for his tree diagram of story superstructure.[15] *Narrative* is divided into *plot* and *moral.* In turn, plot is divided into *setting* and *episode* with episode comprising *happening* and *evaluation.* Finally, each happening is a matter of *complication* and *resolution.* In "Aunt Lympy's Interference," the plot consists of S/1 through S/164 ("So after all Melitte did not go to the city to become a *grande dame*," 517), and the moral resides in S/165–S/169 (summarizing reactions to her decision). Setting may be instantiated by S/1–S/19, if we take setting in the broadest sense to include the norms of Melitte's life. It is here that the imagery of spring and youth is established. "Aunt Lympy visits Melitte" is the first happening of the story, extending from S/20 to S/54; evaluation as such is not overt, although the image of Aunt Lympy moving off in her throne-like buggy sums up the importunate and judgmental tone of her visit. This series of sentences ends in the A cluster of preclosure points.

A causal connection leads into the next happening: "Melitte receives a letter from her uncle." What follows is a complication of responses, as everybody puts pressure on Melitte, ending in a resolution: S/105, "Oh, I'll go!" Here we arrive at the B cluster of preclosure points. The third happening is the encounter with Victor, with a complication in Melitte's coyness, and a resolution through his passion, ending in the C cluster. No further events are dramatized, though Melitte's implied marriage and the summary of reactions to it are the subject of comment on all sides—the D cluster. In short, the statements of the superstructure, following van Dijk's model, divide up the text in exactly the same way as the preclosure clusters do, following the free choices of 180 readers.

A very general truism can be inferred from this correlation: young-adult and adult readers of short fiction have internalized certain broad conventions of narrative structure; therefore they intuitively recognize as wholes those portions of a story that can be blocked out as events and hence retained on the superstructural (most conventionalized, paradigmatic) level. It seems that both the macrostructures and the superstructures, as representations of how a story is chunked in the act of processing, confirm my sense that preclosure choices are another way of arriving at some of the same information—and by means of a simple, direct, nontechnical exercise any teacher can use.[16]

The Conclusions

And so I come to the overall results of my study. I wanted to deconstruct not the story but the reading of story. I wanted to surprise that primitive sense of story in the act of underwriting the reading of a literary text. Unfortunately, there was little agreement on these "simple" recognitions. Does that mean a primitive sense of storyness is, paradoxically, far from universal? Does it mean that "literary" reading, even on beginning levels, dulls or disorients that sense? Is there any way to strengthen that sense, and is there any point in doing so? Granted its limits, I think my study answers *yes* to all of these questions.

Certainly the short story form, with its oral, tale-ended beginnings, still draws much of its peculiar force from its primitive connection with a mode of knowing. We misname or abuse the sense of storyness when we talk only of plot; we forget or underrate it when we exclusively privilege the New Critical, New Historical, neo-Marxist, feminist, or any other approach. I do not mean that we should teach the sense of storyness per se; if the ability to chunk stories in this way exists at all, it is already learned by the time students read Chopin—or any other literature as literature. Rather, we may want to invoke that sense, respect it, and build on and from it.

Those whom we identify as creative writers, those who have tried to make stories, may, through that process have come round again to what the untrained reader still relies on—a way of configuring experience as story. Again, I am not suggesting that we teach story writing to aid story reading. Rather, we may want to keep retying discussions of theme to decisions of structure (how differently would the story "mean" if it ended here, if it began there, if this happened before that, if this were left out). Above all, we may want to keep our students asking what is at stake, and for whom, in a context as free as possible, initially, from ideological frames.

Many people have noticed that some of the most influential statements about the short story come from short story writers. For this genre in particular, a kind of practitioners' criticism coexists with, and may dominate, the body of formal, academic criticism. Much of what these writers have to say is impressionistic; as they attempt to get back to fundamentals, their statements verge on the ineffable because elemental storyness is preeffable, centered not in language but in a cognitive strategy. Folktales, anonymous and conventionalized, have their roots in the unspoken and unspeakable. Modern stories thrust their language upon us, in all the signatures of style, yet they spring from the same source. Poe, Anderson, Welty, Bowen—when it comes to the short story, we turn to them, to the makers and shapers, for insight and guidance. Perhaps that is because we have not yet found a critical vocabulary that is simple enough.

Preclosure study offers a middle ground between an elite aesthetics and a respect for readership in the broadest sense. Why discourse analysis instead of, for instance, reader-response criticism? The crudity of the "responses" captured by my experiment would dismay a Stanley Fish or a Wolfgang Iser. Besides, I am dealing with variously trained readers. The "informed" reader is not a standard in my experiment but simply a variant. There is also the issue of first readings versus rereadings. Trained readers are rereaders; my study assumed a first-reading experience, overruling, perhaps, the very kinds of responses trained readers have been taught (and prefer) to give.[17] One person, among the most sophisticated readers in my sample, said she had not even considered preclosure points in the body of the text (the inner-shell points) because, as a reader of short fiction in particular, she privileged "the whole" and resisted preclosure.

Good readers ignore preclosure. They do so on principle. In asking readers to "break training," I was asking them to deconstruct not so much the web of language (the focus of hermeneutical studies), not so much the joints of narrative (the focus of narratology), as the habits of academic reading. In other words, I was short-circuiting, if not subverting, the materials of reader-response criticism. I was asking readers to look for minimal, short-term storyness, at the expense of duration and complexity. I was making primitives of them.

Does that mean I was making children of them? Consider, for a moment, some of the work done in the last two decades on the developmental psychology of reading. Much of it rests on a surprising shift in the field of psychology itself. R. L. Gregory makes the point that "organisms are controlled by fictions rather than stimuli."[18] Even on the neurological level, "storying"—making predictive scenarios—controls adaptation and survival. And according to James Britton, "it requires an act of the imagination to construct any situation in which we actually find ourselves."[19] In other words, storytelling is not only a recreation, an art, a social activity, but also a primary mode of cognition. A fundamental way of managing experience is to encode it as story. Recognizing story is therefore perhaps the most basic, least sophisticated, *least literary,* of our responses to fiction.

It is not news that stories may be expressions of fundamental drives or ways of interacting with the world. In the late 1950s, Randall Jarrell defined story in Freudian terms as "a wish, or a truth, or a wish modified by a truth."[20] What he did not say, and what I'd like to add, is that storying is a way of chunking fictively represented experience for purposes not just of self-expression or vicarious living, but primarily of cognitive management. Here I am following closely D. W. Harding's view of literature's cultural function. He rejects the idea that literature offers mainly opportunities for emotional identification with characters (the basis for much teaching) and says, instead, that "in entering into the 'virtual experience' of influential works of literature, a child is offered a flow and recoil of sympathies that accords with the culture pattern in which he is growing up."[21] Preclosure study can document a reader's perception of the "flow and recoil" of narrative sequence. For purposes of generating data, the naïve reader is truly the equal of the foremost scholar. It is only when we begin to interpret the findings that our aims, experience, and skill make a difference. Regardless of our critical orientation, reading for storyness can be a useful heuristic for aesthetic appreciation, critical insight, and social or historical inference.

chapter three

Preclosing an "Open" Story by Julio Cortázar

L eaping from Chopin to Cortázar reminds us how disparate are the many short narratives we label short stories. "Aunt Lympy's Interference" is simple, regional, and old-fashioned; "Orientation of Cats" is difficult, cosmopolitan, and postmodern. One is a sentimental love story; the other a fugue on love's failure. Both stories are problematic for students, who may find Chopin quaint and Cortázar obscure. On the other hand, sophisticated readers may, on a first reading, dismiss the first story as a trivial tale, while lauding the second as a puzzle worth solving. In the discussion that follows, I suggest that a preclosure study of the Cortázar story can enlighten the student *and* inform the trained critic.

A year before he died, Julio Cortázar stood before a painting taller than his own six feet, four inches.[1] Someone photographed him pausing at the right-hand edge of a large mural showing peasants at work and play at the edge of a village. The painting was on exhibit in Nicaragua, where Cortázar was visiting in 1983. In the photo, he is looking into the heart of the picture, his right knee bent, his left arm swung slightly forward, as if the intensity of his gaze could fool his body into stepping into the scene.[2]

Even if we didn't know this writer was fascinated by the permeable boundaries between visual art and "real life," even if we didn't know he sympathized, politically, with the vision captured in this pintura *naif*, we could hardly look at the rapt spectator without being caught in a triangulated gaze: ourselves looking at Cortázar, who is looking at the picture, which, in turn, shows us an image—a meaning—that includes his attention. Such triangles, in which a leg is thrown over the barriers between art and life, are common in Cortázar's fiction. They illustrate his belief in the multiple and sometimes exchangeable orders of reality. For example, "Orientation of Cats" is a very short story in which we're invited to "look" at a man, who is gazing at his wife, who, in turn, is so engrossed by a painting she seems to enter it.[3]

What I want to do here is triangulate the critical gaze at a story—"Orientation of Cats"—that is, itself, about lines of vision. My method is the kind of reading experiment that is at the heart of this book. I'll be showing how a group of students helped me to "see" a mighty narrative in a wisp of fiction. In the end, we may have a better understanding of a surprising way in which short stories earn their compression.

The Pedagogical Axis

Putting "Orientation of Cats" on a syllabus for undergraduates is asking for trouble. Most students nowadays are acquainted with modern tendencies to interiorize action, to bend realism, yet these features are hurdles, not handles, for the average reader. I asked 114 readers, almost all undergraduates, to rate their understanding of this story after a first reading, and over 60 percent admitted that some aspects were "confusing"; 13 percent were "totally lost." The teacher, looking at these students, sees a pedagogical problem. One solution, of course, is to re-present the story in more familiar terms. To retell it.

"Orientation of Cats" is a story about a man who wants to know more about his wife. An unnamed husband, speaking in the first person, opens with a description of his relationship to his wife, Alana, and to their cat, Osiris. He admits up front that, "when Alana and Osiris look at me[,] I can't complain of the least dissembling, the least duplicity." Yet he quickly adds that "woman and cat [know] one another on planes that escape me," and while he has "renounced all mastery over Osiris, . . . Alana is my wife and the distance between us is a different one, something that she doesn't seem to feel but which blocks my happiness when Alana looks at me, when she looks at me straight on just the way Osiris does . . . without the slightest reserve . . ." (3–4). He is convinced that, behind his wife's blue eyes, "there's more." Other selves, other Alanas he's never seen. What he wants is to catch his wife in the act—not of betrayal—but of revealing new selves. His goal is to see, to "know," every one of her manifestations.

Alana is best observed when listening to music or looking at paintings: art has the power to fix her attention, to draw out from her the buried selves she never consciously hides because she doesn't know they exist. The narrator tells us, "In my own way I make a stubborn effort to understand, to discover; I watch her but without spying; I follow her but without mistrust . . ." (4). Put one way, he is a seeker, a man who wants knowledge within the bonds of marriage; put another way, he is a stalker, a man who wants "mastery" over the soul of his wife.

He recalls that, seeing her in front of a Rembrandt, he "felt that the painting was carrying her beyond herself," offering a "glimpse of Alana in Alana" (4). And so the action begins with the events of "yesterday," when he took her to a gallery with the specific intention of catching her in a moment of self-revelation. He recounts how he followed her from painting to painting. His quest was going well: "I was watching her give herself over to each painting, my eyes were multiplying the lightning bolt of a triangle that went from her to the picture and from the picture to me, returning to her and catching the change, the different halo that encircled her for a moment to give way later to a new aura, a tonality that exposed her to the true one, to the ultimate nakedness" (6). Here we have the same geometry we found in the photograph of Cortázar looking at a painting in a gallery, although, in that case, *we* were the "male" onlookers. However benign that triangle may have been (and it may not have been entirely so), in the story the role of the onlooker is clearly suspect. For, in the narrator's mounting desire to "know" his wife, there is a murky blend of abstract curiosity and sexual predation.

Then something changes. The paintings begin having a negative effect. Alana's face reveals pain, "repulsion, the rejection of an unacceptable limit" (6). Sketchy details suggest that the pictures hold hints of mortality, that Alana is, finally, losing her innocence but is fighting the import of limit, cessation—death. Suddenly the narrator has to do a little soul-searching himself: what exactly does he want from—and for—his wife?

When Alana stops at a final painting, the crisis arrives. In the picture is a cat, identical to Osiris, who is looking out a window at something hidden from the viewer. Alana is able to identify with the cat and, in doing so, is able to see past the frame of the window. When she looks back at the narrator, he realizes "the triangle no longer existed, she had gone into the picture but she hadn't come back . . ." (7). We're told, in conclusion, that when she *does* look back at the narrator, she sees what the cat sees beyond the window frame. Since we cannot know what that is, we're left in the narrator's shoes. Geometrically, he's been equated with what's invisible from his own point of view. In effect, he has been "zeroed out" by his own logic, his own desire. Selfishly seeking his wife's many selves, *he*'s left with no self he can see. The quest, in other words, has backfired.

Students have no trouble observing the narrator's obsession or the irony of its outcome. They can recognize a traditional conflict between the unconscious, holistic sort of "being" assigned to the woman/cat, and the analytical, possessive way of "thinking" assigned to the husband. Intuition versus reason is a handy explanation for the tension in the story. Today's students, primed on discussions of gender issues, can recognize these stereotypes of male and female "qualities," and may see Cortázar himself as trapped in sexist attitudes, despite the advantage he gives to Alana (and despite his own well-documented love of cats, which aligns him with Alana rather than with the male narrator).[4]

Offering students a paraphrase of the story may be a way of solving the pedagogical problem, but it only tantalizes the critic. The natural move here would be to turn our gaze back to the story itself. Instead, I want to consult a different sort of reader, a new line of sight. The reader I have in mind is no longer the trained scholar, the experienced teacher, nor even those busy stand-ins we like to employ for our critical shows—the anonymous "we," the "informed reader." Rather, the reader I'll be turning to throughout this book is an aggregate "person" composed of a real group of readers, the students themselves.

The Empirical Axis

The materials I am going to use were collected from a population of 114 readers from several different classes taught in the 1980s at the University of Iowa. In all cases, the responses were gathered before I said a word about the story, although, of course, the readers themselves brought a rich and varied mix of prior knowledge and experience to the reading of this text. One other feature of the experiment should be mentioned up front, a refinement occasioned by my findings in earlier experiments. Because sentences that end a paragraph are more easily targeted as preclosure choices, I gave half of the group (57 readers) a variant text, in which the paragraphing had been deliberately altered from the original.

The story, in both variant and original forms, has 34 sentences in

English.[5] As usual, each sentence was numbered, so readers could quickly record their preclosure choices. These records, along with other information about each reader, were encoded in a simple database program for easy access and handling. In the past, I have found that 20 percent agreement on a particular sentence is worth noting. Perhaps because "Orientation of Cats" is such a short text, percentages of agreement were much higher this time. For example, the sentence most often recognized as preclosural was chosen by 67 percent of the readers. There is no need this time to review the many kinds of inferences that might be drawn from the data. Instead, I will just focus on some of the more interesting findings, interpreting them as I go along.

The first anomaly has to do with the ways male and female readers perceive storyness. Students in today's classrooms are often primed to respond to gender issues in fiction. Although important, these responses often reflect the paradigms of other, more ideological study, preempting a more open approach to the text and, perhaps, a fuller appreciation of the author's own way of handling these themes (a problem I will take up in chapter 5). This danger may be greatest when the story, like "Orientation of Cats," highlights sexual stereotypes. In these cases, I have found it useful to look for *gender bias in the choice of preclosure points*. Students are captivated by this kind of evidence because they have generated it themselves.

Among the 114 readers, 32 were male, 80 were female, and 2 left this question unanswered. The ratio of males to females was about 1 to 2.5. Among the readers choosing each of the more favored preclosure points, the gender ratio is roughly the same; in other words, none of these possible endings was noticeably more attractive to one gender or the other—an interesting fact in itself. However, if we look at the small number of readers who chose the *earliest* preclosure points (any sentence between and including S/1 and S/7), there is a clear skewing.

Of the fifteen readers choosing sentences in this group, nine are male, and six are female—making the male/female ratio now 1.5 to 1, instead of 1 to 2.5. If we note that one of the males chose *two* sentences from this group, and another chose *three*, the number of male *choices* becomes twelve out of eighteen—or *two to one*. Given the small numbers involved, this evidence has no statistical meaning. It does, however, raise the question of whether men are likelier than women to accept early closure.[6]

Among this group of early preclosure points, the most popular is S/7. The narrator has been telling us that he accepts his exclusion from the world of Osiris, the cat, but cannot find peace in his relationship to Alana. He then confesses,

> S/7   I've never told her so, I love her too much to break this surface of happiness over which so many days have slipped, so many years. (4)

There are, here, local lexical closural signals that may help trigger a *pre-closural* choice, as the word *shut* (as in "shut the window") may have done in "Aunt Lympy's Interference." Words suggesting absolute or excessive states of being, like *never, too much,* and *so many* (and, indeed, *happiness* itself) have closural force. So do references to the passage of time, such as *days* and *years.*[7] Yet to imagine the story ending at this point, a reader must feel a certain global closural force in a mere statement of the status quo, an apparent willingness to hide discontent, to preserve harmony, for the sake of one's partner. It would be fruitless, if not indefensible, to look at the psychology or the morality of this stance and to correlate it somehow with male rather than female attitudes or sensitivities; however, we can certainly wonder about the gender bias in the *choice* of S/7.

If we had to describe the putative story that ends with that sentence, we might notice that it offers only generalized narrative, explaining a common or habitual state of affairs in the lives of the characters. However, the sequencing of information does have a mini-"plot": into the narrator's happy domestic world intrudes a counterforce, an obstacle to his complete emotional and intellectual fulfillment; he struggles with the paradox that his wife is, to him, both closed and open; finally, invoking conjugal love, he decides to keep silent. If, indeed, a story ends here, it's a *gendered anecdote* about male desire, female mystery, and a compromise on the part of the man: he opts for the status quo because he "love[s] her too much." This outcome may be positive if we see him as a loving husband, negative if we see *him* as the dissembler. Either way, however, the narrative stalls because the narrator is afraid to be open with his wife. Four of the thirty-two male readers could accept this wrap-up, but only three of the eighty women could do so. A far higher percentage of the female readers didn't think things could (or should?) end there.

The very next sentence, chosen by a slightly larger (though still very small) number of readers, offers a dramatic increase in closural signals:

S/8   In my own way I make a stubborn effort to understand, to discover; I watch her but without spying; I follow her but without mistrust; I love a marvelous mutilated statue, an unfinished text, a fragment of sky inscribed on the window of life. (4)

This sentence ends a paragraph in the original text and was twice as likely
to be selected by readers of that text than by readers of the variant text,
in which it opens a paragraph. In both versions, however, it contains certain keywords—lexical units given prominence by the concerns of this
story. Nearly all the verbs have special resonance in this story of curiosity and passion: "understand," "discover," "watch," "love." There is an
even more specialized pair of keywords—"text," "inscribed"—that posit
a metaphor of reading and writing. This husband is trying to "read" his
wife.[8]

What is most remarkable about this sentence, however, is the high incidence of local syntactic cues. A reader who has never heard of tricolons
or anaphora is still going to hear the repetitively initialed and triadic structure of "I watch" / "I follow" / "I love" and "a . . . mutilated statue" / "an
unfinished text" / "a fragment of sky." According to rhetoricians, triadic
structures carry conviction; they round out an utterance. Still, only a very
few readers (11 percent) thought the story could end here, and it is easy
to see why most thought it couldn't. The narrator has not yet found a solution to his problem; he has merely restated it. Yet the syntax of his admission says he has found *something*—a structure for his thought.

This sentence directly follows the gender-skewed choice we looked at
before, but is the same bias present? As it happens, the increment of only
one sentence adds a welter of new closural signals, netting a different kind
of reader. Anyone sensing closure at S/8 needs an "ear" for language, a
sensitivity to rhetorical form. And, indeed, the readers who chose this sentence as a possible preclosure point were remarkable not for their gender
but rather for their level of education: while 60 percent of the whole group
were advanced readers (juniors, seniors, or postgraduates), 83 percent of
those choosing *this* preclosure point were advanced readers. "I love . . .
an unfinished text," says the narrator. For readers accustomed to the literary confluence of desire and textuality, this statement rounds out a comprehension, a *rhetorical conceit*. Gender bias is only one feature worth
noting in a group of readers. Training, as we've seen before, is another.
What preclosure studies do is bring to light the biases and powers of var-

ious slices of the reading population, making these findings available for all to observe and discuss.

Let's look, now, at the overwhelming agreement on the closural force of sentence S/22. On any one of the prior sentences, at most only twelve people felt closure. Suddenly, at this particular point, seventy-six readers came to a stop. While it is true that this sentence closed a paragraph in both texts, increasing the likelihood of choice, it is also true that 67 percent agreement is so unusual in these studies that we cannot fail to learn something—about the text *and* the readers—by looking more closely at this preclosure point.

Husband and wife (in his retelling of the events) have entered the picture gallery. With rising hope and excitement, he has been watching her reveal herself before the first paintings: "my eyes were multiplying the lightning bolt of a triangle that went from her to the picture and from the picture to me." He tracks each new change in her, believing his goal—to know her completely—is finally at hand:

S/22   It was impossible to foresee how far that osmosis would be repeated, how many new Alanas would finally carry me to the synthesis from which we would both emerge fulfilled, she without knowing it and lighting a new cigarette before asking me to buy her a drink; I knowing that my long search had finally culminated and that from then on my love would take in the visible and the invisible, would accept Alana's clean look without the uncertainty of closed doors, forbidden passageways. (6)

Words that denote absolute or excessive conditions, whether positive or negative, are local lexical closural signals. Look how they swell the tide of this sentence: "impossible," "finally" (twice), "synthesis," "fulfilled," "culminated," "from then on," "the visible and the invisible," and, of course, "closed." He is projecting his desire into the future, imagining the experience in the gallery as a conjugation of revelations, which, like a more physical conjugality, would leave them fulfilled as they exit the gallery—she lighting a cigarette, he basking in his achievement. It is possible almost to overlook his condescension ("we would both emerge fulfilled, she without knowing it"), so vigorous and hopeful is his tone.

What kind of story ends here? Is it not a familiar *quest tale*? In this resounding sentence, the "hero" vividly imagines his success, almost as if it belongs to him already. Although he cannot tell how many Alanas may reveal themselves, the focus in this sentence is on the series as completed, every Alana accounted for, the goal achieved. Although he believes he is expressing a copious love, the speech-act force of this sentence is to flaunt the complacency of the rational animal, who abhors what is indeterminate, hidden, or "forbidden." What ends here is a goal-oriented, positivist parable, in which enumerated, observable evidence conquers mystery and evasion. It is the template for a familiar kind of success story.

The next important finding is that one of the favored preclosure sentences, S/27, makes a strong showing *even when buried in the middle of a paragraph*. It is a difficult sentence to decode even on the surface, offering problems of interpretation that may be hard to separate from a slight awkwardness in the translation. Nevertheless, 46 percent of the readers chose this sentence.

In their tour of the gallery, the husband and wife have moved beyond the first paintings, which brought so much pleasure and variety to Alana's face. Alana has begun to pick up negative signals from the paintings she is now encountering. She seems distressed. The narrator, jarred, is afraid she will catch him looking at her and will turn her gaze on *him*.

> S/27   I remained in back, knowing that it would be impossible for me to bear her look, her interrogative surprise when she saw in my face the bewilderment of confirmation, because that too was I, that was my Project Alana, my Alana life, it had been desired by me and reined in by a present tense of city and parsimony, finally now Alana, finally Alana and I from now on. (7)

Here, for the first time, the narrator is in the object position, imagining how he will feel if Alana looks at *him*. Since we have no access to her mind, we cannot know what she would see—only what her husband imagines she might see. For readers of the translation, the wording is strangely obscure here, almost as if the narrator were trying to protect himself from *our* gaze, *our* understanding, at the moment when he himself goes on view. The "bewilderment of confirmation" is a two-way mirror. It suggests that Alana would be confused by seeing in her husband's face a confirmation of the repellent message she has found in the paintings and that the narrator is himself confused by a new realization: his need to "know" Alana is really a way of making her finite, of imposing the kind of limit she is rejecting in the paintings. "That too was I, that was my Project Alana," he goes on, adding "it had been desired by me." Each new "that" or "it" deepens the ambiguity, and the sentence ends with a crescendo of longing—or of desperation.

Granting that other interpretations are possible, let me offer a paraphrase for this crucial and difficult sentence: "I knew I couldn't bear her questioning surprise when she saw in my face the same thing she had been seeing in the paintings—an intimation of limit, a closing off of infinite prospects, or, in other words, death; for I suddenly realized that my effort to know her completely—my Project Alana—was a reductive enterprise, geared to the values of a mundane reality and aimed at total possession of her being." Although he now realizes his dream is in some way diminishing to his wife, he clings to it. The final words of the sentence are poignantly loaded with (wishful) closural words, which I'll italicize: "*finally now* Alana, *finally* Alana and I *from now on*." What he wants is to wrap his wife into a vision that is wishful, private, abstract. Two keywords, "I" and "Alana," are crisscrossed syntactically in the chiasmus at the end of the sentence: "that too was I . . . Alana, finally Alana and I . . . " The lyricism is strained by the simple fact that, at this moment, Alana and her husband are more polarized than they have ever been in the course of their marriage.

Were the story to end here, those final ten words would arc into the empty space of the page, an inverted epiphany in which denial and desire hold reality at bay. We'd be left with a marital impasse, a loaded tension, an existential moment from which, conventionally, nothing could follow but a sadder adjustment to a grimmer life. I cannot help thinking that this sentence's extraordinary power to arrest my students—despite the ambiguity of its wording; despite, in some cases, its middle-of-the-paragraph location—comes from their recognizing, at this point, a familiar story-template. This "ending" has the open, ambiguous, yet deflating tenor of the *modernist ficcione*.

The very next sentence, overall the second-most-favored preclosure point (chosen by 50 percent of the readers), takes the existential moment and holds it, by the very force of wishful thinking, until it resolves in romantic imagery:

S/28   I would have liked to have held her naked in my arms,
    love[d?] her in such a way that everything would be clear, everything

would be spoken forever between us, and that from that endless night of love (as we had already known so many of them) the first dawn of life would be born. (7)

Against the heavy emphasis on closural words—*everything* (twice), *forever, endless, so many*—comes the lineup of inaugural words—*first, dawn, life, born*. An easy, conventional reading finds here a hint that the childless, self-involved marriage could move to a new register, transcend itself, bear fruit in a "happy ending." Although the new life might simply be a more fully shared union of thought and feeling within the shadow of mortality, one doesn't have to be a romantic to see a reference to childbirth. *This* "night of love," after the watershed experience in the gallery, would be different, and the difference might change sensuality into fertility, leading to a more responsible, more venerable form of self-reproduction. The fact that half of the readers thought (wished?) the story could end here, and that most of these readers were only two or three years out of high school, may simply mean that undergraduates are optimistic.

Yet the story that ends with this sentimental imagery offers a dollop of nostalgia. This is the way stories *used* to end—with the distractions and distresses of the modern world melting away before the prospect of "baby makes three." To the cooler eye, remembering the hip, urban, sophisticated setting of the story, this ending would be always already suspect. To the careful reader, of course, the lines are immediately undercut because the narrator is only dreaming. "Wouldn't it be nice if . . . " Yet, the text that would end here would have at least the shape of an *old-fashioned love story*.

It is time to look at these preclosure choices in relation to the "given" ending, the one Cortázar himself provides. After the effusion just quoted, the narrator goes to the exit door of the gallery, hoping for fresh air and a chance to collect himself. Meanwhile, Alana has stopped before the very last picture, the one in which the Osiris-like cat is looking out of the window at something the viewer cannot see. The narrator notes her separateness from the other visitors and "from me, who went over indecisively." His failing self-confidence can be seen in the reference to himself, for the first time, as an object. For Alana, through her identification with the cat, has stepped into another dimension, once and for all eluding her husband's chary, selfish, possessive curiosity.

S/31   In some way I felt that the triangle had been broken; when Alana turned her head toward me the triangle no longer existed, she had gone into the picture but she hadn't come back, she was still beside the cat, looking beyond the window where no one could see what they saw, what only Alana and Osiris saw every time they looked at me straight on. (7)

The "I" perspective has returned, but only to admit its failure to achieve the goal set earlier in the story. Instead of harmony and union, there is disruption—broken lines of connection, a new triangulation (Alana, cat, X [what they alone can see]), a shift of power from the husband to his wife. *She* is now the one with more knowledge.

Significantly, she has not sought it through strategy, deception, or reason, but has simply found it through the powerful sympathies of her nature. To the narrator, what she has discovered must remain forever the unseen X. In a final twist, this very "X" turns into a signifier for the narrator himself. When his wife looks at him, she sees not the "I" of the story, but the "X" in the picture. The man who wanted to know his wife completely hasn't learned how to see with her eyes—so if he looks at himself, trying to see X, he won't see a thing. He is erased to his own view and, to a certain extent, ours. What we have now is a brilliant, almost mathematical deconstruction of rational, goal-oriented action, of male hubris, of the "I" itself. What we have, in other words, is a *postmodern parable.*

The Critical Axis

In the first section of this paper, following the "pedagogical axis," I looked at my students, assessing their needs as readers of the story. Then, shifting to the "empirical axis," I followed their gaze, trying to discover what *they* "knew" about the story. I wanted, for the moment, to align myself with their age-old competence and learned experience as readers of literature. Preclosure study was the method I chose for getting at this unconscious wisdom. Of course, as I admitted earlier, as soon as I began codifying the data, I began interpreting it, which means I was already sighting along the "critical axis." It was necessary to do so at the time the data was presented, for the sake of clarity and economy. Now, in the final section of this chapter, I would like to draw together some of those interpretations, looking for what they reveal as I, myself, look back at the story.

After the most favored preclosure points are studied individually, it is instructive to look at them *as a series.* In effect, what we are then doing is looking at a series of putative stories leading up to the actual story, which is the text as printed. At each of the stopping places marked by the empirical data of the preclosure study, I chose a label for the putative story unfolding to that point. The two earliest, chosen by relatively few readers, but interesting for their biases, were *gendered anecdote* and *rhetorical conceit*. As these terms imply, neither is really persuasive as a complete story. The next four, however, are recognizable templates for short stories: *quest tale, modernist ficcione, old-fashioned love story,* and *postmodern parable.*

The question of who "authored" (or authorized) each of these putative stories is both obvious and complicated. As we've seen, readers were reacting to closural signals when they selected the sentences that "end" these stories; since Cortázar inscribed these signals, clearly he is responsible, in some degree, for the way readers divided up his text. On the other hand, readers respond to these signals and respond to these story units, in both individual and aggregate ways, based on experience, personal preferences, and culturally encoded story schemas.[9] In a practical sense, therefore, the readers have "created" the putative stories by marking them in the text.

Ambiguity of authorship is not such a strange concept today, when hypertext fictions give readers a choice in shaping the plot. My role, too, is admittedly invasive and coercive; I have labeled these templates in accord with my notions of short fiction theory, practice, and history. For all these reasons, it is hard to say in what way these putative stories "exist," whose story sense they encode, and what ends they serve—Cortázar's, the reading group's, or mine. The most honest answer is that we have all played a part, and, more importantly, so have the culturally encoded models that have shaped our perceptions of storyness and of genres of storyness.

I believe preclosure texts are valuable because of their peculiar status. As "stories," they are textually definitive (unlike most folktales or other communal fictions) but, at the same time, are not simply invented by the person who studies them (as are, often, the lab-generated stories used by cognitive scientists). Therefore, putative stories offer a somewhat (although not wholly) objective window onto the cultural perception of storyness. As a short story theorist and critic, I am interested in the way this cultural perception plays off against the particular features of a given short story. How might it reinforce—or countervail—the ostensible themes and styles of the text in view? How might it enrich our experience of reading the story and interpreting its meaning?

To engage these questions, I have found it useful to view the putative stories *as a sequence.* Regardless of Cortázar's plan or awareness, the text marches us through these stories, modulating our reactions by the order and intensity with which we experience each of these preclosures on the way to the "real" end. What is it like to read a quest tale that turns into a modernist *ficcione,* then an old-fashioned love story, and finally a postmodern parable? Do these story types themselves construct a narrative of assumptions, emotions, meanings?

I believe they do, and I believe that tracing this quite different sort of metanarrative can help us appreciate one of the most powerful ways in which "short" fiction packs "much in little." Quest tales offer the reader a familiar format and the promise of simple fulfillment: a goal achieved. In Cortázar's story, that traditional, confident, normative feeling is available at the end of the first putative story widely recognized by the readers. It is also a feeling that supports the narrator's initial optimism, his early assumptions about his private situation, and, hence, the world of the story. All he has to do (he thinks) is stay on the trail long enough, and he'll win the prize.

When we stumble head on into the end of the next major putative story, the modernist *ficcione,* we're captives of a different frame of reference—one where doubts, ambiguities, and tensions abound. I certainly do not want to see this transition simply in terms of a historical shift in literary norms. However, I do suggest that the cultural grounding of this shift underscores the significance of this unnamed character's experience *and* the disturbing impact the story has upon us at this point, as we wonder what the narrator really wants, really means.

Next comes the strangely appealing yet desperate story that ends with a wishful dream of a new "dawn" or birth. This putative story comes as a respite, an invitation to false hope, a textual mirage, if you will, that we credit too easily if we're prone to nostalgia for romantic sentiment, for old-fashioned love stories. In terms of the narrator's tale, this moment is one of almost painful longing, unrelieved by self-knowledge. In terms of the metanarrative, this is a moment of emotional and intellectual counterpoint, as we meet assumptions about narrative—and the world—in which we no longer believe but for which we still yearn. These realizations are not, of course, likely to be registered in these terms by the reader, who is caught up with the surface issues of female intuition and marital power games. Their presence, however, thickens the texture of the reading experience and adds to the heft of this very short story.

I mentioned earlier that there is a point at which the narrator loses his confidence and acts "indecisively." In a way, the story swings around this pivot and heads thereafter to an ending the narrator never imagined. That ending, the actual closure of the story, makes a final separation between husband and wife. For her, the ending is "happy": her temporary pain is healed through her alignment with a suprahuman vision, one that melts boundaries between reality and art, cat and human, life and death (the god Osiris, for whom Alana's cat is named, dies and returns to life in an endless cycle). In Cortázar's work, there are other instances of transspecies bonding; while they are not always so comforting and domesticated as here, these alignments strongly appeal to him.

However, the husband has no access to this axis, this "orientation"; so, for him, the ending is punitive. He is left behind, excluded, "zeroed out"—like all rationalists of the twentieth century who cannot give themselves to the unknown. Put in these terms, the ending reads like a lesson on hubris and, especially, male inadequacy before female mystery. What we hear is the echo of our own time, the lonely click of the disconnected self. Considering, however, the route by which we arrive at this conclusion— the series of putative stories that wrench our emotions in culturally coded ways—the ending is heavily freighted. My students have revealed and I have codified a plurality of stories that "load" this slender text with many times its apparent weight. In the process, we've laid bare one of the most powerful strategies by which the short story achieves its definitive compression, its "much in little." I'd like to think, too, that we've thrown a leg over the barrier between formalist aesthetics and the culture-driven interests of our profession today.

chapter four

Preclosure and the History of the American Short Story

B y "storying" our experience, we learn to adapt, to look after our welfare in a world of pains and pleasures—from burnt fingers to harmed psyches. We've always realized that storytelling was a primitive human activity, keeping clans and cultures together; on the most basic level, chunking experience into story units is a mode of knowing what that experience means and passing on that knowledge, with some variation among cultures but with much bonding as human beings. Storying is a form of cognitive management. Closure is the proof that storying has happened.

If there is something primal underlying short storyness, how do we get in touch with it? Can we use it to explain why the short story not only *does* but also *is* something different from longer forms of narrative? In 1983, my own answers to these questions were based on a phenomenology of short-span reading experiences, wherein the reader's response to the sentence—its typical syntactic and lexical features, its tension between closural and anticlosural features—became the model for the experience of entering, moving through, and getting out of the story.[1] As it turns out, the most promising aspect of that argument was its emphasis on closure. There have since been many studies of the way stories end. Yet there has not been, within the discipline of literary studies, a way of moving from the analysis of closural features and effects, to a test of the primacy, the necessity, the uniqueness of the short story in the family of genres. That is the project of this book.

Discourse analysts, in particular those of the Amsterdam school headed by Teun van Dijk, have studied the way readers—that is, human text processors—build the meaning of a whole discourse. According to Van Dijk, as you may remember, the serial propositions of the text are combined—by means of processing rules—into a smaller set of more general propositions, called *macrostructures*. The formation of these macrostructures is a cognitive strategy for processing the text, for making sense of it.[2]

For over a decade, psychologists have been working with many of the same ideas, but from the other direction. They have been positing "story grammars," or systems of notation for the structure of storyness. In the 1980s there were ongoing debates about the theoretical and practical value of these grammars.[3] Some psychologists thought processors recognize stories primarily for other reasons. According to one group of theorists, storyness inheres in the difficulty and/or importance of the goals for which human or humanlike agents strive. William F. Brewer, on the other hand, argues that storyness inheres in the sequence of affective states produced in human processors when they are reading a tale as opposed to cuddling up with a good encyclopedia.

In general, there has been a shift away from the formal, culturally unmarked, linguistic models of story structure and story comprehension— that is, the story grammar approach—toward the more data-driven, culturally determined, hands-on models of generating and processing "stories."[4] Before children reach school age, they tend to produce "sequential lists of events" when asked to "tell what happened." They recognize the differences among a retelling of a film they've just seen, a news story, and a "more embellished" story of their own—but they can't choose or vary their narrative stance in relation to these subgenres of narrative.[5] Some researchers, assuming that autobiographical memories are the earliest materials of story, say that "event memory" begins early but narrativity comes later, after exposure to adult talk about past and future scenarios. Margaret S. Benson argues for a developmental progression in the ability to use plotted narrative. Three-year-olds can recount events, but without a central theme. Four-year-olds may supply a theme, but without purpose or goals. A goal-plan does appear in stories by five-year-olds. Older readers, beginning at about nine, are able to construct hierarchical goal-plans—and thus full-fledged stories, by one commonly accepted definition.[6]

Perhaps the most interesting research into the way we process stories has to do with the mental models we use in order to comprehend what we read. The story grammarians and those working with artificial intelligence helped us understand how story schemata and event-scripts organize, make sense of, and store incoming information. In the 1980s, the focus shifted to causal and/or goal-outcome relationships. However, to my way of thinking, the most suggestive work for the literary scholar is the more recent development of "situation models." Processing a text is not a matter of decoding one sentence after another, stringing together a sequence of "locally cohesive" units; rather, it is a multilayered, multifaceted process of constructing and revising mental representations of "situations" suggested by spatial, temporal, causal, and emotional information provided by the text.[7]

Cognitive scientists can offer a more flexible, reader-response-oriented, "situational" framework for talking about the reciprocity between the sequentiality of print literature and the networking, interactive, model-building activities of the human mind. The burden of many of these studies is that readers bring all sorts of prior knowledge to the act of reading a given text: story schemata learned at a very early age,[8] scripts for repeated, commonplace activities in their culture,[9] "goal-plans,"[10] "just-world" expectations,[11] and the kind of personal association and inference making that causes different readers to describe the appearance of a character differently, often in terms not found in the text.[12] Scientists are more and more often using "natural" stories (those occurring in the real world rather than fabricated in the lab); they are looking at models for emotional and aesthetic, as well as cognitive experiences in reading. They are attending to the culturally coded assumptions readers bring to the text, with perhaps less of the ideological weighting sometimes found in cultural studies by humanists.

There is much that is daunting for the literary scholar who peers into this territory. The models of inquiry, the rules of evidence, the very nature of what is regarded as knowledge seem alien. It is, I believe, a matter of trading heuristics. Psychology, after all, has turned increasingly to the concept of narrative to explain human behavior. I am arguing that short story critics can profitably turn to cognitive studies. At the very least, we gain an experimental approach to essentialist, honorific concepts inherited from Poe: unity, totality, and single effect. Instead of asking how stories are composed, or even how stories "mean," we can ask how storyness is recognized, by what cognitive strategies it is processed.

I have learned from the story grammarians that the perception of storyness is a gestalt; each of us, as a human story processor, has internalized a story schema, a set of expectations about what stories offer. It is this story schema, rather than any real stories, that the grammars represent. The question is, how are these schemata deployed? How can we watch them in action? Van Dijk's theory of macrostructures allows me to put the question another way. How do readers chunk a text into meaningful units above the sentence level? When do these chunks become story size? Enter, preclosure study.

When I conducted my first experiment, I was unaware that William F. Brewer, a much respected cognitive psychologist, was using *his* students in reader-response tests of short story affects. He was dividing up stories into sections, asking questions after each section to determine how surprise, suspense, and curiosity "stage" a reader's response throughout a story. He was also looking at the way feelings of "completeness" and "outcome satisfaction" influence judgments about "story-liking" and "story-likeness."[13] However, my approach was different. I wanted to let readers do their own chunking in a way that would document, very pointedly, their sense of whole-storyness. Also, I remained convinced that the experience of storyness is tied more directly to closure than to any set of story components or story affects.

The problem with studying the ends of stories is simply that the author is in control. He or she makes chunking at this point not just easy but inevitable. That is why I decided to study those points in a narrative where *readers* feel the story *could* end. By collecting intuitive preclosure choices from various groups of readers, I have been able to speculate about the influence of different kinds of training and experiences on trends in preclosure choices. In the previous chapters, I focused on individual stories, laying out the theory and practice of preclosure study. Now I would like to focus on preclosure sentences themselves and what they can tell us about the nature of storyness in general.

Therefore, on this occasion, I reversed the ratio of readers to stories: instead of having many readers read one story, I myself read forty-five well-known American short stories. Limiting myself to widely anthologized texts, I used fifteen from each of three major periods in the history of the genre: 1820–50 (Early), 1920–40 (Modern), and 1960–80 (Contemporary). My choices were highly conventional and weighted toward the classics, which seemed appropriate at the time, although I would surely use a wider range of stories if I were to repeat the experiment.[14] Regardless of the texts I chose or might have chosen, what I was doing was making explicit my own sense of storyness. The data, therefore, were far from objective, but the effect of my biases remains constant across the sample.

Because the quantity of data quickly became unwieldy, I decided to use just three sentences from each story: the preclosure point nearest the beginning of the story, which I called *anterior closure;* the preclosure point closest to the end of the story, or *penultimate closure;* and the actual last sentence of the story, or *closure.* Once I had collected the 135 targeted sentences, I analyzed them in a variety of ways, cataloging their features, global and local, syntactic and lexical. This time, the aggregate evidence would yield, I hoped, some insight into those features of storyness that remained constant over time (discussed in the first part of this chapter) and those that varied by historical period (discussed in the second part).

Let me briefly review the kinds of information I collected for each story. I divided the features of closural sentences into global and local phenomena, and on each level, into syntactic and lexical features. I'll illustrate with the last line of Poe's story, "Ligeia": "'Here then, at least,' I shrieked aloud, 'can I never—can I never be mistaken—these are the full, and the black, and the wild eyes—of my lost love—of the Lady—of the Lady Ligeia!'"[15]

Global

1. *Syntactic:* These signals occur when the target sentence completes a narrative structure such as the overcoming of an obstacle, the return to an earlier state or event, the achievement of equilibrium, or the rendering of antithesis or paradox.[16] Ligeia's reappearance in the body of Rowena illustrates an obstacle (physical law) overcome, a return to an earlier state (life), and a paradox rendered (life-in-death; horror-in-love, etc.)

2. *Lexical:* These signals occur when the target sentence includes a word naming an end state in relation to the story as a whole, such as sleep, death, parting, or what John Gerlach calls "natural terminations." There is nothing very "natural" about the ending of Poe's story, but the presence of Ligeia's eyes confirms that Rowena is not only dead but displaced, that is, "gone for good." Note that this category includes the *natural-event terminals* and *image recursions* discussed in chapter 2.

Local

1. *Syntactic:* These signals have to do with the design of the target sentence itself, including repetition or parallelism, and inversion (as in the subject/verb order of "At last came his dying breath"). Parallelism may work on the level of a single letter (as in alliteration) or of a word, a phrase, or a clause. The relation may be identical (dog, dog), coordinate (dog, cat), or disjunctive (dog, apple). The degree of repetition may be double, triple, or serial. The Poe sentence is rich in parallelism, including a double triple at the phrase level.

2. *Lexical:*

    a. *Closural words:* Some words are patently closural, either by naming such a condition (end, final, last, etc.), by positing an absolute or excessive degree of some condition (all, nothing, every, none, etc.), by closing a logical relationship of either sequence or opposition (then, thus, but, however, etc.), or simply by marking a temporal shift (then, after, [in] future, etc.). All four kinds of closural words are intertextual; they have closural force in any story. The sample sentence includes the closural words *then, never,* and *lost.*

    b. *Keywords:* These are words that have been privileged in the given text because of natural prominence (characters' names), special "loading" (symbols), or significant repetition (recurrent images). Most of them can be classified by what they refer to: a person, a thing, an action, or an idea. Like a lexical refrain, they arrest us. In the sample, the keywords include *eyes, love,* and *Ligeia.*

For this experiment, I also asked a number of qualitative questions of the target sentences, such as: Did the keywords primarily identify things or ideas? A fuller list of these questions will appear in the second part of this chapter.

By coding these signals, and entering them into a simple database program, I was able to learn, very quickly, their distribution. In "Preclosure by Stages," I'll look at all anterior sentences, then all penultimate sentences, then all closural sentences, to see what generalizations I can make about these three stages of closure, regardless of the period in which the stories were written. In "Preclosure by Periods," I'll study the workings of closure in each of the three chronological periods.

Preclosure by Stages

As I looked at the three stages of closure, certain findings were predictable. Anterior sentences, coming earliest in the sequence, are least authoritative. For example, among sentences registering a global syntactic feature, especially "obstacle removed," those expressing a *character's* point of view are more often anterior sentences (characters who were also narrators were excluded from this category), and usually the character is revealing a false or temporary perception. These sentences are points of transition in the complete story the author wrote.

By contrast, penultimate sentences, being the last preclosure points before the end, very often show a gain in authority and stability. "Returns," when they do appear, are more likely to be in the penultimate slot, while "paradoxes" are *least* likely to occur there. The global syntactic antiplot of "goal *un*reached" almost never appears in the penultimate position. Sentences signaling obstacle removed from a *narrator's* point of view are much more likely to show up in penultimate sentences. Narrators may be unreliable, but they exert a cumulative and finally tremendous pressure on the tale, especially *just before* the author ends the story.

Looking for those times when a global syntactic signal (such as obstacle removed or "equilibrium achieved") was left up to the *reader's* perception (rather than a character's sense or a narrator's claim), I found that most of them occur in the final slot (recall that the narrator's point of view prevails in the penultimate slot). At the actual end of stories, syntactic figuration is least evident; these sentences are the lowest in repetitions and parallelisms, and none contain a subject/verb inversion. Alliteration occurs half as often in the closural slot, compared with the anterior and penultimate locations. On the other hand, local *lexical* signals abound. Final sentences have the highest incidence of keywords and closural words. It's as if the global markers subside, unneeded in the presence of the blank space ahead, while the local markers step forth for a parting flourish.

Overall, the data suggest a normative staging of closure. There tends to be a congestion and/or complication of meaning in the anterior slot, an almost lyrical or rhetorically stable high point in the penultimate slot, and a multidetermined field in the final slot. Is this metascenario just a reflection of one reader's choice of preclosure points? Is it just a restatement of time-honored plot diagrams, such as complication, crisis, and denouement? Does it occur in real texts, or is it only an extrapolation? Let me delay my conclusions for a moment for a brief look at "Rappaccini's Daughter" by Nathaniel Hawthorne.

Recall, if you will, how Beatrice, organically poisoned by tending the plants her father has created, yet pure in heart and spirit, drinks the antidote offered by her doubting lover and dies as a result. Her cry of reproach is my anterior preclosure point: "Oh, was there not, from the first, more poison in thy nature than in mine?"[17] We're brought up short on the horns of a moral and physical dilemma—who, and therefore what, is the true evil in this perverse Eden? The target sentence is a generalization from a character's (Beatrice's) point of view and, while it implies a *yes* answer, offers no real solution to the conundrum of guilt.

A more authoritative voice, the narrator's, resonates in the highly figured penultimate slot. Note the alliteration: "To Beatrice,—so radically had her earthly part been wrought upon by Rappaccini's skill,—as poison had been life, so the powerful antidote was death; and thus the poor victim of man's ingenuity and of thwarted nature, and of the fatality that attends all such efforts of perverted wisdom, perished there, at the feet of her father and Giovanni" (209). The sense of paradox remains, of course, but rather than the cruel impasse of a lover-turned-murderer, it is a judgment on man's hubris. The rhythmic alliteration, the balanced syntax, turns this sentence into a rising affirmation of the moral order. We respond to cadence as much as to plot. Had the story ended here, it would have been a morality play. It would have intoned its message.

However, the story *doesn't* end there. It ends here: "Just at that moment Professor Pietro Baglioni looked forth from the window, and called loudly, in a tone of triumph mixed with horror, to the thunderstricken man of science,—'Rappaccini, Rappaccini! and is *this* the upshot of your experiment?'" (209). There are many global syntactic signals here: the structures of return (Baglioni reappears after a long absence from the story), equilibrium (Baglioni's revenge cancels his feud with Rappaccini), and paradox (Rappaccini's greatest achievement is his greatest loss). Obstacles are removed: Giovanni's doubts and Beatrice's earthly suffering. The global lexical features include the parting of the lovers and the end of an experiment and a life. On the local level, there are closural words (stricken, triumph, upshot) and keywords (Baglioni, window, horror, science, Rappaccini, experiment). What a glut of closural signals, many at cross purposes! This is multidetermination with a vengeance.

The staging of closure in this particular story does, indeed, illustrate the normative pattern I outlined. Of course, it does so in a distinctively Hawthornian way. We can see him mapping his own notions of human fallibility onto the sequence of anterior complication, penultimate high point, and closural multidetermination—which means, in his case, ambiguity.

Yet if preclosure points are primarily evidence of the *reader's* way of encoding storyness, we could say that we are staging our own reception of the story. The cognitive strategy of storying is at work even as we process what is given to us *as* story. The sequence ending with Beatrice's betrayal is, cognitively, a usable chunk. We can store it, in scenario form, as information that bears on well-being: don't trust the Giovannis of the world. We can do the same with the sequence ending in Hawthorne's sermon: Rappaccini's fate horrifies, warns, and moves us. What we're experiencing as readers is a complicated interplay between our own capacity for storying and the peculiar sequence of confirmations and revisions the text has to offer. We are modifying the structure of the text even as we read it, and, in turn, it is modifying, enriching, specializing our perception of the story—and of life.

Do the results above simply confirm traditional diagrams of dramatic structure? If so, we would be left with a chicken-or-egg proposition: Do the diagrams reflect some primal cognitive structure, or are our reading strategies the product of long exposure to rule-bound stories? R. L. Gregory's suggestion that "organisms are controlled by fictions rather than stimuli" supports the notion of primal circuitry, while studies of the way children learn to recognize and tell stories can support either claim.[18] My preclosure studies certainly can't resolve the debate. Their value, it seems to me, is as an interpretive tool for individual stories and as a window on the ways in which the short story genre differs from other narrative forms. Traditional plot diagrams of the stories I've reviewed would highlight crisis points, whereas the above preclosure analysis highlights, at the penultimate preclosure point, a rhetorical emphasis in relationship to stylistic features that couldn't be predicted from the standard "plot" model.

The upshot of my unfashionably formalist analysis is that the sense of storyness is not a product of aesthetic experience as traditional formalists might argue, but rather a primary act of cognition—if you will, a management strategy in aid of understanding. That it should be called into play, triggered, thwarted, exercised in the process of reading is, of course, an aesthetic as well as a moral and, some might say, a political experience. Trying to describe what is unique to the short story form, critics and artists alike have borrowed from the discourse of poetry and religion. Perhaps the discourse of cognitive psychology is no more precise. Yet when people ask me why brevity should so consort with power, why short stories are different from other narrative forms, I suggest to them that it is because, in the configuration of its movement toward closure, the short story models most closely the neural basis of storying.

Preclosure by Periods

For the second part of this study, I looked at the data through the lens of historical period. I found that sentences that triggered my sense of storyness in the Early period (1820–50) are more than twice as likely to come at the end of a paragraph as the preclosure sentences in either the Modern (1920–40) or the Contemporary (1960–80) periods. The higher coincidence of closural sentences and paragraph endings in the Early period certainly has to do with well-known features of nineteenth-century stories: the authors' more intrusive (and expository) treatment of information and the more prominent and clearly jointed movement of plot. It also has something to do with the changing conventions of paragraphing itself: the trend has been away from the paragraph as a block of thought toward the paragraph as a visual aid. This is a change to which the text processor, whether human or artificial, must adapt. In twentieth-century stories, signals of closure are less reliably encoded as indentations in the text.

Does this shift hint at a general decrease in syntactic markers of closure as we move through the history of the American short story? I did find that closural sentences in Early stories are more likely than those in Modern or Contemporary stories to have an inverted subject-verb order. The relative incidence was 4:2:0 (a notation system I use from now on to indicate the real number of occurrences of a given phenomenon in each of the three periods). The anterior preclosure sentence in Washington Irving's "The Legend of Sleepy Hollow" is an example: "In one part of the road leading to the church, *was found the saddle* trampled in the dirt; the tracks of horses' hoofs deeply dented in the road, and evidently at furious speed, were traced to the bridge, beyond which, on the bank of a broad part of the brook, where the water ran deep and black, *was found the hat* of the unfortunate Ichabod, and close beside it a shattered pumpkin" (emphases mine; this sentence, by the way, ends a paragraph).[19]

Closural sentences in Early stories are also more likely (17:1:12) to display the local syntactic feature of alliteration. Note that in the sentence just quoted, *d*s dominate, and a string of *b*s creates a striking—and braking—effect: bridge, beyond, bank, broad, brook, black. Triple parallelisms also appear more often in Early than in Modern or Contemporary stories (13:0:7)—another predictable finding, given the association between tricolons and formal, "old-fashioned" prose style.

Let's slice the data another way, focusing on parallelism as a formal property within closural sentences. We might expect to see it decline as we move into and through the twentieth century. However, that is not true for my sample. Instead, there is an overall drop in the Modern stories, followed by an overall—and equally dramatic—upswing in the Contemporary texts (31:13:33). It's worth taking a moment to comment on what seems like the first surprising twist in the data. The high total in the Contemporary period includes an unusual number of repetitions at the serial degree, repetitions in the identical relation, and repetitions on the level of clauses. Here is an example of a word-level, coordinate-relation, serial-degree repetition in the final sentence of John Cheever's "The Swimmer": "He shouted, pounded on the door, tried to force it with his shoulder, and then, looking in at the windows, saw that the place was empty."[20] Here is a clause-level, coordinate doublet, with several word-level identities, in the anterior closural sentence of Ann Beattie's "A Clever-Kid's Story": "He really thought *that he would always be* in control, *that he would always be* the storyteller" (emphases mine).[21] Linguistically speaking, all of these features suggest a general shift to paratactic as opposed to hypotactic structures. Cognitively speaking, they suggest that closure in contemporary stories is less integrative and more iterative.

Though less highly figured in conventional stylistic ways, closural sentences in the Contemporary period do seem more like their Early than like their Modern predecessors in relying on the surface structure of language to signal closure. But it is significant that Early stories rely more on doublets and triplets, as opposed to the serial repetitions found more often in Contemporary samples. Pairs and triads build relationships; serial repetition is a step toward what we might think of as cognitive entropy. The rising incidence of serial repetitions in the closural sentences of Contemporary stories may suggest modifications in the cognitive model for storyness, as we shall see later.

Let me turn, now, to the lexical features of closural sentences. As you recall, these are divided into two main categories: closural words and keywords. Closural words suggest an inherently terminal status, while keywords are those that have been privileged in the given text. Overall, the highest incidence of lexical features occurred in the closural sentences of the Early period (78:59:57). There were slightly more time-related closural words (10:3:6) and noticeably more face-value closural words like *end* (18:8:10). We would expect these findings, for, as we know, nineteenth-century stories tend toward greater resolution on the level of plot.

What would we expect in the Modern period? Thinking of Ernest Hemingway's stories, we would look for the highest incidence of thing-related keywords. Interestingly enough, when coding keywords in this period, I found myself often torn between the categories *thing* and *idea*. References to things, pure and simple, occurred least often in the Modern period (11:4:12); however, references to things-as-ideas occurred most often there (4:17:8). So, for example, in Sherwood Anderson's "I Want to Know Why," the penultimate closural sentence gives us a keyword, *[race] tracks*, that refers as much to a complex of ideas (the previously idealized world of horses) as to a physical place: "At the tracks the air don't taste as good or smell as good [as it did before]."[22] Maybe we've only confirmed the modernist dictum: "no ideas but in things." And yet, if we look at keywords referring to ideas *not* in things—that is, abstractions—we find they occur nearly as often in the Modern as in the Early periods. Where they decline is in the Contemporary period (45:43:26). These data, like the high incidence of syntactic replication in Contemporary stories, may eventually lead us to a more precise understanding of the "difficulty" of stories in this period—and of the cognitive adjustments required.

Turning from local to global features, let's consider the three stories defined by each of the three targeted sentences: anterior, penultimate, and final. The final story is, of course, the one we normally think of, the one designated by the title. The local features of the preclosural sentences may be enough to signal the end of an anterior or penultimate story; more often, however, these features reinforce the global signals, resulting in the cognitive chunking of the text into story units. We must therefore look at the closural sentences *in relation to the stories they terminate.*

It's time now to list the qualitative questions I asked of each closural sentence. Did it refer to a specific action or idea, or did it summarize a state of affairs previously developed? Did it represent the point of view of a previously introduced character other than the narrator, a first-person narrator, an implied author speaking from a limited point of view, or an implied author speaking from an omniscient point of view? Did the sentence offer a return to an earlier action or state of affairs, or an achieved equilibrium, or an unresolved paradox? Did it represent an obstacle removed, a problem solved, or a goal achieved—or the inverse of these outcomes—and for whom? Did it refer to a natural terminus like death, sleep, day's end—or to a conventional terminus like parting (the end of a visit) or [re]joining (a homecoming, a marriage)—or to a perceptual terminus like satisfaction of a need (even a minimal one) or being in the status quo?[23]

Closural sentences in the Early period exhibited the highest incidence of references to death (13:3:6) and of problems solved (23:9:13)—as perceived by the reader rather than explicitly realized by a character or stated by a narrator (11:2:3). So, indeed, we'd expect of more "plotted" stories. The Modern period offered the highest number of inverse outcomes (0:9:5), the lowest incidence of omniscience in point of view (10:1:7), and the most frequent reliance on a character's perspective (13:19:13)—all suggesting the Hemingwayesque withdrawal of the narrator from a position of authority in a world where generations can be lost and only individuals may, if lucky, survive.

In the Contemporary period, terminals based on satisfaction (the weakest of the positive closural states) were most frequent (5:4:13). This finding is consistent with what we have discovered about Contemporary stories so far. It is no news that stories after 1960 often avoid the clear joining, logical progression, and neat resolution of conventionally plotted fiction; however, it is interesting to consider whether the processing intelligence comes to rely more on local than on global signals, or learns to detect more successfully the fewer, fainter signals we have noted. Or does it need to reconfigure itself in some primary way so that it responds to different signals altogether? That is a question toward which I have been pointing throughout this discussion. More work needs to be done before it can be answered, but the present experiment allows us to take one more step.

We can look at the anterior, penultimate, and final closural sentences *as a sequence*. This is what I call the staging of closure. Describing this process means taking into account all of the features discussed above and putting them into relationship as three stages of closure within a story. We've already seen that Early stories are more discursive, rhetorically and stylistically figured, and highly resolved than stories in the later periods. Looking at the anterior sentences in relation to the penultimate sentence in relation to the final sentence in story after story in this period, I asked myself whether I could identify a normative cognitive progression, a typical way in which closure was staged. What these stories offered, it seemed to me, was a cognitive adjustment from wonder to wisdom: *Has this really happened?* → *This is what's happened.* → *This is the way things happen.*

In the Modern group, anterior closure sentences tended to make simple, naïve declarations. Here are some examples from Anderson's "The Egg," Hemingway's "Indian Camp," and F. Scott Fitzgerald's "Babylon Revisited": "The egg broke under his hand"; "He couldn't stand things, I guess"; " . . . I lost everything I wanted in the boom."[24] Penultimate closural sentences tended to make statements of fact that were more loaded, triggering a degree of cognitive processing hardly suggested by the surface features of the discourse. Here are the corresponding examples from the same stories: "The question got into my blood" (Anderson, 147); "The sun was coming up over the hills" (Hemingway, 21); " . . . they couldn't make him pay forever" (Fitzgerald, 341).

Final sentences in the Modern period were, as many people have noted, often tinged with irony on the part of either the narrator or the implied author: "And that, I conclude, is but another evidence of the complete and final triumph of the egg—at least as far as my family is concerned" (Anderson, 147); "In the early morning on the lake sitting in the stern of the boat with his father rowing, he felt quite sure that he would never die" (Hemingway, 21); "He was absolutely sure Helen wouldn't have wanted him to be so alone" (Fitzgerald, 341). According to my sample and my preclosure choices, Modern stories often move the reader along from a naïve world view toward a skeptical one: *This is the way things are.* → *This is the way they are if one reads between the lines.* → *This is the way one thinks they are, but they really aren't.*

Now let's look at the Contemporary period. I'll illustrate with Joyce Carol Oates's "Where are You Going, Where Have You Been?," Ursula Le Guin's "Schrödinger's Cat," and Raymond Carver's "Why Don't You Dance?" The anterior closure sentences were about four times more likely to be evaluative comments than statements of action: " . . . they don't know one thing about you and never did and honey, you're better than them because not a one of them would have done this for you" (Oates); "'We used to think so,' I said, 'but really we should use larger boxes'" (Le Guin); "'You must be desperate or something,' she said" (Carver).[25] Penultimate sentences were more than twice as likely to offer a character's subjective reaction than a summary comment: "She watched herself push the door slowly open as if she were back safe somewhere in the other doorway, watching this body and this head of long hair moving out into the sunlight where Arnold Friend waited" (Oates, 54); "He gazed about him in mute bewilderment, and did not flinch even when the roof of the house was lifted off just like the lid of a box, letting in the unconscionable, inordinate light of the stars" (Le Guin, 49); "There was more to it, and she was trying to get it talked out" (Carver, 10).

Final sentences were about four times more likely to show a character at risk but adjusting in a strange world, rather than either fully integrated or truly embattled within it: " . . . the vast sunlit reaches of the land behind him and on all sides of him—so much land that Connie had never seen before and did not recognize except to know that she was going to it" (Oates, 54); "I wonder if he found what it was we lost" (Le Guin, 49); "After a time, she quit trying" (Carver, 10). In the Contemporary stories, the staging of closure reversed the direction taken in the Early period, now moving the reader away from rather than toward cognitive control: *This is the way things seem.* → *This is the way they feel.* → *This is the way it goes.*

As I mentioned at the beginning of this chapter, studies of closure helped turn short story criticism into short story theory. Studies of preclosure, as I have designed and performed them, push even further toward a theory of storyness. Those conducted with many readers of one story offer more objective evidence to work with, but in any case the training and sensibility of the investigator are necessarily in the picture. Happily so, I would argue, if we are interested in the value of these experiments to literary study.

That value, it seems to me, is at least threefold. Looking for preclosure is, first of all, a pedagogical strategy. It turns even the most naïve student into a valued analyst—which is good for morale. Second, it is a critical tool; the collation of many readers' preclosure choices within and across stories turns intuitions into data. These data yield insight. Third and most important, it is a theoretical heuristic, prodding us to think about literary response as cognitive management. By now, you are familiar with the mantra: *storying is a way of processing experience in the interests of*

chapter five

Katherine Mansfield and Sandra Cisneros

The two stories considered in this chapter seem worlds apart. They are separated by seventy years and a hemisphere. There is a mandarin quality in Katherine Mansfield's work, even in this story about a life-battered charwoman, that is out of fashion today. We prefer the earthy ethnicity at the heart of Sandra Cisneros's lyricism. Yet both stories have a lot to say about the social influences on identity formation. So vividly do both stories portray the constraints on female expression, autonomy, and fulfillment, that they appear to be documentation for a feminist argument.

In today's literature classroom, where the emphasis is so often on matters of race, gender, and class, these stories are eminently usable. It is a failure of responsibility to study and appreciate them fully without regard to their "messages." There are times, however, when the social significance is so much in the air, so much a part of the context in which the stories are read, that the cultural index precedes the narrative experience. In these cases, preclosure study is, in my view, a healthy alternative. It offers a way of starting with the story and ending with the relevance, an approach that is fairer to the author and truer to the art form. Here are two cases in point.

Early Twentieth-century London, a Literary Gentleman's Apartment

She's a widowed charwoman. Yesterday, her loving little grandson, the light of her dreary life, was buried. As servant, wife, and mother, she's the generic British working-class female at the turn of the century—cowed by drudgery and burdened by loss. Her husband, a baker, died of "white lung" disease, and those children who survived the high rate of infant mortality fell victim to other ills of the late-Victorian underclass: emigration, prostitution, poor health, worse luck. This is the life of Ma Parker, who comes to work after her grandson's burial, stunned by a grief she can barely stand. Her employer, a "literary gentleman" out of touch with humanity, hopes "the funeral was a—a—success." What a day! What a life! If only there were someplace to go—certainly not a room of her own, but a corner, a stoop—where she could "be herself" and have, for the first time in her life, "a proper cry." As the final line says, "There was nowhere."[1]

Katherine Mansfield's "Life of Ma Parker" is an unabashed tearjerker. The old cleaning woman keeps her eyes dry, but *we're* not supposed to. In fact, the emotional bribery is so patent, the assault on pity so bold, it's hard not to dismiss this story as an embarrassing lapse, one of quite a number of stories in which Mansfield's tougher insights and cooler ironies fail to control her sentimentality. The story is dissipated in the emotive response, which is triggered too simply and spent too quickly.

At the same time, there is a quantity of sociological detail, an imaginative empathy, a spare iconography of working-class life that make the story a perfect set piece for cultural studies. Indeed, in today's climate of social awareness in the literary classroom, it is very hard to find readers—either students or teachers—who will not approach this story primed to talk about gender and class issues. Such readers, one would think, are just the ones to appreciate the story.

What often happens, however, is that the issues, valid and important as they are, frame the reading process so exclusively that the story becomes an ideological product. Like Ma's employer, the literary gentleman who takes a passing interest in "this product called Life," such readers hypostatize the "life" represented in the story (capitalizing Women and Working-class). While they do so with much encouragement from Mansfield, and with considerably more insight and sympathy than her male character displays, they, too, are allowing the story to dissipate and escape them.

As a short story theorist and a teacher, I want to know what we can find in this tale when we do not "spend" it too quickly as sob story or, for that matter, as protest story. The question might be worth asking simply because "Life of Ma Parker," composed in 1920, dates from the same period as those firmly controlled masterpieces, "Miss Brill" and "Daughters of the Late Colonel." However, it is also worth asking because the sins of this one little story—exaggerated affect, subordination of character to type, social pathology, oversimplified message—have all, at one time or another, in various guises and degrees, been charged against the *genre* of the short story.

While it is obviously true that this one text does not stand for all stories, nor even for one category of fictions (modernist, impressionist, working-class, feminist, etc.), I am once again suggesting that my approach fits many a tale that claims our attention yet resists our engagement, either because (as in chapters 2 and 3) the story presents special difficulties to the student or because (as in this instance) it can be grasped *too* easily. I want to slow down the reading process in order to track it more carefully, to net more value from a short[er] fiction.

As a context for what I am about to do, let me first mention two of the more usual ways of approaching Mansfield's story: formalist and biographical. "Life of Ma Parker" is rarely anthologized and hardly ever taught, and then only, one supposes, as a checklist of modernist techniques: controlled point of view (it shifts deftly from one character to the other in the first half-page), free indirect discourse (we often hear echoes of Ma's speech in the narrator's voice), cinematic flashbacks (with implied fade-ins and fade-outs), a pair of famous impressionist images (in the rainy street, "the men walked like scissors; the women trod like cats"), and the signature open ending that withholds resolution. Calling students' attention to these technical achievements, to the ways in which the *sujet* is transformed into the *fabula,* is certainly worth doing, although there are better examples in the Mansfield canon. Yet, in the case of this rather slim artifact, I'm inclined to agree with the cultural historians: a formalist approach, used alone, is unsatisfying.

More inviting, especially to those who see Mansfield as a tragic figure, are the biographical echoes. The grandson who dies of pleurisy (one of Mansfield's own diseases) evokes Charlie Walter, the sickly little boy sent to Mansfield, like an emotional care package, while she was recovering from a miscarriage at a German spa in 1909.[2] Ma Parker, one of a number of working-class, female isolatos portrayed with genuine sympathy and understanding in Mansfield's work, may well derive from one of the servants Mansfield employed over the years, a class of woman she seems to have observed closely.[3] It is tempting to see the unnamed literary gentleman as a sly joke on her occasional roommate, fellow writer, and eventual husband, John Middleton Murry, whose delicate aversion to "this product called Life" often frustrated Mansfield. Or the portrait may be an even slyer, gender-bending parody of her own inadequacies. The literary gentleman is royally insensitive but also awkward, misguided, and alone in the world.

However, the relationship at the core of the story—the coy and tender interaction between a child and a mothering grandparent—reaches back into Mansfield's childhood. These scenes strongly resemble more famous ones between Mrs. Fairfield and Kezia in the autobiographical stories "The Prelude" and "At the Bay." All biographers of Mansfield agree that she never received the love she needed from her withdrawn and self-centered mother, finding some modicum of steadiness and affection in her maternal grandmother, Mrs. Dyer. Thus, in the relationship between Ma Parker and little Lennie, the childless (and eventually sterile) Mansfield inhabits the position of the loving mother she did not have and could not be, as well as the position of the beloved child, which she never was and could not have. A story we disparage for overflowing sentiment looks suddenly efficient, encoding vast amounts of hurt in 202 sentences. The biographical approach shows us, in particularly succinct terms, how art can transform an excess of self-pity. Yet, again, there is more to the story.

It's easy to find that "more" in the social content of the tale. Flashbacks from Ma Parker's own history—her cruel apprenticeship as a cook's helper, her husband's death from an occupational disease, her family's diaspora into the byways of poverty, emigration, and prostitution—read like a lesson in demographics. The good student, therefore, will speak feelingly and expertly about the absence of a welfare net, about the limited social and economic choices for the working-class family, about the class-coded barriers to communication between the charwoman and the literary gentleman, about the gender-coded expectation that Ma should swallow her suffering. These readers will know what the author is telling them: that women like this one were marginalized by society. End of story.

"Not so fast, not so fast," I want to tell them. But, in teaching as in writing, it is better to illustrate. So—naturally—I ask them to do a pre-closure exercise. I give them a transcription of the story with the sentences numbered and paragraphing removed (though, in this case, section breaks were marked by Mansfield's ellipses). I ask them to list the sentences that give them a feeling of closure—as if the story *could* have ended at that point. I turn my students into a distributed reader. As I have elsewhere shown, this empirically defined reader, no matter how naïve the constituent real readers may be, has a kind of wisdom no scholar can offer.

In the present case, I gave the exercise to two different undergraduate classes at the University of Iowa, for a combined total of 51 readers.[4] The ratio of females to males was 38:13, or almost exactly 3:1. Altogether, 149 preclosure points were chosen. As usual, I will focus on one or two choices with special relevance, and then on the set of most-favored choices.

My first discovery was a noticeable gender bias in some of the results. Just as I found in the Cortázar experiment, readers choosing the earliest preclosure points were disproportionately male. The very earliest choice, defining the very shortest putative story, occurred at sentence S/15. The sentences leading up to it describe Ma Parker's arrival at her employer's flat, his awkward attempt to acknowledge her personal tragedy, his culminating faux pas, and Ma's response to it. Here is what happens:

S/9   He could hardly go back to the warm sitting-room without saying something—something more.
S/10   Then because these people set such store by funerals he said kindly, "I hope the funeral went off all right."
S/11   "Beg parding, sir?" said old Ma Parker huskily.
S/12   Poor old bird!
S/13   She did look dashed.
S/14   "I hope the funeral was a—a—success," said he.
S/15   *Ma Parker gave no answer.*
S/16   She bent her head and hobbled off to the kitchen . . . (484)

Although only one person chose S/15 as a preclosure point, it is not an eccentric choice. The previous sentence ends with inverted syntax ("said he" rather than "he said"), a linguistic marker associated with closure. The sentence after it denotes a change of venue—one of the most common and powerful markers of narrative initiative, back-signaling closure in the previous sentence. The target sentence itself, S/15, includes a lexical closural signal, the negative absolute *no*.

If we look at the putative story that would end at S/15, it is a minimal one, indeed. Not much more than an anecdote. What "happens" is a failure of communication caused primarily by class difference (note the employer's assumption about "these people") but also by the difference between a peremptory male and a grief-burdened woman. Although this is not the subtlest of Mansfield's portraits of social and gender difference, it has her deft economy, her needling wit, her fluid sympathy. In the first fifteen lines, the viewpoint is *his,* not hers. I found it interesting that the only reader who could imagine the story ending here was a male.

Five readers chose S/24, still very early in the text (12 percent of the way through). The literary gentleman has returned to his breakfast, Ma Parker is removing her hat, her coat, and the boots that cruelly pinch her feet:

S/22   To take off her boots or to put them on was an agony to her, but it had been an agony for years.

S/23   In fact, she was so accustomed to the pain that her face was drawn and screwed up ready for the twinge before she'd so much as untied the laces.

S/24   *That over, she sat back with a sigh and softly rubbed her knees. . . .* [Mansfield's ellipsis]

S/25   "Gran!" [Here begins a remembered scene with her grandson.] (484–85)

Once again, a change in venue—this time a dramatic flashback—signals a new beginning, giving closural force to the sentence before. That sentence also features the strongly closural word *over* (in the sense of completed, done), and a heightened lexical feature (the assonance of *that, sat,* and *back* combined with the alliteration of *sat, sigh,* and *softly*). At first, this putative story seems to add little to the anecdote mentioned above, simply following each of the characters into his or her separate world within this one dwelling, and zeroing in—very much as a cinematic close-up might—on the telling image of the aching feet. Note that the viewpoint has shifted. Now it is *hers,* not his.

Nevertheless, of the three readers choosing this preclosure point, two were male and one was female. Overall, if we look at the choices of sentences prior to S/25, we find that four were made by four different men and two were made by the same woman. This 4:1 ratio of male to female readers is all the more startling when we remember that the ratio of male to female readers was 1:3. At least within the limits of *this* distributed reader, there is clearly a gender bias in the choice of early preclosure points. Male readers were more willing to accept the story as "over" much sooner.

As I mentioned above, it is not my intention to avoid or downplay the importance of social issues in this or any story. My objective is to keep students from plugging in ready-made concepts and responses that say more about their prior course work than about the story at hand. Preclosure exercises are a way of engaging one part of their knowledge, their story competence, while temporarily suppressing another part of their knowledge, their issue awareness. The purpose is to bring them back to the issues via the reading experience of this particular story.

When I reported my findings to the readers who had generated them, I had their attention. They were as full of questions as I. Why would male readers be more receptive to *these* putative stories? Why the shortest ones? Why the ones with anecdotal force? Why the ones that depict an encounter between two persons of unequal power and sensitivity, an encounter that encodes the difference without resolving it or absorbing its emotional fallout? (Here, in response to revelations from the reading experience, was the place for the lexicon of gender relations.) Our answers, our further questions, brought us back to the literary gentleman's treatment of Ma. Why is he so willing to wrap up his response to her, to dismiss it—and her—summarily? To readers who have just been confronted with their *own* gender bias, the answers to these questions can seem much more telling.

Gender bias on the female side is evident in another choice, which happens also to be the most-favored preclosure point. By the time we reach S/167, we know all about the financial and emotional deprivations of Ma's life; we know that Lennie was the focus of all her love, all her joy, all her hope. Now, for apparently the first time, she acknowledges to herself that she has had a hard life. As this thought gains momentum, as her misery deepens, she realizes she has never cried in front of people. All her life, she has internalized her sorrows, accepting them, going about the business of serving her family and her employer. For what?

S/162 Lennie gone—what had she?

S/163 She had nothing.

S/164 He was all she'd got from life, and now he was took too.

S/165 Why must it all have happened to me? she wondered.

S/166 "What have I done?" said old Ma Parker.

S/167 *"What have I done?"*

S/168 As she said those words she suddenly let fall her brush. (489)

Thirteen readers (25 percent) chose S/167. Twelve were female, one was male. Even with the higher percentage of women in the group as a whole, the gender bias is clear: women were more likely to choose this preclosure point and, consequently, the putative story it caps. None of the other highly favored preclosure points shows this degree of gender bias. Most show little or none. Not only were women more likely to respond to this sentence, but they did so in large enough numbers to make it the most popular choice overall. Why? If male readers were more willing to wrap up the story as a telling anecdote, why were female readers more willing to end it with an open-ended question that is either plaintive or assertive—or both?

Before we can speculate about these questions ourselves, we need to look at the results of the experiment as a whole. Interesting as it may be to study individual choices that are especially revealing, the wisdom of the distributed reader is to be found, as always, in the *series* of putative stories defined by the most-favored preclosure choices. In determining these, I had to decide whether to look only at the individual sentences, or to count, as one slightly vibrating point, a cluster of two or three neighboring sentences that were highly favored. As I've done in the past, I decided to follow the second course, using only the top five clusters. I've listed them in the order they appear in the story, noting some of the preclosure signals that helped to trigger these choices:

1. *Ten readers chose one of the sentences that end Ma's interaction with her employer. Possibly to redress his own feeling of inadequacy in dealing with Ma's grief, he has just accused her, indirectly, of stealing a spoonful of cocoa:*

   S/136   And he walked off very well pleased with himself, convinced, in fact, he'd shown Mrs. Parker that under his apparent carelessness he was as vigilant as a woman.
   S/137   The door banged. [closural word] (488–89)

2. *Eighteen readers zeroed in on the words bursting from Ma's lips after she reviews her hard life. As noted above, S/167 was chosen overwhelmingly by women:*

   S/167   "What have I done?"
   S/168   As she said those words, she suddenly let fall her brush. [syntactic inversion] (489)

3. *Twenty-two readers chose the moment shortly after, when Ma wanders out into the London streets:*

S/172   She was like a person so dazed by the horror of what has happened that he walks away—anywhere, as though by walking away he could escape. . . . [Mansfield's ellipsis]
S/176   And nobody knew—nobody cared. [repetition; negative absolute]
S/180   Gran wants to cry. (489–90)

4. *Eleven readers focused on her growing need to cry:*

S/185   She couldn't put it off any longer; she couldn't wait any more . . . [repetition; negative absolute] (490)

5. *Nine readers chose the next-to-last sentence:*

S/201   And now it began to rain. [change of space/time/condition] (490)

There is no doubt that the true ending is grim. Unfortunately, it is muddied by overdone pathos. Ma looks everywhere for a place to cry, but even her family offers no refuge, for it needs her to be strong. There is no public or private space for her to be by herself and for herself. She's utterly alone. "And now it began to rain." Whether a naturalist fillip or a London verity, the drizzle is too much. And yet the very last line, the *actual* closure of the story, has an echoing bleakness: "There was nowhere." It is Mansfield chiming in with the empty universe.

The actual story is very sad, indeed. But what of those putative stories we have discovered along the way? Here is my list of them.

Social Vignette. When the employer strides off, pleased with himself and letting the door bang behind him, we're left with a story whose "point" is to reveal the character of these two parties to a relationship: male and female; employer and employee.

Epiphanic Tale. When Ma asks "What have I done?" she is, for the very first time, questioning life's equity. This is the primeval "Why me?" At first, the words suggest a desire for information: did she in fact do something to deserve this kind of life? However, as the question echoes in the reader's mind and in hers, it becomes a protest, for she *hasn't* deserved her pain. There is a dawning awareness of in-grained injustice, although the full epiphany is reserved for the reader as part of the emotional and intellectual modulation effected by the story.

Existential Parable. This is the story that ends with Ma becoming Everyman who suffers. She is compared, rather objectively, to "a person so dazed by the horror of what has happened that he [note the generic pronoun] walks away. . ." The closural force of the negative absolute ["nobody knew; nobody cared"] echoes the existential themes of loneliness and abandonment.

Feminist Exemplum. Realizing her loneliness, Ma thinks of her grandson, Lennie, and imagines herself talking to him: "Ah, that's what she wants to do, my dove. Gran wants to cry." Throughout her life, her wants have rarely been satisfied; more to the point, they have rarely been acknowledged, even by herself. Now, however, in the short declarative statement that ends this story, Ma states what *she* needs. Behind the third-person of *she* and *Gran*, an urgency is developing, an *I* is emerging. From a feminist perspective, this is a tragically meager, yet relatively great achievement for a woman like Ma.

Psychological Case Study. In another pair of negative absolutes (not any longer, not any more), we're told that Ma has arrived at a crisis: she *must* cry, and she must cry *now*. Desire becomes decision. The story that ends here brings Ma through diffidence and depression to a point of built-up pressure that threatens to explode. She is on the brink of a crying jag, a flood of tears that would, in both feminine lore and post-Freudian psychology, offer healing release.

Each of these putative stories is different, even though the basic roster of characters and events remains the same, and even though portions of the text are identical from story to story. Each *acts* on us differently, both emotionally and intellectually: we are wryly, maybe poignantly amused by the social vignette; moved by the epiphany that questions the moral universe; chilled by the bleakness of the existential parable; stirred by the feminist exemplum, the gain in self-consciousness; satisfied, perhaps cheered, by the everyday truth of the psychological study.

Our experience of these stories in succession is an integral part of what it means to read "Life of Ma Parker." I believe this to be true even though, obviously, other experiments might yield a slightly different configuration of preclosure points, and even though my choice of just five putative stories is arbitrary (those chosen by at least 15 percent of the readership). And, of course, under "normal" conditions, we are not conscious of ticking off preclosure points and, therefore, of making our way through a series of putative stories. However, we can raise that consciousness by activating story competence. I must leave to the psychologists the question of whether putative stories register cognitively in normal text processing, any more than story grammars or other macrostructures do. What interests me is their power, *once hypothesized*, to uncover and characterize the much that lies hidden in a "little" text.

The sequence I sketched out above creates a metastory, one in which Ma Parker questions her fate, stands for existential humanity, takes a step toward self-assertion, and reaches a critical mass of emotion. Nothing in this sequence changes the sadness of the outcome, but everything in this sequence changes some valence in Ma's life. Momentarily, at least, the emphasis shifts from tallying her losses to appreciating her gains—those barely noticeable ways of "be"-ing more aware, more centered, more dramatically interesting than she has ever been before.

That seems to me the likeliest explanation for the dominantly female recognition of the *epiphany story*. It is the first moment in Mansfield's text where this downtrodden woman says, in effect, "Hey, wait a minute." It is hardly the sort of breakthrough we would call forceful or heartening, nor does it change any balance of power. We cannot know, finally, whether we hear "What have I *done?*" or "What have *I* done?" Guilt or resentment? Submission or resistance? Perhaps the reason women were more likely than men to respond to this line has something to do with their life experiences or their tolerance for ambiguity. I do not know, for I am far less wise than my distributed reader.

I do know, however, that the putative stories give me a perspective on the story that raises it in my estimation. Enriched by the added (or, I should say, the elicited) putative stories, "Life of Ma Parker," like Ma herself, begins to assert itself. It becomes more complex, less easily dismissed, less tidily summed up. We know that it is not enough to cry for Ma Parker. Our emotions—both the jerked tears and the social outcries—are modulated by the putative stories, not just through a changing sense of what the plot is but by a serial subjection to different *types* of stories.

I still regard "Life of Ma Parker" as a minor work by a sometimes-great writer, but I do not let my students "spend" it too quickly, as either a sob story or a protest story. For me, it is the tale of a Frank O'Connor–style heroine, a female descendent of Nikolay Gogol's Akakey Akakeivitch, a member of a "submerged population" for whom life, after a given moment, never looks the same.[5] Her lonely plight, foregrounded in the existential parable, reminds me of Elizabeth Bowen's comment on the short story in the modern world: "The short story . . . [places its character] alone on that stage which, inwardly, every man is conscious of occupying alone."[6] Every woman, too.

Late-Twentieth-Century Chicago, an Hispanic Neighborhood

She's an impregnated teenager. Eighteen weeks ago, she was sent to her Mexican relatives to escape her "shame" and await her baby. Addressing an unidentified listener for whom the reader is a stand-in, the girl tells her own story. She's the daughter of a Mexican mother, who was exiled to the United States for a similar reason—to give birth to an illegitimate baby. That baby becomes the narrator. The city is apparently Chicago. There the narrator was left with her grandmother and uncle, sent to school, and eventually put to work selling food from a pushcart. One of her customers is a mysterious man called "Boy Baby."

She's not sure we would like him—a "bum," with "greasy fingernails he never cut[s]," and a bed in a cubbyhole behind an auto repair shop.[7] To everybody else, he's a grease monkey. To her, however, he identifies himself as Chaq Uxmal Paloquín, the heir of a glorious civilization destroyed by white conquerors. As some readers may know, Uxmal is a real place, the site of Mayan ruins, including the Pyramid of the Magician. In the story, Chaq claims his father took him to the "Temple of the Magician" and "made him promise to bring back the ancient ways" (30). According to Chaq, his own future son is destined to rule an empire.

There are two wishful scenarios: the girl yearns for a sexual initiation that will be not tawdry and quick, but "like a tent full of birds" (28); the man speaks of reclaiming his ancestors' heritage. He takes her to his shabby lair, reverently shows her the guns he has stashed there, and deflowers her on a cot. It is a "holy night," but it is also no "big deal" (30). Like every Girl Baby, she has waited and waited to learn about sex. Now she knows. But there's more to find out. Her lover having decamped, she is sent to her mother's family in San Dionisio de Tlaltepango, where the news finally reaches her: Boy Baby is just an ordinary Mexican whose real name means "fat-face." Not only does he have "no Mayan blood," but, according to later news clippings, he may be a serial killer of young women.

History, myth, and desire come together in this story of a girl who is touched by a love that is identity changing, life altering, and either glorious or sinister—or both. Her impregnator is the male principle (he's baby, boy, and man in a timeless present), the personification of a tawdry fate (unwed pregnancy is both a sin and a commonplace in the narrator's family), and the incarnation of a Mayan king-god. His touch, like that of Mexico's later God, can make a virgin into a mother on a given holy night. The reader may have Mary in mind, but the girl identifies herself as Ixchel, the queen of "Tikal, and Tulum, and Chichén"—and (although the story doesn't mention this relevant detail) the Mayan goddess of childbirth. Virgin Mary? Mayan consort? This girl is an eighth grader. In the end, she is just another pregnant teenager, if you go by sociology. But if you go by mythology, the sexual body, the dreaming soul? This girl *has* been touched. She has received a powerful and ambivalent gift she calls love. Perhaps it is the same old trap that has snared women for centuries. Perhaps it's a transcendent experience.

The story I have been summarizing is called "One Holy Night," and it appears in the short story collection *Woman Hollering Creek* (1991), by Sandra Cisneros. Like other stories in that volume, it has been praised for its sensitivity to the female psyche and for a lyricism that dignifies while it does not mitigate the tension between Mexican and American identities. Unlike Mansfield's "Life of Ma Parker," which may strike some readers as well-intentioned but sentimentally simplistic and patronizing, Cisneros's work is likely to be viewed as timely, vital, and politically correct. My contention is that *both* stories can be packaged too easily by our interest in their issues.

Mansfield's story is a consciousness-raiser, showing the plight of the British working-class woman in the early twentieth century. Cisneros's story is a diversity-enabler, showing the mainstream American reader what it is like to live in a Mexican-American barrio, or a Mexican village. It is also a gender-sensitizer, showing these same readers what it is like to be female in a place that may be alien culturally but can be, and should be, emotionally accessible. While the older tale may suffer from its author's fading image, perhaps the newer one suffers from its author's—and its issues'—visibility. Like other stories by writers identified by their ethnicity, it is overdetermined by its author's success. It is replaced by what it stands for. Is there a way to retrieve its "original" storyness?

Perhaps—if we enter the story with eyes peeled for closure. We never know where we will find it, or what sentence conceals it. We may see it coming, or we may stumble into it. Every reader's adventure is different. On this occasion, I was my own sample reader and will tell you my experience. Previously, I had read only this writer's story "Mericans," but I was generally aware of her reputation and themes. I was ready for an encounter with a sensitive and thoughtful Chicana, but I had no idea what else to expect. This was my first preclosure point:

> So I was initiated beneath an ancient sky by a great and mighty heir—Chaq Uxmal Paloquín. (30)

You will have to take my word for it that, while doing this exercise, I looked only for whole-storyness. Only after the sentences had been identified and listed in isolation did I begin to dissect them. In the sentence just quoted, the most obvious preclosure signal is a global syntactic one: the end of an arc from innocence to knowledge. It is one of the most familiar narrative types in short fiction, and it is named for us in the sentence: initiation. On the local syntactic level, there are two forms of repetition: the parallelism of the two adjectives ("great and mighty") and the identity of the two apposite nouns (heir = Chaq). There is also a faint inversion created by the passive voice: not *he initiated me* but *I was initiated by him.* Lexically, the sentence offers several closural words: the excessive-degree terms *ancient, great,* and *mighty,* and the logical-conclusion term *so.* The sentence ends in four keywords.

Self-evidently, the narrative that ends here is an initiation, although it has been presented atypically as a flashback. This is a story schema modeled on the rite of passage, making us think of anthropology, of close-knit cultures, of ancient observances marking natural cycles. Using this Urscript, Cisneros is extraordinarily effective in mapping one girl's story onto a biological template *and* a Mexican heritage.

My next preclosure choice followed immediately:

I, Ixchel, his queen. (30)

If Chaq is a Mayan king, or at least the descendant or representative of one, then his mate is also Mayan royalty. On the global level, this sentence completes the naming process begun in the previous sentence: heir = Chaq Uxmal Paloquín; I = Ixchel = his queen. In its elliptical simplicity (without the copulative verb), this sentence offers a three-way parallelism of identical terms, with *Ixchel* a keyword because it is Mayan. With the addition of just this three-word sentence, we have a wholly new putative text. It's no longer an initiation story. It's a *revelation*. The model is not anthropological. It's Aristotelian. The "I" discovers its unforeseen identity, causing a leap from ignorance to knowledge (anagnorisis) that changes her life. "He said he would love me like a revolution," confides the narrator at the beginning of the story. Just as guns and the phallus are transparently equated in a story about the advent of a lost empire's savior, so the breaking of the hymen is a revolution, a recognition of a newly defined self. "I" am "Ixchel." That is a revelation, indeed. Once, "I" was a lonely, imaginative, Chicana virgin; now "I" am a Mayan queen, a woman, and [soon] a mother. That is peripeteia.

My third preclosure sentence is the one that caps the narrator's discovery that her hero is a fraud. "He was born on a street with no name in a town called Miseria." His parents are poor working people, a knife-sharpener and a fruit vendor. He, himself, is nearing middle age (he's thirty-seven), with a laughable cognomen (meaning "fat-face"), and, of course,

There is no Mayan blood. (33)

Once again, on the global level, there is a dramatic reversal. The pretender is unmasked, the tall tale is leveled, and "truth" is revealed. On the local syntactic level, the expletive bumps the subject behind the verb. Lexically, there's the absolute *no*, the keyword *Mayan*. Short and declarative, the sentence has a ring of finality. We may forget that it is not the narrator who authorizes this truth. She merely relays what her relatives have learned about Boy Baby. Yet, for the reader, the information creates what Thomas Leitch calls a "debunking rhythm," a closure through disillusionment.[8] It is a variant of the initiation story, except that the knowledge acquired here is an *un*knowing of what was previously known or thought to be true. Leitch claims this pattern can be found in many American short stories, and surely the unmasking of Chaq ends in the potential for disillusionment. For lack of a better term, I'll call it a *reality check*.

As a moment of truth, however, it means more to the reader than to the narrator. For *she* doesn't care about the "facts." *She* has a "truth" of her own. She loves "fat-face" or Chaq, regardless of his name—perhaps regardless of his crimes, if he has indeed killed the women whose bodies have been found "*on the road to Las Grutas de Xtacumbilxuna . . .*" (34). Pregnant and rusticating among her cousins in Mexico, the narrator thinks of her lover as neither king nor bum, reality nor myth. He is something of all, yet essentially a "man." That is magic enough. Referring to the girls who know nothing about sex, the narrator tells us:

> They don't know what it is to lay so still until his sleep breathing is heavy, for the eyes in the dim dark to look and look without worry at the man-bones and the neck, the man-wrist and man-jaw thick and strong, all the salty dips and hollows, the stiff hair of the brow and sour swirl of sideburns, to lick the fat earlobes that taste of smoke, and stare at how perfect is a man. (34–35)

This was my third preclosure point. There is a knowledge here that countervails the ignorance shown by "they," the virgin cousins. Since the narrator herself was a virgin not so long ago, there is a kind of image recursion, too. Is this a more advanced initiation story? No, not exactly, because the narrator has already acquired this experience and is now remembering, summarizing, delivering, and reliving it.

The sentence is overloaded with local preclosure signals. Repetition is everywhere, from the many alliterated *s*es to the central parallelism of four verb predicates: "to lay," "to look," "to lick," and "[to] stare." As resounding as a Hawthorne finale, the line ends in a verb/subject inversion: "how perfect is a man." Meanwhile, the words *sleep, dark,* and *all* are closural, and *man* is a keyword.

What kind of story ends in this sensuous, lyrical, yet earthy inventory of the male head and torso? Before I hazard a label, let me remind you of the normative pattern for preclosure progression discussed in chapter 4. According to the historical survey conducted there, anterior closure offers a tentative conclusion. In my reading of "One Holy Night," anterior closure is reached in the initiation scene. And, indeed, although the narrator believes in her transformation into Ixchel, she is wrong, in the literal sense,

about her lover's identity and will modify her claims later. Penultimate closure is reached in the survey of the lover's body. Characteristically at this
stage of closure, an obstacle is removed; now, indeed, the narrator can
"see" in the "dark." It is also common for sentences at this stage to reach
a high point of lyrical and rhetorical stability, and that is strikingly true
of the elaborate syntax and vivid imagery of this meditation on the male
body. It is almost as if Cisneros has internalized the normative progression I discussed in chapter 4.

Yet it is hard to identify the putative story ending in the penultimate
preclosure point. Following the earlier revelation about Boy Baby's identity ("no Mayan blood"), the narrative seems to subside. What follows is
reflection. "I don't think they understand," says the narrator about her
cousins. What they don't understand is "how perfect is a man," but also
how attentive is love. This story—the one that ends in the memory of a
nighttime vigil over the sleeping body of the lover—is a *testimonial* to the
loneliness and intensity of female devotion.

The actual story ends with a declaration of and about love. After telling
us "[t]his is how it is with me," the narrator clarifies what "it" is:

Love I mean. (35)

According to the survey in chapter 4, there should be local lexical signals
at the point of actual closure, and that is indeed what we find. Subject and
verb are in normal order, but the predicate is bounced to the front of the
sentence, causing a noticeable dislocation and emphasis. Every word is a
keyword.

This time, when we ask what kind of story ends here, we are no longer
talking about putative narratives, but about the text as written, studied,
loved, and remembered. This, finally, is *Cisneros's* story. If you recall, the
three stages of closure typical of the Contemporary period (1960–80) follow the sequence: *This is the way things seem.* → *This is the way they feel.*
→ *This is the way it goes.* In "One Holy Night," published about a decade
after the last story in my survey, the pattern is still visible. Indeed, it *seems*
that the auto mechanic is a noble Mayan. Indeed, the reverie on the lover's
body is about how things *feel* to the narrator. And, if we look at the next-
to-last sentence that is so closely linked with the elliptical "Love I mean,"
we find even greater conformity. I admit to being shaken by how closely
the actual sentence ("This is how it is with me") follows the model (*This*

is the way it goes), which I had formulated years before I read the Cisneros story.

"One Holy Night" is from the late twentieth century, but it is in many ways a traditional narrative. It embeds one of the oldest story schemata, the initiation familiar to anthropologists; it moves on to a revelation with echoes of anagnorisis; next, there is a reality check, a classic American type. Is her lover a sordid criminal with a con man's appeal, or a people's savior disguised as a tramp? We must take the narrator's lead here. She loves the man who made her a woman, and this is a story about that love. Finally, perhaps, we're drawn away from narrative altogether, toward lyrical exposition featuring lists and definitions.

Looking back from this perspective, we notice how often the narrator struggles to define the essence or nature of things. She tells us early on that she's different from the girls of Allport Street. She didn't want sex to be a fumbling grope in an alley or a car: "I didn't want it *like that* . . . I wanted it . . . *like* gold thread, *like* a tent full of birds. *The way* it's supposed to be . . ." (28; emphasis mine). Later, trying to describe Boy Baby, she concludes, "[H]ow do I *explain?*" Speaking about her cousins, she doesn't "think they *understand how it is* to be a girl," or "*how it is* to have a man," or "*what it is* to lay so still [and watch him] . . ." (34; emphasis mine). The answer she gives them is that the thing they're curious about—sex—is "a bad joke" (35). To herself and to us she tells a different truth, ending with "This is *how it is* with me." (35; emphasis mine).

Perhaps she has just given us one more testimonial? In a sense, yes; however, it follows not only the rejected Allport Street notion of love but also two alternative definitions that carry more weight. According to one of her closest friends, love "is like a big black piano" falling on you; according to another, "it's like a top" that spins all colors into white. Without commenting on these analogies, the narrator moves past them. For *her,* love is like having a harmonica always at your lips, through which you breathe in and out, so that your every breath is amplified, not as music but as life itself. The story is, finally, an *anatomy of love,* ending in a privileged definition.

The narrative has subsided into an exposition that has been heralded along the way by the narrator's many attempts to define meaning. In this way, both the narrator and the author can abort the narrative expectations raised by the question of who finally impregnated the narrator—an impoverished drifter, a serial killer, or the incarnation of a Mayan king.

Instead, the question becomes a far more general one: what is love? Love is what allows the narrator to conflate Chaq + "fat-face" + criminal into one core identity, the only one that matters: he = the man she loves. Because of the narrative momentum established by the earlier preclosure points, the meditative turn at the end of the text fakes narrative closure. Let's refer to the normative sequence again: from anterior congestion and/or complication (borne out in this story), to an almost lyrical or rhetorically stable highpoint in the penultimate slot (amply demonstrated here), to a multidetermined field in the final slot. Assertively simple as "Love I mean" is, these three words are the point at which the narrative question (who's Chaq?) impregnates the expository question (what's love?) to conclude, by example and by definition, that love—the transformer of identity and circumstance, the hum in the breath—is divine inspiration.

Unlike Mansfield's "Life of Ma Parker," the Cisneros story does not need to be raised in anyone's estimation. In today's literary and academic environments, it is highly regarded. Socially and pedagogically, it is a useful work of art, appearing on reading lists for courses in Chicana literature, and in general anthologies for ethnic diversity. I would not leach from this powerful and beautiful story one iota of its cultural and ideological relevance, impact, or mission. Still, in a sense, the story no longer belongs to Cisneros, nor even to its narrator, but rather to the feminist critics who have framed so much of the discussion that surrounds—and sometimes precedes—our acquaintance with the text.

According to Katherine Ann Payant, "[t]he 1980s and 1990s . . . have been the decades of the Chicanas [as opposed to the Chicanos, who spearheaded political movements in the 1960s], and "Cisneros is perhaps the best known of these Chicana writers."[9] It has been this author's mission, says Laura Gutierrez Spencer, to "criti[que] the fate of the heroine in Western patriarchal literature . . . by reveal[ing] the truer-to-life consequences for women who are socialized to live their lives waiting for the happy ending."[10] Sometimes overtly, and almost always by implication, the narrator becomes a "site"—of multicultural tensions, of revisionist storytelling, of negotiated discourses. The subtitle of an article by Maria Szadziuk captures the common view. Cisneros writes about "Becoming a Woman in Biethnic Space."[11]

There is no doubt, of course, that Cisneros is deliberately rewriting domestic and public histories from a woman's point of view. Still, three sample readings of "One Holy Night" show how easily assumptions about female subjugation to social norms, male rhetoric, and physical violation can be mapped onto the plot of a given short story. Jeff Thomson thinks "the narrator is correct in believing that her seduction is also her initiation into a society of women—'We were all the same'—however the society is one of seduction and abandonment and not the glorious rise of the Mayan Sun Kings as Boy Baby would have her believe."[12] Elaborating on this theme, Payant finds that the narrator is seduced by a false rhetoric, a calculated abuse of the ancient legends for inglorious and sexist advantage. "Here Cisneros wryly combines traditional native myth with the harsh realities for a teenager growing up in an American barrio . . . Unlike in the title story [of the collection] and 'Bien Pretty,' where native myth is a source of empowerment, here it is falsified and used to seduce." She goes on to explain that "[t]he protagonist is not only seduced by the romance of the myth, she seeks sexual experience to possess the knowledge of adult women . . . [but winds up illustrating, once again, how] the cycle of female oppression continues."[13] Note that in both of these interpretations, Boy Baby's story about his ancestry is viewed as patently false, malevolent, and manipulative. It has no other value or purpose than to subjugate his young victim.

That view reaches an extreme in Mary Pat Brady's analysis of the story. She argues that women are socialized to believe that they are at risk in public places—such as the street where the narrator is selling her mangoes and cucumbers. Almost by definition, it is a predatory male who approaches her there and lures her into his cave-room.

> "One Holy Night" illustrates the myriad discourses that help to naturalize this spatial logic and render it invisible. One of the most interesting means of obscuring this use of spatiality is the discursive refusal to characterize the narrator's sexual encounter as rape, even though it involves a young, vulnerable, clearly naïve girl and a much older man . . . [S]he avoids describing her experience as rape by emphasizing her own agency. She thus builds a case for her own culpability and suggests that this assault was what she desired because she was "in love" with Boy Baby.[14]

Rape? Assault? As we have seen, preclosure analysis leads me to a different interpretation of the encounter between these two people. While I hold no brief for Boy Baby, I do not see him as a quondam rapist, nor am I so sure he isn't to some extent the victim of his own fantasies—even if that means he really is a serial killer of young girls. Although he disappears temporarily, he does return, seeking the narrator at her grandmother's house. To say that he abandons the girl he seduced is to forget that the old woman chased him away with a broom. Perhaps he has returned simply to add another victim to the list of murdered girls; perhaps he has come to redeem himself from the generic charges leveled at his sex—"the infamy of men." In my reading of the story, this point is left moot. In the space of this indeterminacy, we are free to remember that, in the observance of their religion, the "real" Mayans killed young women. Like ancestor, like descendent?

Be that as it may, when it comes to the narrator's fate, I sharply disagree with the critics I have mentioned. Payant sees the initiation into womanhood as "[leading] to stasis and entrapment" (98). As we have seen, the sequence of preclosure points highlights the story's turn toward meditation, toward an exploration of the meaning of love. Perhaps the narrator is "entrapped" by the mores that punish unwed mothers. Yet her thoughts are active, even aggressive, in coming to terms with her situation. Payant gives her no credit for her description of her own feelings, telling us the girl "was 'in love,'" with ironic quotation marks. The critic is denying the girl credence, discounting her voice—a response that may be justifiably cynical from a feminist point of view, but, oddly enough, smacks of "male" disregard for the narrator's inner life. I prefer to trust the shape of the story, which tells me that this girl has, indeed, been caught in the "same old story" of the women in her family, but which shows me, too, that her imagination gives her a leverage and a freedom I want to appreciate.

While I do not agree with the interpretations of Thomson, Payant, and Brady, I do not quarrel with their right to bring their own assumptions to the story. As critics, we all find what we're looking for. When I interpret the pattern of preclosure choices for a given story, I have no illusions of objectivity, nor of privileged access to the "real" story. In the case of "One Holy Night," perhaps I am only jettisoning the feminist template in favor of a pattern of serial preclosure that is far less neutral than I wish it to be. However, it does seem to me that we are closer to the grain of the work itself if we come to it without words like "site" and "rape" at the ready. I can see no harm, and believe there is great benefit, in using preclosure study as a check on the current tendency to map issues—and politically correct attitudes towards those issues—onto a text, even when, *especially* when, the text invites a socially conscious reading.

In Cisneros's work, love is not invalid because it is wrongly bestowed or abused by the male. Her better-known story, "Eyes of Zapata," gives us a much more mature heroine, a woman in many ways subjugated and betrayed, yet capable of luminous integrity in her fortitude, her constancy, and in her reverie on the sleeping and naked body of the revolutionary hero—a companion scene to the inventory of the lover's body in "One Holy Night." In this author's work there is something deeply affecting and inflaming about the sufferings of women, but there is also something that was missed or devalued by the feminist critics I cited. There is something powerful and definitive about the capacity to dream, to savor, and to love. Cisneros's vision is greater than her agenda. Preclosure study is not the only way to arrive at this understanding, but it is a very effective and direct way of doing so.

Whether the text is a forgotten one on the shelf like Mansfield's, or a recent one in the spotlight like Cisneros's, if we read first for social relevance, we shortchange the story, stereotype the author, and cheapen the issue. By reading first for storyness, we do not lose or diminish topicality. Neither are we distanced from the characters. We are actively "in" the story, discovering its themes within the folds of the narrative.

Loving (?)
Raymond Carver

R aymond Carver is arguably the most influential and imitated short story writer
of the last quarter century. Teachers, writers, and aficionados of the genre
are as likely to be familiar with his spare, lowbrow, and strangely resonant idiom as they are with Hemingway's clean, mannered, and highly
codified style. In his own time, each writer immortalized an American psyche that is wounded, inarticulate, yearning, and doomed. Yet Carver, dead
of cancer at fifty, was no Harry at the foot of Kilimanjaro. He was a recovering alcoholic with a soul mate by his side, a career at full tilt, and a
deepening vision. So goes the legend.

I am, to an extent, a believer, as I think anyone would be who was ever
in the presence of those hovering shoulders, those wingspread eyebrows.
At one of his Iowa City appearances, I heard him read "Why Don't You
Dance?" and became a devotee. I should be as ready as anyone to take his
word as gospel. Describing the two-year break before his "late" phase, he
once wrote, "I found myself in a period of stocktaking, of trying to discover where I wanted to go with whatever new stories I was going to write
and how I wanted to write them."[1] As befits a legend, there is a hint of
apocrypha about the genesis of the transitional story. "Cathedral," based
on a visit by the blind Jerry Carriveau to the author and Tess Gallagher in
Syracuse, was written either at his desk one morning, as he claims, or in
a train from Syracuse to New York City, if you believe Tess Gallagher.[2] Either way, it marked a turning point: "I knew it was a different kind of
story for me, no question. Somehow I had found another direction I

wanted to move toward."[3] In an interview with David Sexton, he famously added, "and all of the stories after that seemed to be fuller somehow and much more generous, and maybe more affirmative."[4] Critics have agreed with him, as a sampling of titles will suggest: "Conditions of Possibility: Religious Revision in Raymond Carver's 'Cathedral'"; "Insularity and Self-Enlargement in Raymond Carver's 'Cathedral'"; "Knowing More Than One Imagines; Imagining More Than One Knows"; "Raymond Carver's Therapeutics of Passion"; "'The Possibility of Resurrection': Re-Vision in Carver's 'Feathers' and 'Cathedral.'"[5]

Carver was, indeed, in a generous mood—to the critics. He gave them an attitude toward this text. Perching their words on his prose, they've accepted his guidance. They've agreed that this tale is "really something," that it marks a "new direction." An ideology has grown up and the story has been canonized. In the last chapter, we rescued a pair of texts from their social agendas, at least until we could appreciate them as stories. In the case of "Cathedral," what I am trying to circumvent is the critical aura itself. What I am looking for is a different way "in" to a work of lay scripture.

I am looking for preclosure. The discussion that follows is more subjective than usual, and it foregrounds the readers more prominently. There are only four, and they are persons I know well. None are academics. Two men and two women, they are white, middle-class, and very well educated. They cannot be called a "sample," for they represent no one but themselves. Each has agreed, as a personal favor, to read "Cathedral" and to mark preclosure points. As a courtesy, I will use code names, for I am going to typecast these persons in ways that are woefully inadequate and simplistic. What follows is not who they are but rather what they've let me make of them—only for now, only in these pages.

To classify them, I could use one of the available methods of profiling, such as the Myers-Briggs typology. To do so, however, would be to invade their privacy even further and to give a false impression. I am not a psychologist. Under the circumstances, it is more honest to improvise. Let us say that we interpret our experience with reference to (p) relationships with people, (i) ideas about day-to-day reality, (m) systemic patterns or models, and (s) spiritual frames of reference. We see a young woman shoplift a scarf. If we think, "That's my best friend's daughter, and she'll hate me if I tattle," we are coding our experience in terms of (p) our relationships with people. If we say to ourselves, "What I've witnessed is a crime, and it's my duty as a citizen . . . ," we are coding our experience in terms of (i) concepts and ideas. If we conclude, "I'll bet she also runs stoplights, so they'll catch her eventually," we're coding our experience in terms of (m) predictive models. "There's some bad karma," we may believe, or "God sees and decrees," and if that is our response, we are coding our experience in terms of (s) transcendent faith.

Of course, these modes overlap. We rely on all of them in some fashion or degree. Yet, if I rate my own tendencies from a not-so-prominent 1 to a very-prominent 5 in each of these categories, I get a kind of profile:

p=2   i=4   m=5   s=1

My "pims" tells me I'm a cerebral type, not very social, and not at all religious. Yet I know myself to be often illogical, deeply attached to certain people, and dedicated to principles that some might call transcendent. In short, the grid I am proposing is a weak index to personality and no guide to behavior. At most, it offers some comparative reference points. It's also important to keep in mind that 5 is no "better" than 1, and that the "pims" categories are not necessarily the ones to provide the most accurate or full picture of any one of these persons. Among my sample readers:

Jill cares for and needs people, and is highly sociable; she is also deeply religious. As a diagnostician in her work, she relies frequently on models, and as a reflective person, she conceptualizes on occasion. Roughly, her profile is
p=5   i=3   m=4   s=5

Pete is just as people-oriented and sociable; religion, too, is important in his life, although perhaps slightly less pervasively. He is analytical in a situation-oriented way. Again in approximate terms, his profile is
p=5   i=3   m=3   s=4

Fran, a family mainstay, is interested in people and their accomplishments, but there are inner and outer circles of regard. Although not religious or given to modeling her experience abstractly, she is curious about the world and keenly evaluative. Loosely, her profile is
p=4   i=3   m=1   s=1

Jim is intellectual and alert to systemic features of experience. Highly organized, he is nevertheless tolerant of uncertainty. He values human greatness but sees mostly human weakness. Taking a stab, I'd say his profile is

$p=1$ $i=5$ $m=4$ $s=2$

These are the readers to whom I gave the 708 sentences (paragraphing removed) of Raymond Carver's "Cathedral." I, too, read the text for storyness so I could add my perspective.

From the very beginning, we hear a familiar American vernacular: "This blind man, an old friend of my wife's, he was on his way to spend the night."[6] The eighteen monosyllables in a row and the overdetermined pronouns ("*this* blind man . . . *he*") are markers of informal oral communication used mainly to point, to assert information, to buttonhole someone in the schoolyard, at the street corner, on the neighboring barstool. We're hearing from a husband who is uneasy about the impending visit of his wife's former employer, a blind man named Robert.

Two things make the narrator uncomfortable: the knowledge that his wife has sustained an unusually close though nonsexual relationship with this person, and the fact that the man cannot see. When she was young, the narrator's wife had a job reading to the blind man, and the experience left a deep impression—especially his final gesture of passing his hands over her face in order to remember what she "looked" like. Over the years, she has stayed in touch with this friend, telling him all about her life. Carver is in top form as he lets the narrator's jealousy and ignorance show through. We sense the bafflement so typical of males in Carverdom, and also a wounded vanity as helpless as it is petty. While his wife is fetching their guest, the narrator tells her story.

The summer before she was to marry her childhood sweetheart, while her fiancé was completing officers' training school, she worked for Robert in Seattle. "So okay," the narrator sums up at one point: "I'm saying that at the end of the summer she let the blind man run his hands over her face, said goodbye to him, married her childhood etc., who was now a commissioned officer, and she moved away from Seattle" (210–11). Later, she tried to write a poem about that tactile farewell (the narrator dismissively recalls her showing it to him; he didn't "get" it), then telephoned the blind man one night and began an exchange of audio tapes in which the two spoke freely about their lives. Eventually, her marriage failed—"she didn't like it that [her officer] was part of the military-industrial thing" (211) recalls the narrator, casually invoking the 1960s cliché—and she attempts to kill herself. Saved, divorced, and later married to the narrator, she nevertheless has continued to express herself through two channels that exclude him—the yearly poems she writes and the confessional tapes she sends to Robert. We can infer, and the husband may on some level grasp, that his exclusion is the result of his own self-centeredness. He can feel his own entrapment—numbed with alcohol and "cannabis"—but cannot empathize with others. "Cathedral" is narrated by a man who unconsciously reveals his selfishness and ignorance, the scared and puny self that crouches in us all. Yet there is about his wife a hint of moral superiority that may have contributed to his tetchiness.

As in a host of classic stories, a mysterious stranger arrives to rattle the cage. Robert is first at the door, then in the house, finally on the sofa. The narrator, having been put on notice by his wife—*if you love me, you will welcome my friend*—is awkwardly polite to his guest, although there are half-intentional faux pas. The visitor is unfazed, and his bluff good humor and simple pleasure in the reunion endear him to the reader. Dinner unites husband, wife, and visitor in a mock-heroic feast: "We didn't talk. We ate. We scarfed. We grazed that table. We were into serious eating" (217). This is a ritual the narrator can understand. As we'll note later, it stimulates his first effort to craft his words. He even begins to appreciate his visitor, who, despite being blind, "ha[s] right away located his foods" on the plate (217).

After dinner, the social drinking continues. Then the narrator offers marijuana. Realizing that Robert has never smoked it before, he watches as the blind man willingly tries something new, quickly masters the technique, and then stops when he has had enough. Master of the "dope," the narrator praises its quality: "It doesn't mess you up." Robert's reply—"Not much it doesn't, bub"—could be an amusing reference to his bout with drowsiness, but could also mean that he has been briefed on his host's drug dependency (202). Certainly *we* know by now that it is the narrator who is "messed up."

The wife leaves the room to change into a robe and later returns to fall asleep on the couch, seated between the two men, whom she leaves to their own devices. The blind man tries to make conversation, and the narrator admits he is "glad for the company." After food, alcohol, and marijuana, the next diversion is TV. The narrator turns it on. At this late hour, all he can find is an educational program on European cathedrals. In a blunt yet rare show of interest, the narrator wonders if his blind visitor has any conception of cathedrals. When Robert asks for a description, the narrator tries but can't find the words. He has no imagination or inspiration. When asked if he is religious, he says he is not: faith is another capacity that "just isn't in [him]." This narrator is trapped inside a body with no window on meaning. He is that classic human type, the sighted man who can't see.

Robert, of course, is the blind man who *can*. He tells the narrator to fetch paper and a pen, and instructs him to draw a cathedral. As Robert had once learned the wife's face by touching its contours, he will now "learn" what a cathedral looks like by placing his hand on the husband's while he draws. Is the blind man simply curious—eager, as always, to learn something new? Or is he aware that his former employee needs his help once again? Her second husband may not be "part of the military-industrial thing," but, as a person without friends, hope, or ideals, neither is he part of the human community. Has Robert arrived to reclaim him? Be it so, if you will, as Hawthorne might say. Directed by Robert, the narrator turns a corner in his life. He draws a cathedral. Starting with a sketch of his own house, he adds spires, and, when told to do so, he adds people. Directed to close his eyes and keep drawing, he does. Allowed, when done, to open his eyes—he does *not*. By his own decision, he remains in the darkness of new light. He can locate his body, he knows where it is, but for the first time, it doesn't confine him: "I didn't feel like I was inside anything" (228). He has touched another person, grasped an idea, floated free of the body—and of the low-roofed caves of ignorance and fear. *That,* to quote the narrator, is "really something." It is more than any other Carver character has achieved until then.

I asked Jill, Pete, Fran, and Jim to read Carver's story, to mark preclosure points, and to tell me very briefly what they liked most and what they liked least about this short story. When the four copies of the text were returned to me, I covered the names of the respondents and, closing my eyes, shuffled the copies until, when I looked at them again, I could no longer tell to whom they belonged. Then I recorded the responses. I did not link the choices to the readers until I had finished analyzing *all* of the preclosure points in local and global terms. However, in the discussion below, I identify the readers along the way.

The first sentence chosen by anyone was

S/74   In time, she put it all on a tape and sent the tape to the blind man. (211)

This sentence concludes the back story about the narrator's wife and her relationship to Robert. The repetition of *tape* is, perhaps, a low-frequency preclosure signal. Lexically, there is a time-shift phrase (*in time*) and an absolute-degree term (*all*). *Tape* and *blind man* may function as keywords. Yet on the global level, has anything ended? We have a sense of the narrator's character, we know that he resents his wife's closeness to Robert, but the husband is reacting to his internal anxieties, not to the blind man in person. Will his fears be corrected or confirmed? We don't know. He isn't the protagonist of the events recounted.

His wife is. *She* is the one whose experience has been chunked in a significant way by this segment of narrative. Admittedly, she is viewed at a distance through a cracked and grainy lens more interesting to us than she is, but still she is the heroine of a familiar kind of story. The conventional dream scenario (marriage to a first love in an officer's uniform) turns into a nightmare, plunging her into despair, from which she recovers when, inspired by a blind social worker, she finds her own voice. It is a *1960s parable,* a story of salvation. Told by the wife or by Robert, it might have been saccharine. Told by this narrator, it is far more complicated. It is revealed as a sentimental stereotype, but it also has the power to convict its teller of emotional inadequacy. In terms of plot, it is, indeed, the wife's story; yet in terms of tone, perspective, and ambient meaning, it may after all be the narrator's. It is *his* consciousness, in all its shallow yet real angst, that blooms on the page.

Even as we rejoice at the wife's recovery of meaning through her friendship with the blind man, even as we groan at the husband's mockery of her need to "connect," we may feel, on some level, that he does have a point. He may not be worthy of knowing, or capable of appreciating, his wife's inner thoughts—but there are consequences inherent in her sending them to another man. The superior yet distant wife; the selfish yet baffled husband. We've met them before in the earlier stories. In its wry, unflinching unprettiness, the tale that ends here is like the harsher, less "affirmative" ones Carver is supposedly outgrowing. Because of the distancing lens, because it is the *pattern* of the scenario that matters, this sentence has a higher model quotient than people quotient. The only person who chose it was Jim (m=4; p=1), who wrote that he did not care for the second half of "Cathedral" because the prose seemed less precisely and memorably crafted.

The next sentence chosen was

S/407   "Your bed's made up, Robert, when you're ready. (221)

This is the wife speaking. Immediately thereafter, she falls asleep and effectively exits from the story until near the end, when she will wake up, bewildered and excluded. There are local preclosure signals. Balance is achieved by the movement of Robert's name to the middle of the sentence. If a bed is "made up," if a person is "ready," certain processes have been completed. There is a time shift in *when*. On the global level, what has happened? In reminding Robert that his bed is ready, the wife has her final moment of authority. This is the gesture of the hostess and homemaker, and it captures the warmth and respect (the bed awaits *his* readiness) of her relationship with Robert.

But that is old news. What has *really* "happened" so far is that Robert has been given food, alcohol, and marijuana, and in the case of the drug, he has entered—and mastered—new territory. Indeed, if we look at the story up to this point, it records an *initiation,* with Robert as its hero. Just as the wife was the changed character—that is, the putative protagonist— of the story ending at S/74, Robert is the main character of the story ending at S/407. This deferral of the *narrator's* story is significant and will be discussed later on. For now, however, let's look more closely at this sentence. Its people quotient is high. Still, the offer of the bed is a metonymy for hospitality; it instantiates an idea/l of generous behavior. The one person choosing this sentence was Fran (p=4, i=3), a woman of alert intelligence who has lived primarily within the home, in service to its values.

Fran's second choice, as it happens, is the next sentence in the overall list of preclosure points. With his wife asleep on the couch, the husband has asked his guest whether he'd like more strawberry pie or whether he wants to go to bed. Robert replies that he'd rather stay up and talk with his host. The narrator should be rolling his eyes at the prospect. A tête-à-tête with Robert! Whose mere existence makes him squirm! That would certainly have been his reaction at the beginning of the story. However, now he says, "That's all right," in an offhand way.

S/436   Then I said, "I'm glad for the company." (222)

For someone like the narrator, that is saying a lot. On the local level, we have the time shift *then*. The keyword *company* has at least two implications: on the surface, it reminds us of social rituals (having company for dinner); through its root, it suggests the more personal *companion*. The two meanings mark the beginning and end of a narrative arc in which the narrator's perceptions of Robert change. Originally, the narrator saw him as an unwelcome but socially mandated guest; now he seems ready to view the man as a fellow human being who might share his psychic space. In other words, the story that ends here is tending toward epiphany but is more properly a *recognition story*. Importantly, the narrator, for the first time, is the protagonist. It is also worth noting that the domestic frame of reference, the emphasis on human warmth and fellowship, once again suits the profile of the reader—Fran—who chose the sentence.

Interestingly, she did *not* choose the next sentence in the text, although other readers did. Following his statement that he was glad for Robert's company, the narrator confirms this surprising admission:

S/437   And I guess I was. (222)

For her, this sentence did not carry closural force. Perhaps it simply paled in comparison to the admission in S/436. Maybe the spoken words of that previous sentence were more decisive because they were "real" communication. Only words said aloud can bring people together in the way she would like—a point worth remembering.

To choose, instead, the inward-turning S/437, a reader must be comfortable with ambiguity. Despite the summary formula (I = someone who is glad for Robert's company), the sentence carries different meanings depending upon which word is stressed. If the narrator is thinking, "I *guess* I was [glad]," then he is still in a grudging mood. However, if he is thinking, "I guess I *was* [glad]," then he is owning up to a change of heart. Night is encroaching; his wife is asleep. Perhaps anyone's presence would be welcome right now. He has told Robert that he is glad to have his company. Now he tells *himself* that perhaps he really meant what he said. Something is dawning on him. What we have here is, indeed, an *epiphanic tale*. So, who thought the story could end here?

Pete did, and I did. Pete's profile (p=5, i=3, m=3, s=4) is consistent with alertness to human solidarity but suggests that he responds more readily to the unseen than Fran does. He flagged a possible sign of inner awareness, the narrator's appreciation for the *value* (not just the physical fact or the social norm) of companionship. My profile (p=2, i=4, m=5, s=1) is quite different from Pete's (and, indeed, from Fran's). It is less people oriented and more model based. However, in choosing this sentence, I was not reacting to the new friendliness of the moment. What figured more prominently for me was the very shift, itself, from offhand remark ("I'm glad for the company") to interior double take ("And I guess I was"). As I read those words, I heard the narrator thinking, *It's weird—but even though I wasn't keen on his coming, I am glad this blind man is here with me.* I saw a crucial if minuscule gain in the complexity of the narrator's thought. I saw a quantum if tiny leap forward in the way he was processing the moment, for rarely do Carver's men reflect upon, interpret, and thereby "own" the meaning of their experience.

We can guess that he values Robert's company because the alternative is worse. In the lines that follow, that point is made clear. We learn how the narrator ordinarily spends his evenings. After his wife goes to bed, he smokes marijuana and tries to stay awake, dreading the sleep that is ravaged by nightmares. The dreams must be frightening because he sometimes wakes from them with his "heart going crazy." In Carver country, unfocused anxiety is the norm. Although this character is a few rungs higher on the economic ladder (as was Carver by this time), he is just as lost as his predecessors—until he begins to realize that companionship matters.

What comes next is something like a real conversation. The two men are looking at the TV special on medieval cathedrals, and suddenly the narrator has his first unselfish thought: "Then something occurred to me, and I said, 'Something occurred to me. Do you have any idea what a cathedral is?'" (223). Robert doesn't, so the narrator tries to describe these monumental structures. He knows he is failing, but he keeps on trying. Finally, he admits he is "no good at it." Readers familiar with Carver's work will not be surprised; the inarticulateness of his characters is a critical shibboleth. Robert could have drawn a similar conclusion, but he does not. Instead, he asks the narrator whether he is religious. Awkwardly but honestly, the narrator lays out his anticredo. He cannot believe in religion. He cannot believe in anything. "It's hard," he says, hinting that the vagaries and frustrations of life invalidate any faith in a higher meaning or purpose. Encouraged by the blind man's sympathetic silence, he keeps talking, focusing now on the cathedrals, and admitting that they "don't mean anything special to me. Nothing. Cathedrals. They're something to look at on late-night TV." It's an anticatechism, and its final sentence is the next preclosure point:

S/589   That's all they are." (226)

Another copulative verb. Another summary definition. Cathedrals = objects on TV. Nothing else. Nothing more. There is a flat, declarative honesty about this line, without shading or temporizing or delicacy. The two male readers chose this preclosure point. Pete's profile is p=5, i=3, m=3, s=4. Jim's is almost the opposite: p=1, i=5, m=4, s=2. Indeed, it would seem that this is the unlikeliest pairing of readers; the only common denominator is their sex. Once again we must remember the limitations of the profiling method I am using. The categories are too informal, the ratings too subjective, and the sample too small for the results to be anything but a provisional heuristic for discussing reader responses. What the method *can* do, however, is identify rough similarities and differences within its own frame of reference—and that's what it does here.

How important is the gender link? On a number of occasions throughout this book, I have identified readers' sex as a variable that seems occasionally to matter. Because I am neither interested nor trained in gender studies, I have for the most part left these observations on the table, inviting others to make further sense of them. Surely it would be a simple-minded perpetuation of stereotypes to say that the blunt, assertive, and dismissive honesty of S/489 makes it a more salient and closural sentence for male readers than for female readers. On the other hand, this is a rare instance in which the narrator takes stock of his beliefs without fanfare or excuse. If he's bereft of grace, he's not entirely without sand. I'm grateful to my male readers for pointing this out to me.

Eyeing the preclosure signals, I note the absolute-degree term *all*. This sentence ends a series of negative summaries with absolute force: "I'm *just no* good at [describing cathedrals]"; "It *just* is*n't* in me" (emphasis mine). There's so much more that "isn't in" him! Yet honesty is there, in a way it hasn't been before. Responsiveness is there. The narrator is coming clean, almost taking the offensive in stating a negation. The story that ends here is a *confession*.

In an empty vessel, a drop will resound. That is what happens in the next, and last, preclosure point. Finding that the narrator has no existing capacity for faith, Robert has taken another tack. He appears to be focusing on the problem at hand, looking for a practical solution to the narrator's deficiency, so that the original goal—giving Robert an idea of cathedrals—can be reached. Of course, it is difficult not to see another agenda in Robert's actions. As I've mentioned before, he may have prior knowledge that his friend's second husband has disappointed her, too, or he may have grasped the situation after his arrival. Either way, he may be acting as a kind of spiritual diagnostician and healer. Or, on a more mundane level, he may simply be, quite literally, a "social worker" who is always on the job, always mending human beings. Angel or practitioner, he knows that the route to the unconscious is sometimes through a physical experience that models the missing insight, bringing it into being through some form of enactment. Many a psychological and pedagogical theory is latent here.

Robert has rested his hand on the narrator's and instructed him to draw a cathedral. At one point, the wife awakens, wonders what is going on, and is ignored. The story belongs to the two men she brought together. Robert, focused on the act of drawing, tells the narrator to shut his eyes. Obediently, the narrator drops his lids. Commanded again to "draw," the narrator moves his hand. "*We* kept on with it," he says (emphasis mine). He is guiding the blind man's hand, but it is the blind man who has guided him to this moment. Finally, Robert says, "I think that's it." Either he has grasped the mental image he was seeking, or it is time for the narrator to "open his eyes" to what *he* has learned. Right here, the narrator shifts allegiance. The guide has said *open your eyes*, but the narrator does not obey. Instead, he gives *himself* a directive. "I thought I'd keep them [closed] for a little longer."

S/701   I thought it was something I ought to do. (228)

On the local syntactic level, we once again have a summary definition: keeping my eyes shut = something I ought to do. There is the assonance of tho*ught* and *ought*. While *something* is a keyword by virtue of its symptomatic vagueness and its frequency in the story (it's used twenty-nine times), *ought* appears nowhere else in the text. Previous examples of imperative modal auxiliaries are limited to three: the narrator's comment that you "should" sit on the right side of the train for the best view; his belief that blind people "must" wear dark glasses; and the wife's comment that she "shouldn't" have eaten so much. By contrast, the narrator's feeling that he "ought" to keep his eyes closed, even when Robert has released him from this duty, has a protomoral signature that is new to the story—and, of course, to the narrator.

To what virtue is he raising his sights? To the decency of keeping his eyes shut, although Robert now says he may open them? Since the blind man lives entirely and forever in darkness, it is unseemly for the narrator to hasten back to the light. Or, to put it another way, if Robert has invited the narrator into his world of closed eyes, then it is only right to dwell there appreciatively, to accept what it offers. If, on some level, the narrator realizes the unkindness of his earlier attitude toward the blind man, then perhaps there is an element of atonement here, as well. By keeping his eyes closed, even when he does not have to, he is making a gesture. He is making himself "blind." He is identifying with Robert.

Or maybe not. Maybe the narrator has not advanced quite so far morally and is simply responding to the novelty of the situation. *Here's a new kind of mind-bending experience. Maybe it's better than dope. I "ought" to give it a try.* Whatever its subtext, the statement is remarkable for this simple reason: it is the first time the narrator has enjoined his own behavior on the basis of, or for the sake of, a moral (or protomoral) consideration. If he can intuit the possibility that there might be a good reason for keeping his eyes shut, perhaps he can imagine good reasons for more important decisions about what to do and how to live. Although it is only faintly indicated, what we have here is a maturation tale, a moral *coming-of-age story.*

Three readers responded to the closural force of "something I ought to do," making this sentence the most popular preclosure choice. It is the one and only sentence marked by Jill (p=5, i=3, m=4, s=5), and it is one of three chosen by Pete (p=5, i=3, m=3, s=4). Despite the difference in gender, these two readers have very congruent profiles, emphasizing people and religion. As we have seen, various readings of this sentence *do* suggest an abstract recognition, however nascent, of human reciprocity and spiritual transcendence. I was the third reader who chose this sentence. Because my profile is the opposite of Pete's and Jill's (emphasizing concepts and models rather than people and gods), I introduce an anomaly similar to the one we noticed when Pete and Jim, despite having opposite profiles, chose the same sentence. In that earlier case, we could look to the common gender for an explanation. Here, I believe we can look to the richness of the sentence. It encodes generalizations, maps grammar onto action, hints at community, and reaches a higher plane. It offers something for everyone, or more accurately, in relation to the putative story it concludes, it resonates along a spectrum of human interests. Preclosure study

allows us to recognize and articulate the many ways in which this unpre-
tentious sentence emblazons a rich meaning for itself and for the story.

Actual closure comes shortly thereafter. Robert asks whether the narrator is now looking at what he has drawn. We know that he is not. He
still has his eyes closed, although he does not say so. He is confiding to us:
"I was in my house. I knew that. But I didn't feel like I was inside anything." Seemingly a reply to Robert, the next and final sentence is

S/708   "It's really something," I said. (228)

To Robert, it must seem as though the narrator is talking about the drawing. We, however, know that he is referring to an experience inside his
head. For the last time, we have a summary definition: It = something.
Lexically, the line says almost nothing. It is frustratingly vague, an empty
redundancy suggesting, if anything, the poverty of expression we thema-
tize in Carver's work. Yet, if we look at the last sentence of the story in relation to the preclosure points leading up to it, we may find that the
words—and the story—are engorged with new meaning.

In the remaining pages of this chapter, I will discuss what we can learn
from the preclosure choices and from the readers used in this experiment.
Let me start by reviewing the preclosure points and the putative stories
they end.

1. a *1960s parable,* with the wife as the protagonist: S/74 In time,
   she put it all on a tape and sent the tape to the blind man.
2. an *initiation story,* with the blind man as the protagonist: S/407
   "Your bed's made up, Robert, when you're ready.
3. a *recognition story,* with the narrator as the protagonist, as he
   will be in all the subsequent putative stories: S/436 Then I said,
   "I'm glad for the company."
4. an *epiphanic story:* S/437 And I guess I was.
5. a *confession story:* S/589 That's all they are."
6. a (moral) *coming-of-age story:* S/701 I thought it was something
   I ought to do.

In the completed text, we have a *revelation story:* S/707 "It's really something," I said.

This progression looks like a normative sequence. It could be described in the language of religious conversion, spiritual enlightenment, or psychological development. In the language of genre poetics, it represents a modulation of prototypes: hagiographies, tribal scripts, Aristotelian dramas, Joycean short stories, purgation narratives, Bildungsromane, and spiritual journeys. So much narrative. So few words. So goes the short story genre. Of course, I'm not suggesting that Carver had these prototypes in mind, although I can't preclude their influence through some indirect channel. Surely he knew the Joycean short story, and many human scripts are present in the stories and dramas of his beloved Chekhov.

In order to appreciate more fully the serial embedding of story types, we must turn our attention, once again, to the progression of preclosure points. The first two are focused, as I have said, on the stories of the wife and Robert. However, once the focus shifts to the narrator, the preclosure points reveal a kind of oscillation. The line that closes the recognition story is spoken aloud: "Then I said, 'I'm glad for the company.'" The line that closes the epiphany story is an internalized comment: "And I guess I was." This alternation is repeated in the lines that close the confessional and coming-of-age stories: "That's all they are," says the narrator to Robert; "I thought it was something I ought to do," says the narrator to himself. Actual closure moves back into oral language: "'It's really something,' I said."

Perhaps this alternation is purely accidental, for I've derived it from a list of preclosure points that no one reader—not even I—retrieved as a complete sequence. If the rhythm exists, it was "found" not by any one of us, but by the distributed reader we constitute. Yet, of course, the sentences *are* there, and they come in this order. Any number of other patterns are also there, and might be found by other readers, but this is the one I've been given to interpret. When I consider it, I find that the movement from reactive speech to internal musing to evaluative speech looks familiar. It is a basic variant of the cognitive process by which we orient ourselves in relation to what we know.

When the narrator says that he is glad for Robert's company, the recognition comes almost spontaneously, though prompted, as I earlier described, by the encroaching night and the inertness of his wife. It is the cognitive equivalent of a knee-jerk reaction. *The world is empty: I am glad I am not alone.* Again as I have already explained, something happens when the narrator internalizes the spoken word, turning the reflex into a thought: "And I guess I was [glad]." That is a rudimentary process of interpretation, of encoding an experiential datum into a definition that, in turn, represents and stores what is learned. When the narrator confesses that, to him, cathedrals are nothing but things to look at on TV, he is again speaking aloud, but this is not a knee-jerk reaction. It is more like a square-shouldered stance. He is stating a position. The words go nowhere. Later, when he says to himself that maybe he "ought" to keep his eyes closed a little longer, he is complicating his vision *and* the uses of language. He is not just reaching an understanding; he is turning it into a guide for his behavior.

Schematically, what I've just described—the transformation of thought into action—is a model for mature interaction with the world. Dramatically, it is the turning point of the spiritual journey we have been following in the story. And that is why, when the narrator concludes—once more aloud—that "It's really something," we are satisfied, and perhaps even touched, by a final statement that, on its own, is almost laughably vague and understated. In the context of the story, these words will strike almost any reader as a spiritual breakthrough. In the sequence of preclosure points, they can strike us—and this is the surprise—as something more.

Although it has been said that "talk fails" at the end of this story,[7] giving way to a fuller internal experience the words clearly don't describe, I would argue that it is not the content of what is "said" that matters so much as its closer and closer engagement with what is "thought." It is this process that educates the narrator. I certainly do not wish to minimize the role of the physical touch, the real and symbolic "contact" that makes this story so new and powerful in the Carver canon. Most discussions do focus on the interactive relationship between the touch and the understanding, and certainly without that touch, the process I have been highlighting might never have begun, might never have broken through to a new discovery. My reasons for emphasizing the more cerebral side of the equation may have something to do with my profile, but my conscious motives were to avoid the sentimentality that so easily creeps into discussions of this text, and to offer yet another explanation of why this story achieves a fuller rendering of, and a greater faith in, human potential.

One critic's reading of the story has affinities with my own and may be usefully compared and contrasted with my findings. In his article "'The Possibility of Resurrection': Re-Vision in Carver's 'Feathers' and 'Cathedral,'" Nelson Hathcock reminds us that Carver wanted a proactive reader, but knew he had to earn one. Quoting Carver, Hathcock agrees that, "if the words are in any way blurred—the reader's eyes will slide right over them and nothing will be achieved. The reader's own artistic sense will simply not be engaged."[8] If readers pay attention on the level of the word, argues Hathcock, they realize that the narrator in "Cathedral," like Jack in "Feathers," is noticeably evolving.

Hathcock shows how each character is startled into a crude form of rhetorical invention: Jack becomes almost lyrical about the ugliness of his hosts' baby, and the narrator of "Cathedral" rhapsodizes over the "scarf[ing]" and "graz[ing]" that goes on at the dinner table. Perhaps more importantly, the narrator has also been striving for expression through the very act of revisiting the past reflectively—something Carver's characters rarely do. Hathcock points out that the narrator claims he doesn't understand certain things, yet by verbalizing his puzzlement, he is making a beginning. These efforts bring him to the point of sympathy with the blind man's wife because her husband couldn't see her, and they lead him to admiration for the blind man because he knows where "his foods" are. At the culmination of the story, claims Hathcock, the narrator admits the limits of language and, through the "imaginative transfer" from Robert, reaches "an ineffable 'something' beyond a linguistic register, beyond the power of words to inhabit" (38–39).

It is here that my reading diverges from Hathcock's. From my point of view, he too easily drops the idea of linguistic evolution in favor of a pat notion of spiritual transcendence. If we rise above the word-by-word level to consider the putative-story level—as we do when looking at the results of preclosure study—I believe we can see that the narrator has *not* left language behind. Rather, he has made a minimal but important breakthrough by linking interior and external speech. No matter that his final words seem lamely vague. In relation to the series of inner and outer expressions we captured as preclosure points, his conclusion is not just an empty signifier pointing to something beyond itself, some "ineffable 'something,'" as Hathcock suggests. Rather, his remark is an achievement of effability, of getting something "out" into the domain of human communication. The words mean what they say: the nothing in this man's soul has turned into "something."

The progress I have been charting with the help of preclosure study incorporates the spiritual dimension, but not as ghostly transcendence in a glorified sense. Perhaps a spirit does enter the narrator, for surely it is a "higher" faculty that apprehends an inner freedom and shares the wonder with a listener. What he perceives, he must acknowledge. It seems to me that this transition is an even richer paradigm for what the artist himself goes through as he rises through pain and silence and darkness to the point of expression, no matter how parsimonious and elliptical those final words may be. For the narrator, for Carver, the sparest prose is the most "loaded."

But stop. I'm slipping into the groove of acclaim for this story—and my readers are challenging me. None of them was particularly impressed by "Cathedral." All four are college graduates, and among the group are degree-holders in law, medicine, and finance. Significantly, however, none has recently studied in a literature classroom. The authority of their responses comes from an experience quite different from that of my usual readers, college students and teachers. And it led them to heresy.

Everyone did find the portrait of the blind man effective, but Fran, the oldest member of the group, felt there was too much conversation; Pete and Jill thought the husband and wife too distant from their own worlds to be fully sympathetic; and Jim found the second half of the story less artful than the first half. With the exception of Jim, these readers were unaware of Carver's stature and did not know that they were "supposed" to admire his work. Even Jim was free of the conditioning I mentioned at the beginning of this chapter. He did not realize the extent to which this particular story had been defined by a critical consensus founded on the author's own assessment of the story's significance. Instead, by choosing a preclosure point a tenth of the way into the story, Jim was making a statement. He found the putative story of the wife's salvation—with all the wry digs the narrator supplied—a sufficiently interesting tale. Even its upbeat ending, in which the wife finds solace in communicating with Robert, is undercut by the dubious fate of being married to this narrator. In his praise for the style of the early pages and in his failure to be uplifted by the "revision," "self-enlargement," and "resurrection" critics find at the end, Jim may have sensed that Carver's genius had been tampered with—perhaps by Tess, perhaps by success, perhaps by a concession to symbols with a softer, more commonplace outline.

What I was testing in this group were the reactions of mature and highly intelligent people who were not programmed to respond to this story in the usual ways. Although these reactions cannot be generalized to predict those of larger groups of readers and although the selection of these four participants was highly idiosyncratic, I have argued that the preclosure choices of even a single reader are suggestive for the critic. They tell us the myriad ways a story can "mean" what it narratively says. These four readers provided me with a series of preclosure points quite different from my own choices, which overlapped theirs only twice. For that very reason, their responses were a valuable heuristic for me, providing the springboard for analysis. Preclosure study offers a plurality of interpretations that are never predictable but never really random.

My readers' responses would have been useful to me without the information in the profiles. One of my reasons for characterizing the readers more fully was that, for the first time, I *could*. Unlike the other readers I have used in my experiments, these were people I knew well. Another reason, of course, was to vary the possibilities of preclosure study. Correlating preclosure points with reader profiles is something else that can be done. Carried out more "scientifically," such correlations might offer some empirical, as opposed to ideological, insight into gender bias in reading, as well as other forms of influence on the hermeneutic process. Psychologists are the ones to continue the investigation. What I have done is simply to demonstrate, within the looser bonds of an interpretive essay, yet in freshly concrete and specific terms, that readers *do* reconstruct (or redraw) the stories they read in the light (or the dark) of their own proclivities.

By giving me their feedback, these four readers guided me through and beyond the approved take on this story. Through their eyes, I saw that "Cathedral" refracts much more than a mellowing Ray. The sea change the narrator experiences is not just a move from isolation to human contact, although it is surely that. Nor is it just a move from materialism to spirituality, from confinement to freedom, although surely those are themes of the story. As a dis-covering of the generic pattern reveals, it is also a move *from* the potentially endless sequence of self-serving notations to which our nerve ends and emotional antennae are condemned, *to* a cycle of reaction, reflection, interpretation, and storage by which progress is made and understanding enabled.

I share Hathcock's view that "Cathedral" is a rewriting of "What We Talk About When We Talk About Love." In that story, people sit around a table, become slowly drunk, and try to define "love." They tell stories, give examples, trade information. In the end, the light is gone, the bottles are empty, the talk is silenced. Hathcock makes the excellent point that the empty darkness and wordless "human noise" at the end of this story are dramatically different from the creative darkness and true "re-vision" at the end of "Cathedral." I'd add that the "noise" is replaced by a meaningful signal. Robert has enlightened the narrator, setting him free for an instant from loneliness and prejudice. If the last line were missing, that freedom would remain an insular discovery. But the narrator says words his companion can hear. Conversion is conversation. No matter if it is the barest of remarks, no matter if its resonance may fade the next day. All basic plots are irreversible.

There are ancient tales of conquest and discovery, but it is the achieve-ment of the "modern" short story to dignify the smallest of increments in perception and understanding. On one level, I am less concerned with this pivotal story itself than with the short story as a form. I believe this genre works by nesting primal narratives, whose endings become the plot of a metastory. Taken in sequence in "Cathedral," these narratives yield a story about a man learning to think before—and after—and again be-fore—he speaks. Theories of genre can be confining, but they can also be liberating, if genre is conceived as an activity of story making in which the reader can participate. I redrew this story, with the help of four other hands—Jill's, Pete's, Jim's, and Fran's—but it was Carver's edifice we were tracing. His hand guided ours.

chapter seven

Revisiting Ann Beattie

In Carver's "Cathedral," the blind man asks the narrator whether he is going to remain in a job he dislikes, and he replies, "What [are] the options?" He means, of course, that there are none, or at least none that he can imagine or realize on his own. Compared with him, the majority of Ann Beattie's characters have more education and better jobs; they have apartments in the city or houses in the country, and sometimes both. Typically, they have lovers, and/or their spouses have lovers and/or former spouses. It is a world full of options, but there is sometimes little difference among them, no permanent assurance of value, and often no will to make a decision. For many readers, loss and aimlessness are the dominant features of the Beattie universe.

The cliché about this writer is that she is the chronicler of her generation. As Pico Iyer memorably says, she is "perhaps the first and the finest laureate of that generation of Americans born to a society built on quicksand and doomed to a life in the long, ambiguous shadow of the sixties."[1] Although the stories of her latest collection, *Perfect Recall* (2001), are more reflective and slightly more end-directed, it may still be fair to say that her fiction puts the notion of preclosure more severely to the test than does the work of any other writer discussed in this book. If the premise of the stories is that storyness is passé, if closure is a non sequitur, then how can a reader identify preclosure points?

Ann Beattie claims that she writes quickly and never knows where the stories are headed, or how they will end. "I've never in my life sat down and said to myself, 'Now I will write something about somebody to whom such-and-such will happen.' "[2] As Carver had his minimalist editor in Gordon Lish, Beattie had hers in J. D. O'Hara: "It was really O'Hara who, in literally taking the scissors to my pages, suggested that more elliptical endings to my stories might be advantageous" (106). Whether or not we accept Beattie's description of her work, and although surely the O'Hara blade was not wielded on all occasions, we can be forgiven for believing that preclosure study is a violation of the mindset and the aesthetic that produced these stories.

My decision to attempt it is partly for the sake of argument, to test the limits of the method. Partly, however, this is a way of teaching myself to appreciate stories I did not warm to at first glance, by an author who once sat beside me on the floor of a crowded auditorium and would not let me dislodge others from their seats, although she'd been the guest of honor in the same room the day before. By this reference I mean no sentimental praise of her modesty or collegiality, nor any self-congratulation at the propinquity to fame, although on other occasions I might recall the incident for just those reasons. No, what seems relevant here is the standpoint, or in this case, the sitpoint, she accepted in the visual and cultural space she had entered.

It was an evening of readings. John Barth, Jamaica Kincaid, and Robert Coover would stand at the podium. Because I'd had a hand in organizing the event, Beattie recognized me and stepped over other legs to stretch her elegantly booted calves beside my rumpled skirt. From this eye level, the room had no center, only an encroaching horizon of oversized bodies, around which she caught glimpses of the faces at the front of the room. She heard the drone of fortified voices—there was, of course, a microphone—and the rippling responses of laughter or applause. She was almost invisible. The rest of the overflow crowd either did not recognize her in the unusual role of floor-sitter or else were shyly pretending not to notice.

It is tempting to think she could have recalled, at a later time, the odd angles of vision: speakers severed at the neck by a looming audience; herself reflected in the iris of a gawker. This was, after all, Iowa City, town of burgeoning authors. Would she have sized up the room as a whole? "I don't think I have an overall view of things to express," she concluded in the interview I have been quoting (107). What she does have is an eye for anxiety. She discerned it in my face, I'm sure, for her smile kindly said, "This is fun."

So is reading her fiction. I've settled in with "Weekend" (*Secrets and Surprises*, 1979) and "Where You'll Find Me" (*Where You'll Find Me,* 1986), both of which were reprinted in *Park City* (1998). As I've done occasionally before, I've used only myself as a reader, although it seems this time to be a deliberate choice of private engagement before public discussion. I had no desire to get to know the author better through her work, although it is often said that she is a "Beattie character" in the flesh. I did, however, want to get to know her stories better. Going into these reading experiments, I was familiar with only a few of her better-known tales. Beattieville is almost as far from my world as Carverdom, yet I felt more lost in her pages. I hoped that preclosure study would help me to share, once again, her line of sight.

"Weekend" (1979)

First published in the *New Yorker,* "Weekend" shows us a common-law marriage that has lasted for six years. Lenore, thirty-four, has had two children by George, a fifty-five-year-old former professor who was denied tenure and has created a fragile domain for his ego in a house he renovated in the woods. Lenore, the focal character, once overheard him referring to her as "simple," and although hurt, she has closeted her pain in a home and a life she continues to find comfortable.

Every weekend George invites former students—young, pretty, unmarried women—to visit. They accompany him on walks, provide an adoring audience, and possibly gratify him sexually. A rather traditional expository opening lets us see George as vain, fashionably unconventional, and increasingly withdrawn, while Lenore appears vulnerable yet clear-sighted—a woman who has settled for a relationship that is strained but still viable. Whenever she raises the issue with George, he puts her off with cutting remarks or dismissive clichés she'd rather swallow than challenge.

> . . . [W]hen there is an answer—even his answer—it is usually easier to accept it and go on with things. She goes on with what she has always done: tending the house and the children and George, when he needs her. She likes to bake and she collects art postcards.[3]

Although she is living with a man who sees himself as a rusticated artist and local sophisticate, she sounds like a conventional homebody.

Enter: two girls, Friday night. The next morning, George takes Sarah for a walk to the nearby store, but as rain begins to fall and Julie takes the car to look for them without success, the implications seem glaring. Whether suspicious or just worried, Julie says, "Maybe something happened to them." With characteristic plainness, Lenore replies, "Nothing happened to them . . . Maybe they took shelter under a tree . . . Maybe they're screwing. How should I know?" She shrugs and pours her guest a cup of tea.

George and Sarah return later, and throughout dinner there are signs that Sarah feels awkward about her escapade with her host; Julie is embarrassed for Lenore's sake, and George is pontificating about the famous scene of stalled cars in Godard's film about stasis. This foursome is trapped in a social moment that disguises the sexual triangle. After dinner, George and Sarah go out again for a walk, leaving Lenore and Julie sitting by the fire, drinking wine and speaking with the frankness of those left behind. Julie admits her close friendship with Sarah but regrets that Lenore, "such a nice lady," is being treated so badly.

Rejecting this view of herself, Lenore seems resigned to "giv[ing] up [her] weekends" (and her partner, at least temporarily?), noting that "it's good to have something to do." Throughout the story thus far, the question of what "to do" has been a refrain: "But what will she do for the rest of the day?" she wonders in the morning; "What am I going to do?" she shrugs at the likelihood of betrayal; "What can she do about it?" she asks herself, when she hears the story of another student who died in a car crash. She, herself, prefers sitting in stalled traffic. The routine of her life gives her *something* to do, and that is enough.

"For all I know," she consoles Julie, "your friend is flattering herself, and George is trying to make me jealous" (207). Perhaps she is only playing the hostess at her own expense, offering her guest a more palatable scenario. Yet, we've seen that she readily accepts "answers" that, on some level, she knows are false. Now she gets up and adds wood to the fire, the hearth of domesticity. Talking to herself, she reaches a conclusion that felt, to me, like an ending:

When these [logs] are gone, she will either have to walk to the woodshed or give up and go to bed. (207)

This was my first preclosure point. Because this reading experiment is the most recent of those discussed in this book, I can no longer claim that my response to preclosure "signals" is ingrained below the level of consciousness, as I believe is the case for the average reader. By virtue of having identified and discussed these triggers so often, I have either reinternalized them or, if you like, indoctrinated myself with them. I cannot sit next to a text and be innocent of assumptions about its operational strategies. So, in this case, I cannot say that I was not looking for time-shift words like *when,* or absolute-degree terms like *either . . . or* and *gone.* Surely my ear is by now sensitized to the closural force of serial repetition on the level of alliteration and assonance (*w*alk to the *w*oodshed; *g*ive up and *g*o; sh*ed*; b*ed*) and on the level of the phrase (to walk . . . [to] give up . . . to go).

If a car is caught in a traffic jam, does its failure to move mean it has reached a destination? Lenore entered her relationship with George apparently believing that they were genuinely in love. Now she is the keeper of the flame, literally and figuratively. Choices present themselves only in the minimal and resigned form of a decision about whether to get more firewood. There is no indication that Lenore is aware of the symbolic overtones of the choice she has posited: she can keep fueling the status quo; or she can "give up and . . ." do what? Leave? No. The alternative she imagines is simply a retreat to her bedroom. If the story were to end here, it would be an *inverted fairy tale,* in which the princess has become the drudge in her own castle.

If we read on, we discover that Lenore is almost dispassionately curious to know what Julie thinks of the predicament. This is a girl to whom Lenore feels akin. She has observed how attentive Julie is to what is happening around her, and how instinctively she plays the role of the domestic caretaker: earlier in the evening, she caught Sarah's wineglass before it could spill. But Julie confides that she, herself, could never live under the conditions Lenore endures. Survivor of a failed marriage, she nevertheless believes she could not live with a man without being married to him. "I'm not secure enough," she confesses. The answer has a familiar offhandedness:

"You have to live somewhere," Lenore says. (207)

The story will go on to complicate this remark, but the line has a summary quality that brought me to rest again. The bitter wisdom is offered as a truism and may just prove that Lenore is "simple," as George claims.

Maybe, however, it reveals a subtler tendency to use simple-sounding re-marks as a deterrent to "too much communication" (208). Perhaps there's a hint here of a dated and sexist assumption that women must live, whether they wish to or not, where they find male protection—although Lenore's brother, who has continually urged her to leave, comes to mind as a refuge. Perhaps I simply want to credit Lenore with a deliberate if fake toughness, a blasé tone that conceals a duty to accept the consequences of her alliance. At this point, the story is emphatically hers, and despite the flaws in her arrangement with George, despite our resistance to such pas-sivity, we may accept the tale that ends here as an *existential parable,* a distant echo of Godard's.

But, of course, Beattie carries on—and so, therefore, does Lenore. Wanting Julie to accept the situation, she takes the girl into George's study and shows her some hidden photographs. They are portraits that George took of himself, nakedly revealing his tortured soul. Or so the women be-lieve. Julie whispers her amazement at the "photograph of a man in agony, a man about to scream" (208). Lenore, once again, shrugs. Interestingly, she is now playing George's favorite role of the explicator with a captive audience. She says, "So I stay," implying that she tolerates George's infi-delity because it stems from a primal anguish she can't abandon. The women appear to share this recognition: "Julie nods. Lenore nods . . ." (208). Beattie underscores and recasts the significance of this moment by letting us know that

> Lenore has not thought until this minute that this may be why
> she stays. (208)

If we accept this statement, we've reached the end of an *epiphany story.* The time shift is clear: "until this moment" she was in the dark; now she has seen the light. She has arrived at a new insight that explains her behavior—to Julie, to us, but most of all to herself. Like many preclosural sentences, it contains an equation: my reaction to these pictures = the reason why I stay. True, she may again be revealing her simplicity. How does she know that George was not indulging in yet another form of self-dramatization, hiding his petty failures behind a glorified imitation of the tragedian's mask? Yet that very gesture might be the greater horror, and perhaps Lenore understands that duplicity is, as the saying goes, a cry for help.

As usual, the next line pulls back from completeness. Lenore admits

to herself that the pictures are only one of the reasons she stays in this relationship. Far from concentrating her thoughts, the pictures had originally scared and embarrassed her. "She had simply not known what to
do" when she found them. They are a symptom, not an answer, although
perhaps they prepare for the Dionysian scene that follows. George and
Sarah return, soaked with rain and brandy. In front of Lenore and Julie,
George grabs Sarah into his arms, spins her around, and proclaims that
he loves her. It is one of the more dramatic turning points in Beattie's stories. Everything that follows is a reaction to it.

Sarah rushes off to the guest room in tears. Lenore, in response to her
son's cry, leaves the room, comforts her baby, and goes directly to bed.
Julie, in shock, has presumably followed Sarah to her room. Soon she
knocks on Lenore's door to announce that she and Sarah are leaving, and
within moments their car can be heard on the gravel in the driveway.
Lenore tries to fall asleep but cannot.

The only sound in the house is the electric clock, humming by
her bed. (209)

Now will she leave? Or will she patch up her ruptured life with habitual compliance, self-sacrificing pity, or just plain inertia? When I came to
the humming clock in the silent house, I heard it as a closural image. The
absolute-degree term *only* had its effect, as did the buried equation (the
only sound = the clock's humming), and the keyword *bed*. George has in-
sulted Lenore publicly, but in such a way as to make a fool of himself,
alienating the girls he wanted to impress. He will try to pass off his out-
rageous behavior as a joke. What will Lenore do? Options come to mind.
She could accept his phony excuses, make a scene, and/or take her children and depart, playing the wronged wife. In a somewhat coy yet academic way, the story could end here in an oh-so-telling image that leaves
all these options open. This is the kind of ending that substitutes a mood
for an action. It implies that ambiguity is artistically superior to resolution. It says that the love story is now the *relationship story*, and all that
is required is to show the lay of the land.

My respect for Beattie was increased by her decision *not* to stop here.
There is one more scene between the main characters, with a flashback
in the middle. As an outcome, it beggars the options I have mentioned.
Lenore gets out of bed and goes downstairs to find George, angry and

bedraggled, in front of the ashen fireplace. He spits out his animosity against the girls, calling Sarah a "damn bitch" and a "stupid girl." Explains Lenore, "You went too far . . . I'm the only one you can go too far with" (209). It is another of those plainspoken truths that may finally prove George wrong: Lenore's simplicity is *not* stupidity. Her statement has a clarity approaching the phlegmatic wisdom of a detached observer.

As many of Beattie's characters do, Lenore remembers a scene from an earlier and warmer time. She and George were on a beach. He playfully ran off, inviting her to catch him, and when she did, he "turned on her, just as abruptly as he had run away, and grabbed her . . ." (210). As Lenore recognizes, the gesture is a precursor of his grab for Sarah, which had such different and disastrous results. Needing always to be the coveted prize, he must constantly restage and reenact his capture of a woman who pursues him. It is his script for cheating failure and old age. Lenore, I think, has intuited as much. Remembering his dash into the water, she wonders:

> If she hadn't stopped him, would he really have run far out into the water, until she couldn't follow anymore? (210)

For all her understanding of the man, she can still ask herself this question. She may sense that his bravado, his vagrancy, is only a ruse to make her "save" him before he proves a coward. Or perhaps she thinks he *might* throw himself to his demons, if he should once succeed in "going too far" for her love to reclaim him. The story that ends here is an *open-ended mystery,* for we do not yet know whether he has crossed that line. Will she, or will she not, put out her hand one more time?

Still lost in anger, George "wouldn't care" if the girls died in a car crash, like the student they had talked about at dinner. Lenore rejects this cruel wish but seats herself on the floor, joining him in listening to the rain. Actual closure is reached in the following sentence:

> She slides over closer to him, puts her hand on his shoulder and leans her head there, as if he could protect her from the awful things he has wished into being. (210)

Her decision is made. There will always be "awful things" in her life with George because he will always be selfish and tyrannical. The irony, whether tender or harsh, is that he cannot protect her from himself, but she will make it seem "as if he [can]," and by that very gesture she will save him from the undertow of self-destruction—and herself from the empty beach.

Is she a passive female, trapped by fear of independence, or is she a survivor, a woman dominated by a weak man but stronger than she realizes? Commanded to look the other way as George flaunts his infidelity, is she the browbeaten hausfrau, or the grownup who abides? By leaving questions like these open, Beattie moves the story beyond a feminist parable, giving *us* some options for our behavior as critics.

Like Lenore's brother, we may chafe at her failure to challenge the demeaning aspects of her life. Like George, we may find her a little boring. What we should not do—and what the above preclosure analysis may help us to avoid—is dismiss the vagaries and mysteries of love, or impose a model of female self-fulfillment that shortchanges Lenore, regrettable as her life may be. We must remember that George's failings are revealed to us through Lenore's observations. Glaring as those faults may be, they are human weakness writ large. Vanity. Failed ambition. Self-deception. Fear of old age and death. Anxiety expressed as cruelty. Who has not a tincture of these sins? In a secular world, who will forgive us for these failings?

Those who love us, answers the completed story. In Beattie's world, there is precious little honor and fidelity, but there can be a mutual neediness that fills in for loyalty. What we have in the end, then, is a story that includes and progressively transmutes an *inverted fairy tale* courtesy of Cinderella, an *existential parable* à la Godard, an *epiphany story* in the modernist vein, a *relationship story* with textbook savvy, and the *open-ended mystery* of the sexual power game. None is a model for the final story, yet their presence, in tandem, creates a distinctive fusion of the blasé and the wishful. From the angle they provide, we get an unforeseen glimpse of a *revisionist love story*. It is a tale without sentiment or precept, but not without beauty.

"Where You'll Find Me" (1986)

"Where You'll Find Me," appearing nearly a decade later, is another story about a visit, told this time from the guest's point of view. With an injured arm confined to her side like "a broken wing," the narrator arrives at her brother's house in Saratoga for the Christmas holiday. Howard, a veteran of two failed marriages to "pale" women, is living with the more color-ful and decisive Sophie, whose ex-husband sends their children large stuffed animals to add to "Mom's zoo." After noting Sophie's somewhat feckless behavior, the narrator admits she isn't in a position to "stand in judgment."

> I am a thirty-eight-year-old woman, out of a job, on tenuous enough footing with her sometime lover that she can imagine crashing emo-tionally as easily as she did on the ice [when she broke her arm].
> . . . I am insecure enough to stay with someone because of the look that sometimes comes into his eyes when he makes love to me. I am a person who secretly shakes on salt in the kitchen, then comes out with her plate, smiling, as basil is crumbled over the tomatoes.[4]

Compared with Lenore in "Weekend," this narrator is less rooted; she has no real sense of home, and her lover, although important to her emotional equilibrium, is tangential to her life. Her relationship with Howard, like some other brother-sister pairings in Beattie's work, seems more durable and appealing than many a love affair.

With deft realism, Beattie creates the scene in this Saratoga kitchen. In preparation for a Christmas party, there are "mushrooms stuffed with pureed tomatoes, [and] tomatoes stuffed with chopped mushrooms" (388). Sophie, the sister-in-law, is amused by the culinary joke, afraid it will go un-noticed, not realizing that she has created a parody of her mate-swapping generation, who are endlessly recycling the same hopes and disillusion-ments. Sophie's young daughter, Becky, enters on the fly and is scolded for bad manners. She ought to have said *hello* to those present. Whether we're in polite society or just Sophie's "zoo," her notions are the rule.

Sidelined, Howard chats in a desultory way. The conversation takes a somber turn, and suddenly he begins talking about Dennis Bidou, a boy who once picked on his sister. Howard recalls standing up for her but re-maining frightened of Dennis. Later, after learning that Dennis had been killed in Vietnam, Howard was haunted by images of the boy that are now resurfacing. To put these dreary thoughts behind him, Howard proposes a trip to the Christmas tree lot. His sister agrees to go with him. Although Beattie doesn't say so, perhaps the errand offers a faint suburban echo of the masculine roles of protector and forager. Because of the narrator's in-jured arm, her brother helps her into her coat and poncho, safety-pinning her attire as if she were a child he is bundling up. She feels like a bird in a cage, covered up for the night. Protected or enshrouded? The bittersweet images trigger emotion:

> This makes me feel sorry for myself, and then I *do* think of my arm as a broken wing, and suddenly everything seems so sad that I feel my eyes well up with tears. (392)

Lacrimae rerum, the Virgilian "tears of things," the melancholy that arises from the knowledge that time breaks all wings—these are the pervading feelings in my first preclosure point. The story that ends here is an *elegy.*

The scene changes to a short time before the Christmas party. Howard is giving his sister a rundown on the guests. The gossip about lovers and husbands may remind the reader of the interchangeable hors d'oeuvres. Abruptly, the child Becky and her friend pass by again, all giggles and confidences, with an "Oh, hel-*lo*" in mocking obedience to the social decorum the grownups maintain while their lives go to pieces. The narrator draws a distinction between the intimacy of girl talk and the casualness of boy talk. Restless and nostalgic, Howard urges his sister to recreate yet another sort of warmth from the past—by treating him, in effect, like a girlfriend. "'Come on,' he says. 'Confide something in me'" (394).

She does. She's had an adventure in San Francisco. In a restaurant, she repeatedly locked eyes with a man sitting with another woman. Afterwards, he found an indirect way to give her his business card and ask her to call. Howard becomes engaged in the story, wanting to know if she ever called (she has not), and then urging her to take steps to reconnect with her mysterious admirer. On a whim, she had sent the man a photograph of herself with a stranger hanging around her neck, a "punk" kid who posed with tourists in a New York street, but she had not included a return address. With surprising insistence, Howard presses her to get in touch with the man. "'Do it,' Howard says. 'I think you need this,' and when he speaks he whispers—just what a girl would do. He nods his head yes."

> "Do it," he whispers again. (397)

The story that ends here—and I had a strong feeling of closure at this point—is a bit of a tease. The close repetition of the keywords *do it* have a subversive if unfocused power, made girlishly conspiratorial and yet unnervingly urgent by the whispered delivery. Perhaps he is simply getting into character, playing the role of the little-girl chum. Can such a gambit be innocent? If we had nothing further to read, we might find ourselves recycling through the previous pages, looking more closely at Howard's behavior.

Suddenly a spotlight might be cast on his brief stint as a screenwriter in Laguna Beach, his own California story. Does he wish he'd never left? During the kitchen discussion, he'd suddenly said he was "depressed" and recounted a memory from his boyhood. "What's wrong with me," he'd wondered, and Sophie had told him to "snap out of it" (389). He'd wanted to know whether his sister keeps reliving her fall on the ice, and he'd wondered what his stepdaughter's little friend was "going to do" about the fact that a pen pal of hers turned out to be in prison. So, when he tells his sister to just "do it," to take a risk, to change her life—is he venting frustrations of his own? Is he hoping for vicarious happiness? The narrative that ends here is a *mid-life crisis story,* in which the happy husband is secretly discontented.

Indeed, the hints of trouble in Howard's marriage are significant. He and his sister go on another errand, this time to buy ice cubes for the party. The frozen element that caused her to slip and break her arm is tamed here for use in people's drinks. But danger remains in another form, as Howard drives the narrator on a detour to a pond. There he reveals that he has fallen in love with a graduate student, a girl he has met only a few times. "There was so much passion, so fast," he says. He is completing the circle of confidence, telling her a secret.

He and the girl, Robin, have had some chilly picnics in the winter weather, and, with the help of a stray dog who adopts them, they have found a surrogate domesticity that offers everything his home with Sophie does not: romance, youth, and freedom. As an old, old story, this confession has its absurd, even pathetic aspects. Yet, because it is confided in good faith, it may earn from us, as it does from the narrator, a sober consideration. Robin is scheduled to leave town in January, and apparently no plans have been made for continuing the love affair. It is a more fully realized idyll than the stalled romance between his sister and her San Francisco admirer, and yet the parallels explain why he so urgently wanted her to trust the "kinetic energy" she felt between herself and the stranger. If she could be persuaded to take the leap, perhaps he, too, could shake himself free from his current entanglements.

Younger readers might urge him to do so. Older ones might shake their heads knowingly. He has already had two wives before moving in with Sophie. Ultimately, none of his liaisons have given him what he is looking for. Perhaps none could, but his relationship with the girl did give him a "feeling" that was "real." He threw rocks for the dog's amusement. He called the dog Spot, and the girl called him Rover. They—but wait a minute. What kind of scene *is* this? Sketched by Norman Rockwell—a boy and a girl and a dog and a pond—it has an air of old-fashioned wholesomeness.

It is nostalgia incarnate, at least for those old enough to recognize the clichés and to long for what they promised. Howard insists that the feelings were real, although poignantly fleeting. He would like to believe that his experience with Robin is a genuine alternative to his life with Sophie. We have, of course, no confirmation that Robin exists. It is possible that Howard has conjured up his little romance, playing a game of "me too!" with his sister, although such a reading seems unnecessarily precious. In either case, we must remember that Beattie chose the sister, not the brother, for her focal character.

The narrator asks Howard more or less the same question he asked *her*, although his case is more immediate and consequential. "What are you going to do?" she wonders. "Get ice," he replies.

> He backs up, and as we swing around toward our own tire tracks I turn my head again, but there is no dog there, watching us in the moonlight. (400)

There are many preclosure signals here. The backing movement of the car reverses the forward movement that carried them to the pond, and the image of retracing their "own tire tracks" underlines this closure. The alliterating *t*s—four in close sequence—adds a note of finality. More emphatically, there is the repetition of the keyword *dog* and a reprise of the closural image of a dog watching a car disappear down a road. The absolute-degree negative—"no dog"—is, of course, the salient point here. It may be an example of the absence-as-presence so beloved by deconstructionists, but here it signifies more narrowly as the inversion of the scene Howard has just described to his sister. What he has said about the dog suggests that its presence made the liaison seem innocent and conventional—legitimate in some fashion. When the lovers leave the pond, they have to abandon the vision of themselves as a grown-up Dick and Jane playing with a dog named Spot. The dog's steady farewell gaze is sentimental—the dog is losing *his* idyll, too—and paradigmatic. It signifies the return gaze of one's remembered and idealized self. Howard mentions that his girlfriend did *not* look back at the receding image of the dog. Yet his sister *does* look back, even though she "knows" there is no dog at the pond now. Why does she half expect—or want—to catch its eye?

There are many ties between Harold and the narrator. The parallel between their secrets is underscored and revised by the parallel between his last visit to the pond with Robin and his visit there with his sister. As I've been suggesting, Howard is in the grip of a discontent that looks rather like a mid-life crisis. His sister's presence has triggered various throwbacks, involving youthful issues of masculinity, an eagerness for the illicit collusions of childhood, and some mildly manic-depressive mood swings. What he wants is a rejuvenated emotional life. Whether or not Robin is a figment of his imagination, the longing for what she represents is patently "real," it is backward-looking, and it is agitated by the presence of someone who has known him since boyhood. Perhaps what Howard wants, what he has been searching for as he has moved from woman to woman, and what a psychiatrist could diagnose all too handily, is a relationship that combines adult sex ("so much passion, so fast") with childhood innocence, with the time-defying simplicity and trust of fraternal companionship.

When his sister asks him what he's going to do, and when he says he's going to "get ice," he may be switching off the fantasy, although he acknowledges that her question is really about his future. We've seen that ice is associated with the ordinary round of social life in Saratoga and with the slick pavement that caused his sister to break her arm as she was running after a bus. Although he urged her to take a risk and run after the man in San Francisco, maybe he is accepting the fact that life breaks arms and spirits and all one can do is fantasize or confide. Perhaps the sister looks back over her shoulder, *as if* the dog might be there, because she, too, is aware that something was left behind. Maybe she can almost believe that what's missing from their lives could materialize as a dog. Perhaps she is just that much more hopeful than Robin. *But.* The conjunction can hardly convey surprise, but it does seem to carry a burden of regret. We may wish, we may hope, "*but* there is no dog there." To use a label from the Cisneros discussion, this is a *reality-check story.*

There is a break in the text at this point, underscoring the preclosural force of the departure from the pond. If Beattie were a different (and perhaps lesser) artist, the story *would* end here, just as "Weekend" would have ended with the image of the electric clock "humming" in Lenore's bedroom. Both of these preclosure points contain salient and resonant images that beg for New Critical exegesis, such as I've been guilty of initiating. Newer paradigms—most notably psychoanalytic and feminist— have their own templates for decoding these images. Perhaps I am reflecting only my own limitations, but I believe that such analysis leads typically toward the meticulous hairsplitting and ready-made sophistication, the postmodern chic, of much that is intelligent—but also predictable and artificial—in contemporary criticism.

So it was with relief that I followed Beattie beyond this point. Howard and his sister return from their errand, she trying to avoid slipping once again on the ice underfoot, he wielding two bags of ice, looking—she suddenly realizes—like "the statue of a blindfolded woman holding the scales of justice . . . but there's no blindfold" (399). Here is another image that rings with implications. These two people know that there was "no dog" at the pond they've just visited, and perhaps that is because they are now wearing "no blindfold." They arrive at a flagrantly ordinary scene of partying adults, sleepy children, cigarette smoke. Howard's little stepson makes a dash for the open air, but Howard and his sister move into the enclosed space—a crisscrossing of generations that is echoed in other scenes throughout the story.

Entering the room, the narrator hears that "Sophie's choice of perfect music for the occasion," Handel's *Messiah*, has been displaced by the sappy and nostalgic "Over the Rainbow" from the *Wizard of Oz*. Brother and sister hear Judy Garland singing, "That's where you'll find me." Readers with good memories will also "hear" the surrounding lyrics, invoking a land mentioned in lullabies, a place "over the rainbow," where dreams will come true. Bluebirds can reach this land, and so, wonders the singer, why can't *she*? Perhaps the adult yearning for an idealized love affair is no more than infantilized wishfulness. As such, maybe it is rendered harmless and yet eternally available in this fragment of pop culture. A conclusion something like that may have prompted me to choose the next sentence as a preclosure point.

The words hang in the air like smoke. (400)

Stasis (words suspended in air) and evanescence (like smoke) come together in these eight monosyllables. Beattie's often noted "flatness" and low "affect" prove deceptive in a line like this, which is clearly elegiac. The story that ends here is a *lyrical lament.*

Actual closure bursts upon the scene with Becky's final salvo. Gleefully, she embroiders on her own inflation of adult etiquette: "'Hello, hello, hello, hello,' Becky calls, dangling one kneesocked leg over the balcony . . . "

"To both of you, just because you're here, from me to you: a million—a trillion—hellos." (400)

It seems appropriate that the last words should come not from the mid-life adults, not from Judy Garland, but from a child. Half on, half off the balcony, she is hovering between socialized behavior and self-performing anarchy, but she has an orientation. Her greeting links the brother and sister with each other ("both of you") and speaks to them from the lost standpoint of childhood ("from me to you"); it denies any evaluative structure ("just because you're here"—in my house, in this universe); and it has an antic energy, a spontaneous absurdity, even a songlike cadence, that becomes the warmest of welcomes. The little girl is the reminder of Christmas past, the greeter of Christmas present, and perhaps the guide to a more relaxed and free psyche.

Hanging in the air is the afterimage of the narrator as a child, a free-spirited little girl whom Howard projects into Robin, and who speaks through Sophie's daughter. In a way, this tale is a *postmodern ghost story.* Whatever the characters decide to do, even if they let circumstances choose their options for them, such outcomes are less important than the haunting of the present by the past.

By labeling the putative stories I have found, I am, of course, borrowing a series of frames through which to view the story. Before I discuss this series, I want to acknowledge the special importance critics have given to cultural framing in Beattie's work. One essay in particular helps me situate my method in relation to more prevalent critical approaches. In "Frames, Images, and the Abyss: Psychasthenic Negotiations in Ann Beattie," Sandra Sprows highlights the two modes of modern perception discussed by Celeste Olalquiaga: "obsessive compulsive disease" and "psychasthenia."[5] The first involves the endless repetition of cultural frames and formulas, while the latter denotes fusion with the surrounding milieu, or, as Sprows defines it for her purposes, a slippage between frames requiring negotiation at the borders between images or formulas provided by the culture.

She points out that the narrator and Howard in "Where You'll Find Me" "constantly see themselves and others through photographic or filmic frames, constituting their place in each other's lives through a series of images." The Judy Garland song evokes another set of ready-made images.

> Yet, the only way to live with these American movie ideals and often tyrannical images is to appropriate them and live on the borders between the images, in the slippages where movement is possible, rather than remaining inside any one pre-fab frame and fearing movement . . . [I]n the end, it is the daughter Becky who enacts the positive and possibly empowering use of a cultural image as she plays with the guests, and the narrator glimpses this as a transgressive move which can make the place "over the rainbow" work as a discursive strategy by recognizing it as illusory, fabricated, and clichéd but still usable in some way. (151)

I suspect that Sprows would agree that she, herself, has deployed a number of frames that have wide currency today, although she might not see them, as I do, as the "popular culture" of academic humanism in the 1980s and 1990s. *Slippages, empowering, transgressive move, discursive strategy*—these words tag her own discourse, suggesting Foucault (whom she lists in her bibliography) but more loosely the systemic linking of linguistic codes and social power structures to be found across the board in "culture"-based criticism of literary works. As a result, her essay on Beattie inserts this author into the canon of writers to be admired for subverting outmoded conventions of meaning.

The rescue mission is clear from an earlier statement in Sprows's essay:

> Rather than indicting a weakness due to a lack of depth or breadth (as many critics contend), the much-noted "flat" quality of Beattie's texts is important precisely *because* it denies the traditional depth or causal scenarios which enable the very American notion of the autonomous individual hero . . . Those who would criticize Beattie's stories for lacking any ultimate meanings or messages immediately set up a privileging of the systematicity of coherent narratives. (141)

Disputing these points is the farthest thing from my mind. On its own terms, Sprows's argument is not only valid but persuasive. Here and now, I'm adding the notion of "psychasthenia" to my critical understanding of Beattie's work, and I am very grateful for the insight. However, I do not find it as comprehensively useful as the tone of the essay suggests it should be. I do not, for example, believe that Beattie's subversion of "the systematicity of coherent narratives" means that narrative coherence is foregone. What I have proposed instead—recasting the surface narrative as a sequence of putative stories with recognizable shapes—yields, I think, a richer, more fully articulated model for the narrative complexity and thematic range of a story like "Where You'll Find Me."

Of course, the story types I identify are also examples of "frames and formulas" available in the culture outside the given story. The difference is that Sprows identifies schemata from the popular culture of contemporary media, reference points that are overtly mentioned within the story, while I posit the immanence of subgenres from the traditions of narrative fiction, reference points that are *not* identified within the story, and for which I have no authority other than my own reading. Perhaps it is time to say again that the experiments documented in this book are demonstrations of an interactive process each critic—and, indeed, each reader—would perform differently, with differing results. *All* of those results would have validity as reading experiences. The only privilege I accord my own findings is their heuristic value as demonstrations. Their only authority derives from what they are seen to add to an understanding of a given text.

Sprows's interpretation of "Where You'll Find Me" accounts for the frequent use of the constitutive "gaze," the clichéd quality of the two potential romances, the performative role of Becky's *hellos*, and the replacement of the *Messiah*, a staple of traditional "high" culture, with a Judy Garland song from the *Wizard of Oz*, an outtake from the media-saturated culture of contemporary society. What she does not account for are the importance of the sibling relationship between the two main characters, the link between Becky and the narrator herself *as a child*, or the particular relevance of *this* Judy Garland song. These are all aspects of the story that come to the fore in the preclosure study above.

While the putative stories may exist only in my mind, they are derived from a close interaction with the text. In contrast, Sprows approaches the story with certain convictions—and concepts—borrowed from Olalquiaga and Foucault. Skimming for pop-culture frames, she "reads" that Howard met "Kate" in Laguna Beach, whereas it was Sophie. At least once, she attributes the narrator's words to Howard. She "reads" that the narrator is carrying the bags of ice at the end, whereas it is *Howard* who is doing so. She "reads" that, in the final party scene, "a young boy in his mother's arms 'makes a lunge . . . ,'" whereas it is "the woman with red hair [Mrs. Janson] holding Todd [who is *Sophie's* son, not hers]." Do any of these glitches matter?

By Sprows's own lights, it is important who is carrying the ice and who is looking at the carrier, but the other errors are mere accidents, the kind any of us could make. I do not mention them to start a nitpicking contest, nor to play games with Sprows's own concept of "slippage." My point is that reading for storyness *starts* with attentiveness to every single word of an unfolding story. It is a bottom-up rather than a top-down form of processing, and as such it maintains a tighter and more replete relationship between particulars and generalities, between the reading-of and the reading-out.

So we are back, now, to my list of familiar story-types. They include the static and the disruptive: *elegy, mid-life crisis story, reality-check story, lyrical lament,* and *postmodern ghost story.* Are they so different from the frames Sprows identifies? Mine, too, point to popular culture. However, they place that relevance within a complicated narrative progression rather than a matrix of allusions to stock images, movies, or songs. She seems to believe that cultural frames are the key determinants of psychological behavior within the story world, but I disagree. The putative stories make a different case. They suggest that we still encode our discontents by storying them. No doubt my list of putative tales would never have occurred to Beattie; however, they highlight, for our consideration, the human struggle to adapt past childhood. Those putative stories sensitize us to the prevalence—but also the failure—of gossip and nostalgia as scripts for adult life. They remind us of the human yearning to stop or reverse time. I am not arguing for a hidden traditionalism within Beattie's work. Perhaps I am simply revising another popular song lyric: everything new is old again. Everything, that is, that survives as literature.

Undoubtedly, Sprows would be delighted with my opening image of Ann Beattie—sitting on the floor at the edge of an auditorium as a not-quite audience member at the standard campus cultural (in both senses) event of a literary reading. Psychasthenia may be an apt model for a mo-

ment that is freeze-framed in my memory. Quite literally, Beattie was inserting herself on a border between the expectant listeners and the per-
forming artist, filling neither frame completely, yet defining herself via both.
Unfreeze the moment, and story can happen. Beattie's characters are often
adrift between normative life choices, but that does not mean their experience is too amorphous to be chunked in narrative arcs. It means—and
here I am quite close to Sprows—that no one plot can do the job alone.

I could say that "meaning" resides in the spaces between the putative
stories, but I have made a different argument in this book. I've urged you
to look for meaning in the metanarrative these stories create. Beattie's
characters may be trapped or confused, they may be unsure of what they
want, or betrayed in their reach for it, but they still have something at
stake. They are oriented toward what lures them. Stories tell us whether
they find, lose, or revise what they want.

Before slipping out of the frame myself, I notice, with a backward look,
that the putative stories in "Weekend" and "Where You'll Find Me" create sequences that turn on a point of stasis (the hum of the clock) or denial
(the absence of the dog). These preclosure points highlight the deflation
of meaning, the "flat," almost programmatic acceptance of postmodern
anomie and disillusionment. Yet, *given their place in the series*, these moments become actively and richly transitional—in other words, anything
but empty or defeatist. Haunted by story types that used to deliver meaning, like fairy tales, parables, and epiphanies, they are pregnant with others, like love stories and ghost stories, almost wistfully reimagined. When
Ann Beattie got down on that dirty floor and craned her neck, her gaze
was on the podium, not the exit.

chapter eight

The Largeness of Minimalism in Bobbie Ann Mason

O ne of literature's memorable semiotic moments occurs in Stephen Crane's classic short story, "The Open Boat." The desperate men in the lifeboat see a speck on the distant shore. Eventually the speck becomes a man. He is waving his arms at the crew. Relief! Rescue at last? No, it appears that the man is only giving them a friendly hail, misreading their condition as they misread his signal. This chapter is about other semiotic moments, some of them in "Shiloh" by Bobbie Ann Mason, some of them in the history of short fiction theory.

"But genre criticism . . . Isn't it—*dead?*" I often hear those words (or get that look) when I say I am interested in the short story. Truly, it is too late to ask, "What is a short story?" Instead, I've been asking, "What is storyness?" In 1982, the same year Bobbie Ann Mason published "Shiloh" in a collection, a psychologist I've mentioned before, William F. Brewer, offered one answer. He challenged both story grammars and plan-based comprehension models, saying that neither was truly specific to the experience of reading "stories." Having an understanding of both literary and rhetorical theory, he knew that discourse has to be understood in the context of its function or purpose. So he claimed that stories are a class of narratives meant to entertain, and he developed experiments for testing the arousal, intensification, and release (or resolution) of three affects within readers: surprise, suspense, and curiosity.[1] Brewer was trying to anatomize story processing, trying to determine its stages: the sequence of its cognitive strategies and affective states. He was interested in the way readers determine the "storyness" of stories and wanted to test empirically for this intuition.

I share that goal, although my principles and methods are different. He was looking for serialized affect; I am looking for serialized closure. The searches may be related, but they differ crucially in the nature and uses of the findings. What I am doing is putting readers in a position to activate the cognitive strategies associated with story processing—strategies that psychologists like Brewer have identified—and I am then recording the *evidence that those processes have happened*. Preclosure choices are exceptionally rich evidence because they reveal not only affective responses to a text but also the operation of internalized narrative schemata.

There are many ways a literary critic might use the raw data, but my method has been to recode the putative stories in terms of story types, those fictional scripts supplied by tradition. Doing so has proven to be a valuable first step toward an objective about which the scientist doesn't care but the literary critic does: the reinterpretation and reevaluation of a text worth the effort. On a number of occasions, I've used preclosure analysis to challenge, or at least postpone, ideological readings of short stories that are laden with social messages. Are there times, however, when social history is exactly what preclosure highlights? When it comes to today's interest in cultural study, is it goodbye that I'm waving—or hello? "Shiloh" is a good place to be when that question is asked.

Mason's well-known story is about the impending breakup of a marriage. Leroy and Norma Jean Moffitt live in Kentucky. Like so many characters in the Raymond Carver tradition of storytelling, Leroy is between jobs. He had been a truck driver, but he had an accident four months ago, and since then he has been staying at home. His wife works at the cosmetic counter in a Rexall drugstore, but she has begun a series of self-improvement activities: a class in body building and then a class in English composition. A restlessness that Leroy cannot understand seems to be driving her, and he knows intuitively that he will lose her. Meanwhile, he smokes pot; goes through an endless series of kitschy craft kits; tries to grasp what is happening to himself, Norma Jean, and their marriage; and focuses on the project of building a life-size "Lincoln Logs" cabin. He wants to build something meaningful, a "real home."

There are many reasons for the malaise of these characters. The rural past has slipped over the horizon while the national chain stores, the pop culture of television, and the new suburbia dominate the inner and outer landscape.[2] For the Moffitts personally, there is one tragic memory: the loss of their only child to sudden infant death syndrome. The pain and guilt seem harder to bury now that Leroy does not travel anymore and the Moffitts see more of each other. In fact, Norma Jean is having a hard time adjusting to her husband's return. Like Leroy's building projects, her self-improvement classes are a symptom. Both characters are trying to deal with change and are looking for self-validation in ways that may be banal or comic; however, they are also painfully confused and searching, a state as close to profound as anyone can reach in a world of Rexall drugstores and *Donahue* segments.

Leroy's mother-in-law suggests that he take his wife on a trip to Shiloh. Her own marriage took place in the nearby town of Corinth, and she remembers visiting Shiloh the next day. She is clearly a woman of the past, the kind who is shocked to discover her daughter smoking a cigarette—not because of the health risk but because nice girls do not do such things. Nor do they get pregnant before marriage, as Norma Jean did, nor do they lose their babies unaccountably. It is no surprise that the pressure is building up in Norma Jean. She is trapped between a do-nothing husband and a disapproving mother. The trip to Shiloh brings all these tensions to a head. As they sit on the ground near the graveyard, Norma Jean tells Leroy she wants to leave him, and Leroy has to face some truths about himself. He thinks about changing. At the end, Norma Jean has walked off to a bluff overlooking the river, and Leroy gets up to follow her. He is hobbling on one leg that still hurts from the old injury and one leg that went to sleep under him as he sat. Mason does not like showy symbols, but Leroy is walking on a meaningful pair of legs. They are unsteady, but they are moving.

The reader experiment on "Shiloh" was conducted in an undergraduate class on the short story, which I taught at the University of Iowa. There were thirty-six students in the class, twenty-three women and thirteen men. Twenty-four were seniors, eleven were juniors, and one was a sophomore. Four said they had studied Mason in another course, nineteen had read the story before, twelve simply recognized the title, and one had never heard of it.

The mix of students wasn't ideal, and the degree of prior familiarity was greater than expected. It is also true that the women greatly outnumbered the men. Like most undergraduate classes at Iowa, it looked very white and middle class, although, if one could rate the socioeconomic status of the parents, one would probably find a wide gap between the lowest and the highest. By any standard, and certainly by any scientific gauge, it was an imperfect sample. The biggest liability was that many students had read the story before. Unfortunately, their preclosure choices might be influenced by some memory of the actual closure. On the other hand, knowing the story, they could concentrate on the experiment itself.

Two texts of "Shiloh" were prepared. As usual, the sentences were serially numbered (1 to 476), and again, paragraph and section breaks were completely eliminated. Each story text was prefaced by a different quotation from Lila Havens's interview with Mason at the University of Houston on February 19, 1984, two years after the story came out in a collection. One quotation begins: "Right now I'm generally more interested in the cultural effects on men than I am the women characters in my stories because women are in an incredible position right now." The other begins: "[M]y larger concerns are tending, I think, toward a strong curiosity about the sympathy for the lower classes."[3] One quotation foregrounds gender issues; the other foregrounds class distinctions. About half the students got text A; the others got text B.

Readers were asked to list up to five preclosure points, starting with the one closest to the end of the story and working back toward the beginning. All in all, the group identified thirty different sentences. These were quickly reduced to five target sentences, which clearly stood out as the favorite choices. Each one had been picked by at least 20 percent of the readers, and no other sentences were noticed by more than 14 percent of the readers. These were the five points where storyness became apparent, marking off five putative stories on the way to the end of the actual story. Although no one reader processed the story in exactly these stages, the distributed reader favored this pattern.

The earliest target sentence occurs halfway through the story. Leroy has found his wife crying because her mother caught her smoking. Trying to cheer her up, he suggests that she play a tune on the organ he bought her for Christmas. During a break in the music, he asks her what she is thinking. When she says, "about what?" his mind is already a blank. But then

S/242   [He] has the sudden impulse to tell Norma Jean about himself, as if he had just met her.
S/243   They have known each other so long that they have forgotten a lot about each other.

S/244   They could become reacquainted.
S/245   *But when the oven timer goes off and she runs to the kitchen, he forgets why he wants to do this.* (9)

Cut. This sentence was probably chosen as a preclosure point because it is followed by a time shift to the next day. That is a very strong cue from the author, and a rather mechanical one, at that. But still, up to that point, the narrative segment has emphasized that Leroy's sense of meaning and direction in his life, and specifically in his marriage, is at risk. How can he regain or preserve well-being? The plan—however hazily formulated—is for Leroy and his wife to get acquainted again, to start over in their marriage. By now, however, we know that Norma Jean has begun to make over her own life without Leroy's help. He wants to build a new home; she wants to go to night school.

The main obstacle to his plan right now is not Norma Jean's separateness; it is his own inability to focus and persist. He is neutralized by confusion and inertia. Is there an outcome here? If so, it is the unenlightened maintenance of the status quo. Though not a dramatic ending, storyness is achieved: a marriage is at risk; the husband has a plan for saving it; he does not act, so the opportunity's lost. The essential qualities of the story are ordinary people, a low-keyed plot, an anticlimactic ending, and a marriage slowly disintegrating in western Kentucky in the 1970s. We know what we've got here. It used to be called a *slice-of-life story.*

Mabel, the mother-in-law, drops by. As usual, she has a negative effect on her daughter's confidence and composure. She retells a news story about a baby who died in an accident, and Norma Jean feels a pointed allusion to her own tragedy and her culpability. Later, as Leroy thinks about getting a truckload of notched logs for his dream house, Norma Jean diagrams paragraphs at the kitchen table.

S/313   Norma Jean is miles away.
S/314   He knows he is going to lose her.
S/315   *Like Mabel, he is just waiting for time to pass.* (11)

Cut. Again, the break comes just before a time shift. But, again, we can look with interest at a newly bracketed segment of narrative, one that incorporates the first putative story but now extends to a new insight about the future of the marriage—or, rather, its demise. Now the narrative shows *two* characters whose self-assurance and self-esteem are at risk. Norma Jean feels threatened by her mother's disapproval, and Leroy feels threatened by Norma Jean's new interests. Even for Norma Jean, the goal seems to be merely to fill time (she says night school is "something to do").

Husband and wife sit looking out at the bird feeder; they sit working at the kitchen table. Leroy has been thinking, "Norma Jean is miles away." There is nothing new about that realization. A period and a space and then: "He knows he is going to lose her." Something is *very* new here. Leroy has grasped that the status quo is doomed. That is the segue into the preclosure point: "Like Mabel, he is just waiting for time to pass." What is Mabel waiting for? She is old; she is waiting for death, the ultimate change in the status quo. In this putative story, little has happened, but much has been realized. The narrative up to this point is a *dawn-of-recognition story*.

We arrive now at the most interesting preclosure point in the experiment. Mabel has suggested a cure for the marriage: a trip to the Confederate graveyard at Shiloh, the site of one of the bloodiest conflicts of the Civil War. Although the South might have won, the army was routed in the end by the Northern invaders. Furthermore, Norma Jean has told Leroy that her name invokes not only Marilyn Monroe but the Norman invaders who conquered the Saxons (Southerners?). The trip is on, the drive over to Tennessee is mostly silent, and the first impressions of the park are mixed. Husband and wife look at the log cabin with the bullet hole in it.

> S/389   "That's not the kind of log house I've got in mind," says Leroy apologetically.
> S/390   "I know *that*."
> S/391   "This is a pretty place.
> S/392   Your mama was right."
> S/393   "It's O.K.," says Norma Jean.
> S/394   "Well, we've seen it.
> S/395   I hope she's satisfied."
> S/396   *They burst out laughing together.* (14)

Cut. This is an unusual target sentence for a number of reasons. First of all, it is not followed by a big jump in time or venue, but only by a seamless shift to a few moments later. It is the shortest target sentence and the one with the most active main verb and the most specific, concrete action. It has the lowest incidence of lexical and syntactic patterning except for the dramatic example of redundancy and bracketing: the sentence begins with *They* and ends with *together.* This strategy is appropriate because this is the only sentence showing the man and wife in perfect synchrony, mentally and physically. It is also the only target sentence chosen only by women.

Once I realized this gender bias, I looked to see which text these women had been reading. The overwhelming majority of them—86 percent—had been reading text A, the one with the gender-focused heading. Given the nature of the sample, it is impossible to answer definitively any of the questions that leap to mind. But let's ask them anyway. Was the gender bias in favor of this preclosure point caused by the content and/or form of the sentence itself, by the kind of storyness found in the narrative segment up to this point, or by the prominence of gender issues in the heading, or (as I believe) a combination of all these factors? Perhaps, instead of asking why women favored this point, we should ask why men ignored it. Designing the kind of experiment that will test for clearer answers to these questions is a project, I hope, for a literary scholar rather than a psychologist.

But, getting back to the inquiry at hand, what kind of story ends with this burst of laughter? Looking at the whole text up to this point, we can say it has been leading to the visit to Shiloh. However, Mabel is the one who always wanted to make this trip and then wanted her daughter and son-in-law to go. She is the one who sees it as a "second honeymoon," a restorative for the marriage. Leroy simply latches onto this hope, adopting the plan as his own. But it never has been, and never will be, what Norma Jean wants. That is the truth she is capturing when she says, "Well, we've seen it. I hope she's satisfied!" It is a funny line, but it reminds us that the marriage itself was originally Mabel's idea, the only option she could imagine for a pregnant teenage daughter. Norma Jean's quip is almost a throwaway line, and yet it is the one moment in the entire narrative when the husband and wife communicate perfectly. They have exactly the same spontaneous reaction to the Mabelness in their lives.

Of all the putative stories, the one that ends here is the most hopeful, the most promising for the future of these two fictional characters. We say to ourselves, "Now, if they could just build on this moment. If they could just realize they have to define their own journey instead of retracing

Mabel's." Is this wishful thinking? Do we know this kind of story, the kind that dangles a happy ending in front of hopeful sentimentalists? We saw a fleeting variant of it in Cortázar's portrait of a failed husband. What layers of conditioning would be revealed if I called this a "woman's" story? That term is the trade label for the "love interest" story favored by slick women's magazines, but let's just call it a *genre story.*

The downbeat follows. The next target sentence is blunt and painful. "Without looking at Leroy, she says, 'I want to leave you'" (14). There is no change of time or venue after this sentence. Its preclosure power is self-contained. There are instances of double and triple repetition on the level of a single letter (i.e., alliteration), and the sentence contains two keywords (i.e., two words that link up forcefully with the story so far): *Leroy* and *want.* The sentence also has the single most definite closure word in any of the target sentences: *leave.*

By this point, Leroy and Norma Jean have had their tour of Shiloh and their picnic. Leroy has commented on the battle of April 7, 1862, but

S/406   They both know that he doesn't know any history.

S/407   He is just talking about some of the historical plaques they have read.

S/411   They sit in silence and stare at the cemetery for the Union dead . . .

S/413   Norma Jean wads up the cake wrapper and squeezes it tightly in her hand.

S/414   *Without looking at Leroy, she says, "I want to leave you."* (14)

What is at risk in the story we have just marked off is a last chance for renewal—rededication—maybe through an encounter with the larger human history memorialized at Shiloh. But Leroy does not know any history. He cannot make a connection. We do not know whether Norma Jean can, but certainly from a feminist perspective, she does win this Battle of Shiloh. She takes a real step toward personal authority and freedom. Even though the narrative is told from Leroy's point of view, so that we sympathize more with his loss than with her gain, suddenly the story seems more hers than his. She has taken charge of it. What kind of story is this? Leroy would call it a "woman's lib" story. We shall call it a *message story.*

The last of the putative stories ends with Leroy trying to grasp what is happening and recognizing the limits of his understanding. Efforts to focus on the battle of 1862 lead to a dazed synopsis of personal history:

S/455   The next day [after they were married], Mabel and Jet visited the battleground, and then Norma Jean was born, and then she married Leroy. . .

S/456   Leroy knows he is leaving out a lot.

S/457   He is leaving out the insides of history.

S/459   It occurs to him that building a house out of logs is similarly empty—too simple.

S/460   *And the real inner workings of a marriage, like most of history, have escaped him.* (16)

Cut. At first, this looks like another dawn-of-recognition story, with the pathos underlined by the relegation of Leroy to the object position: something "occurs to him"; something has "escaped him." Whose fault is it that he has failed to understand the "inner workings" of both public and private history? It is a cultural liability as much as a personal one, and Norma Jean has the advantage only because she is more in synch with the times, not because she is made of finer stuff. She has had her revelation that she can no longer live under the terms set for her when she was eighteen, and now Leroy has his: that he has missed the point. What is at risk in the story that ends here is neither the marriage itself (that is almost certainly forfeited) nor Norma Jean's ability to restart her life (she is well on the way to doing that). What is at stake is Leroy's improvement as a processor of experience.

In those terms, the outcome is positive. He has learned something about his limitations as a human being. But they are the limitations of many Americans—perhaps mostly male—who were infantilized by old myths of open-road adventure, log-cabin romance, and dreams of "settling down" in a "real home" with "the woman [they loved]." What has escaped Leroy are the changes in the country since the 1950s; they flashed by the windows of his truck, but now that he has stopped moving, he is parked in the midst of them. The voice we hear at the end of this putative story is almost a choral one, the lament of a generation, a class, a gender—or one part of it that got broadsided by the postmodern world. It is a *sociographic story.*

Yet Mason does not stop there. Leroy keeps hoping. "He'll have to think of something else, quickly." He even tells himself "he'll get moving again" (16). But, as I mentioned earlier, his legs are not functioning very well as he stands and tries to follow Norma Jean, who has walked toward the river. "Norma Jean has reached the bluff, and she is looking out over the Tennessee River. Now she turns toward Leroy and waves her arms. Is she beckoning to him? She seems to be doing an exercise for her chest muscles" (16).

This is another semiotic moment. Is she beckoning and perhaps reincluding him in her life? Or is she exercising her "chest muscles" (a neutering of the female breast), signaling her independence, and thereby re-excluding him from her life? But what if this binary code is itself the trap? What if Leroy's only chance is to accept the ambiguity of her signal: the chance that it might mean either, both, or none of the above? The next sentence is the last one in the text, in other words, the actual closure point:

S/476   The sky is unusually pale—the color of the dust ruffle Mabel made for their bed. (16)

The dust ruffle is beige, bourgeois, Mabel-made, and suggests that the marriage, tagged by such an image, is a sham, too. On the other hand, if we give Leroy even the tiniest bit of credit for making the analogy—perhaps even for intuiting its message—we must give him far more credit than we have ever given him before. In the end, "Shiloh" is about learning to look more sensitively at the signs and signals that communicate meaning. It is a postmodern story not because it depicts a society without depth or structure (although it does that) but because it shows that the slipperiness of the sign is a function not of misinterpretation (as in "The Open Boat") but of optimized interpretation.

The move to closure is a march to Shiloh, site of a historic drama of missed signals, changing fortunes, and civil trauma. We have moved through five putative stories on our way through the actual story, and of course this staged reading has been, in a sense, rigged. That is to say, we cannot prove any one reader divided the story this way, although it is possible one could have. Rather, we can say that the distributed reader, on this particular occasion, tended to do so. As I've done throughout this book, I've characterized the putative stories in terms of conventional types or subgenres of the short story: a *slice-of-life story*, a *dawn-of-recognition story*, a *genre story*, a *message story*, a *sociographic story*, a *postmodern story*.

I do not want to argue for any one of these labels in particular, nor do I want to suggest that Mason has given us an anthology of story types. But I do want to appreciate the extent to which her "new" story is empowered by "old" formulas of storyness. Recognizing the play of storyness over the story named "Shiloh" not only reveals a conservative deep structure but also brings into relief the cultural scripts (represented as clichéd story types) embedded in the discourse. They supply a richness of signification at odds with the plainness of the language, the apparent thinness and triviality of the cultural envelope, the deliberate "flattening" of the characters: in short, the story's minimalism.

The structuralists may have been the last to believe in a text "filled" with a meaning the reader decoded. Since then, we have been encouraged to view the text as, in a sense, "empty," waiting to be filled or constructed or deconstructed by an agent who is no longer a person with a coherent, centered individuality—who, in short, can no longer be addressed as *a* reader much less *the* reader. I have been trying, once again, to "fill" the text, this time by means of the text-processing experience itself, and to reinvent the reader as a human processor—the distributed reader—who comes into being through the differential acts of individually identifiable human beings but who is not identified as any one of them.

Preclosure study is not the only arena for the kind of literary empiricism I have been describing, but it is a natural segue from the 1980s work on closure in short fiction theory. It has the advantage of turning intuitive judgments into quantifiable data, which can, in turn, be analyzed from a number of critical perspectives, ranging from the more conservative genre interests I have espoused here to the more fashionable interests in political and cultural textuality. And I am now, myself, nearing the end of a chapter—a place from which I turn and wave back. Are preclosure studies just a hopeful effort to save genre theory in the new millennium? Or do they presage the end of literary study, its gradual co-option by politics or the soft sciences? The message is what you think it is.

chapter nine

A Short Story
and Its
Nonfiction Counterpart

In the discussion so far, I have been taking for granted the value of calling a text a short story, and of wondering what makes it one. That assumption is by no means obvious today. It is customary to see genre as a loose and shifting cluster of traits subject to changing trends, hierarchies of taste (and of the power to enforce or guide it), editorial fiat, and any number of other circumstantial pressures. Fiction, of course, has always felt free to use the guise of nonfiction (diary, travelogue, etc.) as a mask or a pose. In the last two decades, short examples of "creative nonfiction," with its array of fiction-like techniques and its leeway for imagination, have garnered more attention and respect—and often look like short stories. Can one—*should* one—tell them apart?

This is a practical question I often hear from my students, but it echoes the view of many scholars who think genre theory is a relic of empty formalism. Obviously, I do not share that view and am inclined to shift the charge of superficiality to the other camp. Nevertheless, no one can write about genre today without being a little defensive, without feeling the need to explain why it matters. What better way to test the usefulness of genre theory—including the one this book proposes—than by bringing it to bear on a frequently deliberate and often vaunted confusion of narrative types in the real world? That is the mission of this chapter, which isolates another of Bobbie Ann Mason's short stories, "Detroit Skyline, 1949," and brings it face to face with its near-double, the second chapter of her later autobiography, *Clear Springs: A Memoir*. First, I'll consider the pairing in relation to feminist scholarship on life writing. Then I'll look at it in relation to a cognitive study of genre types.

Stories, Life-Writing, and "I"

Once upon a time, after tossing the works of Annie Dillard on the fire, a student of mine, Paige Wilburne, was indicted for fourth-degree bookslaughter. Well, you know that's not true because I've signaled that it isn't. If "bookslaughter" doesn't fetch you, "page will burn" will. Let me start over: One evening in Dawson Auditorium, after a reading by Annie Dillard, one of my students, Mary O'Donnell, asked the author whether she ever invented scenes in her nonfiction and whether it was ethical to do so. That certainly could have happened, except that I don't know of any Dawson Auditorium or any Mary O'Donnell. It's fiction disguised as fact. What *really* happened? In a paper on ethics and art in nonfiction, one of my students, Carolyn McConnell, said she'd been sorry to hear of Annie Dillard's startling admission: the author had never *really* been awakened by a cat jumping on her chest with bloody paws, as described in *Pilgrim at Tinker Creek*.[1] She'd lied for art's sake. Now, the confession may be apocryphal, but Carolyn is very real, and so was her disappointment. She had wanted to believe in an art *strong* enough to make the truth *good* enough.

I started off with a lie, too, but I quickly admitted it because I didn't want to put certain things at risk: first, your faith in my credibility, which has to do with the kinds of truth-value markers I use; second, your assumptions about the kind of writing I'm doing, which has to do with what are usually called genre markers; and third, your confidence that I will not go too far, literally, and keep on writing forever—in other words, that there *will* be grounds for closure. As I go on now to talk about fiction and nonfiction and the first-person pronoun, I'll be arguing that genre is, among other things, a conclusion we draw from these markers.

Public opinion says that if nearly all references can be verified, a text is nonfiction; if most of them can't, it's fiction. But you and I know it's not that simple. Not only are there many kinds of hybrid genres, new and old, but postmodern theorists have more or less thrown out objective reality. One referent they've tossed on the fire is the unitary "I"—an essential, irreducible, continuous identity. Suppose we are looking at two pieces of writing and wondering which is fiction and which is not. If there is no such thing as the unvarnished truth, or an "I" to hold accountable for it—then are we stymied? Do we stop right here?

Daniel Lehman finds a way to keep going. In *Matters of Fact: Reading Nonfiction over the Edge,* he argues that nonfiction does something fiction does not do: it "implicates" both the writer and the reader in social realities and practices outside the text. As he explains, reading *Lolita* is different from reading the biography of a pedophile whose victims may be helped or hurt by what an author says about them.[2] Responsiveness to real people creates a four-way matrix of writer, reader, text, and world. Thus, Lehman can reject an essentialist "I" on or off the page, yet argue for accountability. If warm bodies are involved, that's a truth-value marker the author must honor and the reader must heed.

I agree with much that Lehman says, but my own approach is different. I'm descended from the ancient tribe of genre taxonomists, those who look for the distinctive traits of historical genres. As you have seen, I've looked at the way short narratives are processed, defining the short story by the way storyness is cognized or re-cognized—and hence, recognized. While doing this work, I've spent a lot of time teaching students how to write *non*fiction, most recently in the University of Iowa's MFA Program in Nonfiction Writing, where the preferred genres are forms of life writing—the memoir and the personal essay. When a student wants to see how somebody else "did" it, genre comes into play as a set of conventions that are there to be learned from, tweaked, reinvented, or sabotaged. For me, then—in theory and practice—genre has been an inference from typecasting markers.

Let me review some of them. The undisputed genre marker for the short story is the imminence of the end. In this book, of course, I've suggested another: the serial experience of putative stories through the agency of preclosure. For the personal essay, the markers are more a matter of, well, personal opinion. In the introduction to *The Norton Book of Personal Essays,* Joseph Epstein calls this genre "intrinsically formless," going on to say that "the personal essay is able to take off on any tack it wishes, building its own structure as it moves along, rebuilding and remaking itself—and its author—each time out."[3] Phillip Lopate, in his introduction to *The Art of the Personal Essay,* says "even an essay that is 'well made' seems to follow a more intuitive, groping path."[4]

Well made is a term not usually applied to life writing, which includes diaries, journals, and letters, as well as more public forms like autobiography, biography, memoir, and the personal essay. In fact, a largely feminist body of theory on life writing celebrates its freedom from, or subversion of, the kinds of logic and consistency found in more formal—that is, more established, male-dominated—kinds of writing. Nevertheless, my sample of life writing here is a personal essay, which, admittedly, is a highly artful form. I've chosen it mainly because of my teaching experience, but also because the personal essay makes for an especially intimate and telling comparison with the short story, while still being suggestive for life writing—and nonfiction—in general. To sharpen the focus even more, and to address the status of the "I" in both cases, I've chosen a first-person short story and a personal essay written by the same author, about the same event.

However, before introducing these texts, I need to say a little more about genre markers. Because short stories are end-directed, because, as I believe, they are processed by means of deeply ingrained models of storyness, they represent time synoptically. Time with a period after it. Loosely adapting a term Frank Kermode borrowed from the Greek, I'll call this time *kairos*—that is, a span of time with internal grounds for closure.[5] Short story time. That's the snack-sized definition. For the banquet, I refer you to Michael Trussler's eloquent essay, "Suspended Narratives: The Short Story and Temporality."[6] There, among other things, he contrasts the short story's dislocated moment of time with the novel's more continuous and fully contextualized sequence of moments.

But novels must end too, for different reasons, and so I want to contrast the *kairos* of the short story's time with the *chronos*—again adapting from Kermode—of linear time that goes on forever. This is not the physicists' notion of time, of course, but the layperson's. Time with three dots before it and after it. I want to suggest that life writing, and in particular the personal essay, is tied to *chronos* in a way that short stories are not. True, lives must end, and some may even be end-directed—or appear so under the glass of biography. It is also true that most forms of life writing focus on a meaningful section of the lifeline—formative years, influential trips, even moments of experience. But there's a difference. Because biology moves in only one temporal direction, life writing inevitably involves the retrieval of a past experience from a present perspective, however flawed or changeable. The distance between the transcribing moment and the lived moment, whether a heartbeat or a lifetime, must be measured against the base line of *chronos*. The dynamic relationship between the writing "I" and the recovered or reconstituted "I" is, in my view, the primary typecasting marker of the personal essay.

In the upcoming examples, the warm body behind the "I" belongs to Bobbie Ann Mason, whom you met in the last chapter. She is a Kentucky-born short story writer, novelist, and now memoirist. The text I'm going to use is called "Detroit Skyline, 1949." Like "Shiloh," this story is from her first collection, *Shiloh and Other Stories*, published in 1982. Here are the opening lines:

> When I was nine, my mother took me on a long journey up North, because she wanted me to have a chance to see the tall buildings of Detroit. We lived on a farm in western Kentucky not far from the U.S. highway that took so many Southerners northward to work in the auto industry just after World War II. We went to visit Aunt Mozelle, . . .[7]

Left behind are Daddy and Johnny, the males in the family.

The bus trip is summarized in a paragraph, noting that the mother vomited during the trip and that "a black baby cried all the way" (34). When we meet the relatives, we learn that Uncle Boone makes car bumpers at the auto plant, and that there are two threats to postwar security—communist sympathizers and the polio epidemic. We also learn that a local bus workers' strike will keep the visitors from going into the city, trapping them, at least for a while, in the suburbs, where children are afraid of catching polio in swimming pools and workers are afraid of being branded as communists.

This story is partly about the postwar boom in *things* and is larded with brand names of the period: Mixmaster and Kelvinator kitchen appliances, Sanforized cloth, Toni dolls, Pep cereal, Fab detergent, but above all, the names of the television shows that dazzle the child because she has never seen a TV before. This is a kind of writing—sometimes called dirty realism—that is nailed in place by verifiable data but nevertheless is not nonfiction.

With the towers of Detroit still beckoning, a plot develops. The red scare makes the child narrator, Peggy Jo, imagine "a band of little red devils marching in with their pitchforks and taking the entire Kelvinator kitchen to hell" (43). Moody and idle, the child is unprepared for a more immediate crisis: her mother collapses in pain, is rushed to the hospital, and loses a baby she hadn't known she was carrying. While she is away, her daughter glimpses the famous towers, but only on a TV newscast that dissolves into static.

Finally, the bus strike does end, the dream can be realized—but Peggy Jo says no: "I don't want to go" (50). Now it's she, not her mother, who defines the trip's goal. Privately, she believes "[t]he reds had stolen the [miscarried] baby . . . You never knew when you might lose a baby that you didn't know you had. I understood it all" (50). She *doesn't* understand, of course, but she's right in a way she can't comprehend. On this trip, she and her mother have risked what they didn't know they had: a way of life that's dying out with the family farm.

Riding the bus home, mother and daughter cling to each other until it's time to get off. As they walk the half-mile to the farmhouse, the mother tells the story of her return from an earlier trip.

> "You was playing in the yard and you saw me walk up and you didn't recognize me. For the longest time, you didn't know who I was. I never *will* forget how funny you looked."
>
> "They won't recognize us," I said solemnly. "Daddy and Johnny." (52)

Through the trees, they catch sight of home. What they see is a barn, not a skyscraper, but it is they who are now the strange sight, having been changed by their experience. The ending of this story is a recognition scene, multilayered and inverted.

The beginning of this story promised three things: (1) a daughter's narrative of a trip with her mother; (2) a goal-directed desire to show, and to see, tall buildings; and (3) a socioeconomic context. A poetics of the short story will focus on (2), on the arc of desire. Closure will be sensed when we learn whether or not, and under what circumstances, and with what significance, *those buildings get seen*. The time between the announcement of the goal and its outcome defines the *kairos* of this story. In any narrative, storyness is achieved—and *recognized*—when a human agent (or its substitute) gains or loses something that is significant for human well-being. *Short* storyness is achieved—and *recognized*—when such a narrative can be processed in detail and as a whole concurrently. That feat of comprehension can happen only with a narrative we can read, to use Poe's immortal phrase, "in one sitting."

That is why people can read a short story word for word, and, at the same time, process, as a whole, the span of text from the beginning to the sentence just read. That is why it is possible to retrieve a series of putative stories embedded in, and progressing through, the actual story. For the pages I'm considering here, I used myself as a test reader and identified eight preclosure points. Several of them I've noted in my retelling of the story, but now I'm going to focus on the final four, and on the stories they close.

The first putative story ends during the bus-ride home. Peggy Jo is re-flecting on her adventure. The last words of the sentence are

> . . . I felt—with a new surge of clarity—the mystery of travel, the vastness of the world, the strangeness of life. (51)

Not bad for a nine-year-old! What's ending here is a classic *initiation story*. The "I" is a child protagonist who enters a larger world and expe-riences a shift in the paradigms of knowledge. The terms are very general and abstract—*mystery, vastness, strangeness*. In fact, they're generic, ap-plying to hundreds of initiation stories. The next preclosure comes three sentences later. Mother and daughter are still on the bus:

> She had been holding me tightly against her stomach as though she feared she might lose me, too. (51)

Had the text ended here, we would have had a story of wishes and penal-ties: a mother promising her daughter the wonders of the big city, but ex-posing both of them, instead, to postwar suburbia—at the cost of a fetus. This putative story is a *modern-day fable*.

Next, in a flashback, the narrator remembers Uncle Boone's parting words, in which he joked about maybe getting fired. If that happens, says Peggy Jo's mother,

> ". . . y'all can always come back to Kentucky and help us get a crop out . . ." (51).

Progress may fail, but the earth will endure. For me, a story could end here. It would be a romantic cautionary tale about the value of country over city, as well as a pointed counterpart to the myth of the North, which had lured Southerners off the farm ever since the Civil War. It would be a *regional parable.*

I've already mentioned my last preclosure point.

["They won't recognize us," I said solemnly.] "Daddy and
Johnny." (52)

More than any other putative story, the one that ends here raises the question of identity itself. If the "I" is in the eye of the beholder, and if the "I" is not recognized, then is the "I" still "I"? Does experience change our very essence, if we have one, or, if we don't, does it alter the mix of allegiances and values by which we—and others—recognize who we are? The story that concludes here has the shape of a consciousness-raising. Changes have been wrought, partly by a trip *to* the North, but also by a trip *away from* the father and brother. This is a *quest tale* in which the returning hero is not a sobered and disguised Odysseus but two wised-up females their men won't recognize.

My contention, as usual, is that our understanding of this text is enriched and guided, not entirely consciously, by our movement through a series of putative stories: an *initiation story,* a *modern-day fable,* a *regional parable,* and a female *quest tale.* All contribute to the impact of the actual last sentence, in which Peggy Jo sees not tall buildings but the barn through the trees. The strong feeling of closure we have at this point comes, yes, from finding out what kind of building she finally sees, but that recognition is loaded for the reader in a way that I believe is peculiar to the short story—by the serial *recognition* of embedded stories that, along with symbolism, selective detail, and so on, intensifies meaning in this literary form. No matter how many brand names are mentioned, no matter how autobiographical the "I," if the text functions this way, it is "fiction," and, in particular, short fiction.

What I've been illustrating is my version of a poetics of the short story. Is there an alternative "poetics" of life writing? In a collection of essays edited by Marlene Kadar, Evelyn Hinz says there is great need for such a poetics, but that none exists.[8] In the same volume, Shirley Neuman argues that a poetics of life writing is "unwritable" because we cannot systematize a form that is defined by infinite subject positions that differ from each other within and across discourses.[9] Or, as Lopate and Epstein would say, personal writing is too fluid and subjective to be ordered by theory. Is that the last word?

Hoping that it is not, I turn to a book published in 1999, called *Clear Springs: A Memoir,* by Bobbie Ann Mason. Chapter 2 tells about a trip she once made. It begins: "In the summer of 1949, when I was nine, my mother and I traveled to Detroit to visit Mama's aunt Mary, her father's sister. Mama had made the trip several years before, and she was excited about showing me the big city."[10] This, too, will be an account of a visit to relatives near Detroit, of life in postwar suburbia, of a failure to see the tall buildings. But it's very, very different.

This chapter of the book, which could stand alone as a personal essay, is less than half as long as the story. Obviously, the author did not simply cut out material that she invented for the story, and call the residue an essay. This is a new work with its own objectives. In the preface to the book, Mason says, "It truly centers on my mother. If she'd had the chance, she might have busted out to the big city years before I dreamed of doing so . . ." (xi; italics removed). In the short story, the author was going, naturally enough, for storyness; in the essay, she's going for evidence, for a narrative that reveals something about her mother and herself—an insight she didn't have, or didn't use, when she wrote the short story.

Gone are the communist sympathizers. Polio is mentioned only in passing. There's no pregnancy, no miscarriage. Instead, there are sentences like these: "We were country people. We didn't ordinarily go on vacations because there were cows to milk, chickens to feed" (17). "During the Depression, country people from the South had begun trekking northward to find work" (18). The presence of so much exposition is, of course, a typecasting marker of the essay. But this is a personal essay, a narrative essay. It, too, tells the story of an "I."

The bus trip, which took a paragraph in the story, expands to several pages in the essay. "Mama and I were escaping . . . Coconspirators, Mama and I were heading for a bigger and better place, one that would somehow transform us." Interestingly, the next line is "Several black people sat in the rear of the bus, and I wondered if they were escaping too" (18). The short story told us that a black baby was crying on the bus, but there was no race consciousness, only a prefiguring of the baby the mother would lose. Here, in the essay, the adult "I" shows her hand by underscoring the comparison between the white child's pleasure trip and the black people's journey. Going north, for them, is an echo of emancipation, however ironic. For a child in 1949, the comparison between her joyride and their exodus is ignorant but kindly; for a Southern adult writing today, it's loaded with historical consciousness and, implicitly, racial guilt. As it happens, the memoir doesn't go on to treat these themes, but this is an example of what I mean by the interplay between the writing "I" and the retrieved "I." Here it is played out against the subsumed chronology of 1949 to 1999, a *chronos* that includes not only the Civil Rights movement of the sixties but the political correctness of the nineties.

Is there a way to track this interplay through an essay, analogous to the way we track preclosure through a story? Helen M. Buss, in Kadar's collection, has done a fascinating analysis of Anna Jameson's *Winter Studies and Summer Rambles in Canada.* Noting the divisions within the self of the author—primarily her given English self and her discovered Canadian self—Buss explains that these divisions are not reconciled or simply opposed, as they traditionally are in male autobiography. Rather, "Anna Jameson slides through various constructions of the 'I.' "[11] The first is Anna the neglected and passive wife. Another is Anna the wry observer of her own passivity. And so on. The life writer moves through a number of subject positions, all of them called "I." What are these, then, but putative identities? Are *they* what we move through as we read life writing texts? Are *they* what we would find, if we did a preclosure experiment on Mason's essay?

Dear reader, they are. But that isn't surprising. Kadar herself speaks of "the process [in life writing] of becoming more subjective in order to subjectivize the truth."[12] According to Evelyn Hinz, this process has a goal: "auto/biography typically works toward or culminates in a 'recognition' scene—frequently the recognition that in the process of articulating the would-be self one discovers the real but hitherto latent self."[13] Hinz appears to be mapping a quest tale onto life-writing texts, but that doesn't make them fiction. Why not?

1. Because warm bodies are involved (Mrs. Jameson's, for example),
2. because the dominant typecasting marker is still the back-and-forth intricacies of a writing "I" negotiating with a lived "I," and
3. because preclosure highlights not putative stories but payoffs in that negotiation.

In Mason's memoir, the "I" who takes the bus ride up north is a reader of *The Bobbsey Twins,* a child who has never heard the word *valise,* and so pronounces it "*vall*-is." The "I" who explains "We were country people" is close to the writing "I" of the present. The "I" who is a "co-conspirator" is once again the child, the little girl who is proud to say "Mama and I," but she's also the adult from whose vocabulary "co-conspirators" comes, and the writer whose theme is the mother-daughter bond.

About halfway into the essay, Mason embeds an anecdote:

> Mama had visited Mary in Detroit when I was two. [On her return, s]he saw me playing in the yard, and she says that when I saw her, I ran straight to the house. My grandmother declared that Bobbie didn't know who her mother was . . . But Mama said Bobbie recognized her and had run into the house to tell everybody that her mama was home . . . Mama still insists that I *did* know her. And I'm sure she's right. (19–20)

In the fiction, as you recall, this scene is saved up and used, in altered form, as the finale. Here, it is merely a staging point. It serves to contrast two interpretations of Bobbie's behavior: her mother's and her grandmother's. When the writing "I" confirms her mother's version of the story, she is taking a subject position that overlaps her mother's. In an essay about the bond between mother and daughter, this is a powerful piece of evidence.

Maybe the essay could end there, but for me the first preclosure point comes a few pages later. After Bobbie has "marveled" at the suburbs, yearned for the tall buildings, and made a side trip to another town, she finally realizes that there will be ". . . no Detroit. It was disappointing." She concludes:

> I did not know how to readjust my desires to the ambiguities I was discovering in my early travels. (21)

You may recall the story "I," who reflected on the "mystery of travel, the vastness of the world." However, that "I" was defined by cycles of expectation, disappointment, and revision, and had no existence apart from them. *This* "I" is defined by and against a writing "I," yielding a precocious child. This rather stuffy little girl is a putative identity, but not the final or most important one. Thank goodness.

The present-day Mason returns in the next paragraph. " . . . [W]hat I remember from that trip more than my disappointment was my mother in this new setting. She was comfortable with her kinfolk, and she let loose with them in a way she didn't always manage to do at home. She seemed happy just to be somewhere different" (21). Later, Mama is playing cards in the kitchen. Bobbie is listening from the living room, but the scene is reported objectively, impersonally. For a space of 172 words, the "I" disappears. It's as if a typecasting marker for the personal essay were suspended. In context, of course, this absence is a stage in perception. The child must separate from the mother, identify her as a separate person, before the unconscious, biological tie can become a chosen alliance. That change is foreshadowed here.

But it is not yet achieved. When the "I" returns, it's still hankering for tall buildings:

> I longed to know what living in Michigan would be like, in a place that had swimming pools, in a lovely house like this on a street with a sidewalk, so close to the magic towers of Detroit. (22)

This, for me, is the second preclosure point. Something comes into focus here. This "I" is more childlike than the one who was "adjust[ing] her desires"; she's more convincingly naïve, forgetting her mother again, lapsing into a dreamy longing for the different, the magical. This is a Southern child—and every child.

The urban home doesn't have a scrapbook of startling headlines as in the story; instead, it has a gallery of family portraits. Seeing a picture of her grandfather, Bobbie remembers the time "he showed [her] a wonderful thing"—how to cook a potato underground. "I stared at his photograph," she tells us.

> Then I opened my Bobbsey book again, and the New York skyscrapers renewed my longing to see the tall buildings of a big city. (23)

Here, too, the essay could end. Here is an "I" who rejects the homely wonder of baked potatoes, and, by implication, the lore of the past, and holds out for the promises in books and imagination. Detroit is now *any* big city. This is the future writer, Bobbie Ann Mason, who, in real life, moves to New York City, only to return eventually to make her home in the South. The essay that ends here gives us an "I" who has failed to see Detroit but has seen past the farm and partway into the future of the writer we know.

My final preclosure point occurs as Bobbie is overhearing her mother and her relatives playing cards in the kitchen:

> I could hear my mother's laughter rising above them all, and I could feel her triumph as she gathered the pile of winning cards to her bosom, raking them across the table in glee. (23)

Finally, and now decisively, the "I" is drawn to her mother. Christine's pleasure is so demonstrably real that Bobbie *feels* it as if it were her own. Away from her husband's farm and her mother-in-law's regimen, Christine is lively, coy, free. For Bobbie, this is a poignant discovery, but compared to communists and polio and failed pregnancies, how ordinary this moment is. How credible. I can't, of course, prove that it "really" happened, but I think my student Carolyn's trust, which was betrayed by a cat with bloody paws, would be vindicated here. Mason's art *is* strong enough to make this scene good enough.

Good enough, that is, to prepare for the real ending.

> Upstairs later, in our cozy pine-paneled loft, she hugged me as though she were sharing a secret with me, something she desperately thought I needed to know. (23)

"As though." "Secret." "Something." The language is vague again, even conventional, yet we're satisfied. The essay has fulfilled the promise of its early compound subject, "Mama and I." To do so, it slides, to use Buss's term, through a number of subject positions that are ultimately embedded in a final identity that knows its indebtedness to an "other" self. To Christine Mason. Who's a very warm body, indeed.

Does this "slide" of putative identities occur in all life writing, or in all personal essays by literary artists? I'm not in a position to make the first claim, but I'll hazard the second. In doing so, I want to confirm the importance of closural markers, not only to the way we process short narrative texts but also to the way we recognize them in the first place, as either short stories or personal essays. All along, I've argued that our sense of storyness, that deeply ingrained ability to chunk experience—and segments of text—into satisfying wholes, is a primary mode of cognition, arising from neural scenarios. Is our ability to recognize a series of subject positions in a personal essay equally ingrained, equally aboriginal? Experience tells me it is not. "I" must live a while as a conscious human being before "I" can meaningfully negotiate between who she is now (the writer) and who she was then (the subject). Since this is a book about the short story genre, I will not speculate about what this means for nonfiction theory. The *distinction* between genres is, however, my concern. Does it matter, and if so, when and why?

It matters, I think, if we view genre not as a filing system, but as an active ingredient in comprehension. Preclosure exercises are nothing but a device for bringing processing strategies to the surface, where we can use them more consciously to tell us what we've read. I believe we can say that yes, there's a difference between fiction and nonfiction. Each is a contract based on truth-value markers, like the warm-body factor. Each has a history traced by typecasting markers, like *kairos* or *chronos*. And each shapes our understanding through closural markers, retrieving stories from narrative, shaking selves out of time. Those are my putative conclusions. They guide me in writing about short stories and in teaching essayists to revise. They are my case of and for genre.

In the next section, I return to these same texts, subjecting them this time to the distributed reader. With his or her help, I will take a few tentative steps toward defining the symbiosis—yet difference—between the first-person short story and the personal essay.

Saving the Short Story from Literary Nonfiction

I've been arguing for genre distinctions as an aid to appreciative reading. Here I want to address the usefulness of genre from a different perspective. I am wondering whether the short story, after holding its own so long against the novel, will be imitated to death by its close relative, "creative nonfiction." Can—and should—the short story be "saved"?

Asking such a question is a form of dramatic license. The short story isn't dying. It's alive and well. What *is* endangered is genre-based theory, criticism, and pedagogy. At my university, there is a famous Writers' Workshop. Its students write short stories. There is also an MFA program in literary nonfiction. Its students write narrative essays. Should the university continue to fund two separate programs that teach small groups of handpicked students to write short, artful narrative prose? That is the institutional side of the issue I'm raising.

I'm more interested here in the theoretical side, and in the wisdom of the distributed reader. However, before I call upon his or her insight, let me review some conventional wisdom. Traditional rhetoric distinguishes between narrative and exposition. Short stories show rather than tell. But narrativity is not a useful marker for distinguishing between fiction and nonfiction, as we have already seen in the two texts by Bobbie Ann Mason. Are there different narrative *strategies* associated with fiction and creative nonfiction? Many of you may know Lorrie Moore's story, "People Like That Are the Only People Here: Canonical Babbling in Peed Onk." It is about a baby with cancer and the mother's ordeal in hospital hell. Moore's own child has had a bout with cancer. Apparently, the doctors at her local hospital thought she was writing creative nonfiction and were highly offended. Asked whether this story "straddle[s] a line between fiction and nonfiction," she replied: "Fiction can come from real-life events and still be fiction. It can still have that connection, that germ . . . [In the story published in the *New Yorker,* t]he whole narrative strategy is obviously fictional. It's not a nonfiction narrative strategy."[14] How do you tell the difference between narrative strategies in fiction and nonfiction?

Throughout this book, I've studied the way adult readers recognize storyness in a fictional narrative sequence. According to many psychologists, storyness is present when a narrative conforms to a story grammar or, in newer theories, to a situational model that generally includes a location in the world, a goal-seeking agent, and a humanly significant outcome. (It goes without saying that the crafted absence of a meaningful outcome is still humanly significant.) Event sequences generally have a three-part structure, usually some variant of Tzvetan Todorov's equilibrium-disequilibrium-equilibrium structure.[15]

In the terms I prefer, storyness is achieved when experience is chunked into an illustrative unit made memorable and tellable by that end-directed structure. I've returned, again and again, to the suggestion made by the British psychologist R. L. Gregory: namely, that the subtext of all stories begins at the nerve ends. It's the narrative by which our body "remembers" that sticking a finger into the fire is bad for us. If you start with the impulse to investigate the flame, you have a three-stage scenario. Convey that information as a cautionary trope, and you have the basis of story-telling. Keep us wondering if the finger falls off, and you have Edgar Allan Poe.

Of course, there are other ways of passing along information about what threatens or induces well-being. There are record-keeping and instruction-giving, the foundations of nonfiction. If the model for the short story is that primal, end-directed, message-encoding neural scenario, what is the model for the true story of how I burned my finger when I was trying to light the grill that time when Bill and Sarah came over? In a volume called *Remembering Our Past: Studies in Autobiographical Memory*, there is an article called "Time in Autobiographical Memory."[16] The authors argue that it becomes increasingly difficult to remember exactly when a particular event occurred in the past, so we have to construct a pathway back to that information.

We do so by using "temporal schemata" (*let's see, we only grill outside in the spring, and it must have been a weekend, so it was probably a Saturday in April or May*); or by using a "landmark event" (*Bill and Sarah moved away the same year we bought the Buick, so it must have been a Saturday in May before 1989*). The authors refer to these landmarks as "temporal reference points that are long-lived and noncyclic."[17] They occur only once, usually at standard transition points in human life, such as the first trip away from home. To be clear, let's call them *timemarks*. Do we recognize a difference between a closure-referencing narrative (short story) and a timemark-referencing narrative (autobiography), and does such a difference correlate with usual ways of talking about these genres?

For this part of my study, I returned to my usual method of sampling reader responses. Half of the readers would be reading the nonfiction text, half the short story. Although the nonfiction chapter is part of a book, not a free-standing entity like the short story, I treated it as an independent unit. Also, because the story is much longer than the memoir outtake, I had to abridge the story much more drastically than its nonfiction partner. Those are some of the concessions that a scientist would abhor. In the end, though, I had two texts of about the same length, retelling the same core event—a childhood trip to Detroit after World War II.

The short story, as you recall, focuses on postwar materialism, the red scare, and the aborted pregnancy; the memoir focuses on the transformation of the harried farmwife into the lively woman, and on the bonding of the mother and daughter as "coconspirators." The very fact that Mason writes a kind of "dirty realism," dropping name brands and sociological data into her fiction, means that the story and the memoir may look unusually alike. For my purposes, of course, the harder it was to tell the two apart, the better my test case would be.

My distributed reader was composed of two classes taught by a colleague and totaling thirty students.[18] These were classes in writing personal essays, and there had been some discussion of the blurred boundary between fiction and nonfiction. The students had not met me before the day of the experiment, but I cannot say they were wholly uncontaminated, since the instructor, a practicing writer of both genres, is herself a former student of mine. Randomly and anonymously, fifteen of the students read text A (the story) and fifteen read text B (the memoir outtake). There were twenty females and ten males.

One of my first questions to the distributed reader was: What genre do you think you are reading? The choices were diary of a trip, short story, chapter of a memoir, recorded oral history, personal essay, or chapter of a novel. Only one person thought she was reading a short story, and she was right. Of the other fourteen people reading that story, three thought it was a chapter of a novel, so altogether four out of fifteen people—less than a third—recognized that they were reading fiction. Of the fifteen people reading the memoir, none thought it was a short story, but five mistakenly thought it was a chapter of a novel. Eight people did recognize that text B was a chapter of a memoir. Clearly, the students were better at identifying the genre of the nonfiction text, maybe because of their current involvement in writing essays, or maybe because Mason's autobiographical style and fondness for period references are unusually deceptive. The point, however, is that, overall, the conventional genre labels were applied accurately by only nine persons, or 30 percent of the distributed reader.

Would another group of thirty students respond differently? Certainly. This was not a representative sample. Distributed readers never are. They are forever in the category of the pilot study, pointing toward conclusions they can never confirm. They are merely a heuristic, but they are real flesh and blood, and they are unpredictable. Would this particular group, for example, find more closure referencing in the short story and more timemark referencing in the memoir?

Hoping to find out, I offered four one-line descriptions of the narrative and asked the respondents to choose the most apt. Two of the choices suggested an end-directed scenario, while the other two suggested a timemarked chronicle. Unfortunately for my theory, six readers of the story *and* six readers of the memoir favored the goal-outcome description traditionally associated with the short story genre: "The cycle of raised expectations followed by disappointment and reassessment." However, since both texts are about a trip to view tall buildings that are never seen, and since this writer is more practiced as a short-story writer than a memoirist, I shouldn't have been surprised that both texts behave to some degree like a generic short story, just as both behave, to some extent, like an account of the times. Choosing look-alike texts was, after all, the point of the experiment. Looking further, I discovered something about the chronicle-based descriptions. These choices were definitely favored by readers of the memoir. Twice as many memoir-readers as story-readers chose the following description: "The adventures of a nine-year-old girl on a trip she made to Detroit with her mother." Something in the memoir had triggered this leaning toward a description that implies a chronicle rather than a scenario.

Another way to test a reader's global impression of a narrative is to propose several sentences that could conceivably follow the last one on the page, and to ask which one seems the best fit. The students were given four choices, each with a different focal point.

1. I knew I was home when I found myself in the barn, scuffing through straw that smelled like celery seed.
2. Looking back on my childhood, I realize now that my mother was the mystery I needed to solve.
3. I couldn't wait for school to start, so I could brag about television to the kids in sixth grade.
4. When the time came, I went North again, seeking the tall towers of art and intellect.

The first two locate the speaker in a place, a mood, or a thought, and are therefore more static. The second two identify a projected goal, either immediate or distant, and are therefore more dynamic. To disguise this pattern, I scrambled the order of the sentences on the questionnaire. The favorite choice of the story readers was the sentence about the television, a goal-directed scenario with the immediate payoff of bragging to classmates. The story readers' second favorite choice was, as I expected, the other goal-directed scenario: future fulfillment in the North. Altogether, 60 percent of the story readers favored the choices that genre theory would predict, even though, just minutes before, only 27 percent of these same readers had realized they were reading fiction, and only one person had realized she was reading a short story.

Turning to the memoir readers, I found that 73 percent chose sentence 2, the static condition of pondering the mystery of the mother. Since the actual concluding sentence of the memoir is focused on the mother-daughter relationship, this choice is perhaps unduly influenced by semantic carryover. Nevertheless, it seems quite clear that readers of the memoir were less encouraged to see the narrative in goal-outcome terms. Altogether, 80 percent of the memoir readers chose either sentence 1 or 2, as genre theory would predict, although fewer (67 percent) had labeled the text nonfiction, and fewer still (53 percent) had correctly identified the text as a chapter of a memoir.

What about character? I gave the readers the following four descriptions of the nine-year-old girl at the center of both narratives:

1. An eager, affectionate, soulful little girl who deeply loves her mother.
2. A typical little Southern girl temporarily seduced by the modernized North.
3. A naïve and loving little girl who encounters a fearful and uncertain world.
4. An imaginative, moody, observant little girl likely to become a writer.

The first two are essay-like states of being in which the narrator finds herself. The second two are story-like engagements with the world with something at risk. Once again, I scrambled the order before asking the distributed reader to choose the best description for the narrator. Two-thirds of the memoir readers chose the character-in-a-state-of-being options, and two-thirds of the story-readers chose the character-on-the-brink-of-change options. The distributed reader was telling me, once again, that genre *labels* might not matter, but distinctions could be made on the basis of genre *signals,* or what I earlier called the typecasting markers of genre.

Although many of the questions I asked were designed for this experiment alone, one of them was tied to the larger project of this book. I asked the readers of both texts to identify preclosure points. I mentioned earlier that I had abridged both texts by inserting bracketed summaries of omitted material. These physical breaks on the page had too large an influence over the particular sentences that were chosen, but the relative prominence of different choices was still informative.

As you know, I've found that a 20 percent agreement on any one preclosure point is a telling result. Imagine my surprise when I found that 80 percent of the story readers had chosen the same sentence. It occurs later than all the talk about the red menace, later than the mother's miscarriage, later than the end of the bus strike, and later than Peggy Jo's renunciation of her desire to see the tall buildings. It *isn't* the confident assertion that she "saw everything clearly, like the sharpened images that floated on the television screen"; it *isn't* her swaggering statement that she "knew better" than to believe that analogy between the miscarriage and the chicken egg that doesn't hatch. The favorite preclosure point was Peggy Jo's conclusion that

The reds had stolen the baby. (50)

Like most examples of highly favored preclosure points, this one is overdetermined with closural signals. It has a high incidence of keywords: "reds" have been a source of fear and a topic of discussion; the "baby" has been a mysterious agent of harm and alienation for Peggy Jo. In style, the syntax and diction have an emphatic simplicity: no modifiers, just subject + verb + predicate. As a speech act, however, the statement is complicated because, for the reader, the tone of confident wisdom is delightfully sabotaged by the childish ignorance, even while the conceit of the stolen baby gathers force as a metaphor. Dazzled by the glamour of the North, the Kentucky farmwife in the short story forfeits her unborn child. Peggy Jo forfeits a sight of the towers, but she gains confidence in her judgment, however misinformed and comical it is in its details. She doesn't "get" what a miscarriage is, but she gets to be a person her father won't recognize.

When the reader perceives that something that has been at stake has been either lost or gained, storyness is recognized. The story that ends at this preclosure point is, of course, different from the one that ends with the return to Kentucky and the glimpse of the barn. Yet, as I've been arguing, it is the embedding of putative stories that gives such concentrated and distinctive power to the genre of the short story. Each contributes its impulse to the larger narrative arc of the whole, like a booster rocket that *doesn't* fall away but is absorbed by the missile. Human beings learn to

recognize storyness very young, and adult readers interpret closural signals as evidence of storyness without even thinking about it. By triggering
that knowledge, I was able to get from my distributed reader a more sensitive response to genre than the label could produce.

Did the responses also confirm the timemark referencing, sliding-"I"
features we might expect in an autobiography? For the memoir readers,
the preclosure choices were more scattered. The favored choice, attract-
ing only 27 percent of the readers, occurs after Bobbie Ann has seen her
first television show. At home, when listening to radio, she always had to
imagine the faces behind the voices.

Now I hoped they didn't look like Howdy Doody. (21)

It's a funny line, with a charming mix of the literal and the fanciful.
Howdy Doody marks a dot on the timeline of television. The sentence also
presents an "I" that is childlike and naïve, even as it morphs into the older,
writing "I," who surely smiles, as we do, at her earlier self.

The second-favorite choice is perhaps more interesting. It occurs after
the comments about the polio scare and the reference to swimming pools.
Mason, regenerating the memories that cluster around this trip she can
date so specifically in 1949, recalls or constructs a thought from that time:

I longed to know what living in Michigan would be like, in a place
that had swimming pools, in a lovely house like this on a street with
a sidewalk, so close to the magic towers of Detroit. (22)

It is an expository passage inserted into the narrative. It captures a state
of mind, a milieu. It lays out a matrix of associations that have acquired
meaning so far in the text. The first nonfiction preclosure sentence began
"Now I hoped." This one begins "I longed to know." Both contribute to
the reconstruction of memories around a pivot on the lifeline. Both mark
points on the "slide" of subject positions.

I've reviewed only a small portion of the data I collected. For example,
it seems to me worth noting that, when asked to identify the genre of the
text they were reading, *all* of the male students labeled it a chapter, a part
of a whole, whether of fiction or nonfiction. Why didn't they see the little
girl's trip as a complete story? Why was it only the women readers of the
memoir who found preclosure in the sentence about longing to know

what it would be like to live in Michigan, and why was it mostly men who chose the sentence about hoping the radio characters didn't look like Howdy Doody? What about the effects of having been trained to write short stories as well as personal essays? These are the sorts of questions that remain to be asked.

The short story does not need to be "saved" from its nonfiction imitators. Genre distinctions need not be battle lines. However, they are more than old scratches in the sand. I believe that the difference between short, highly crafted fictional and nonfictional narratives is more than an accident of venue, or a literary straitjacket, or a kind of truth value. It derives from the way we process information at the most elementary level. Two of the most basic cognitive processes are counting and chunking. Recounting and storying. The first is the basis of nonfiction, the second of fiction. In nonfiction, we save what we know. In fiction, we model how we know. In our cognitive infancy, we learn the scenario of the flames and the flesh. Stories save *us,* not the other way around.

Epilogue

In the history of short story criticism and theory, the "littleness" of the genre has been sometimes extolled and sometimes excused. Short fiction has often been seen as a minor form, with nothing to offer the narratologist *or* the cultural historian that cannot be found in the weightier novel. From various points of view over the years, I have argued that the form's enduring power and interest can be partially explained by the peculiarities of the way it is processed by human beings with story competence. Novels, even those that embed any number of smaller stories, do not offer the kind of reading experience I have been describing. They do not depend so directly on the sense of storyness, nor do they modulate emotions through putative stories that rest within each other, yet operate serially.

Whether all short stories work this way, I cannot say, although I suspect they can be seen to do so, with a little help from preclosure study. The results, I believe, will always add weight to the actual story, no matter how slight, or exaggerated, or type-bound it may seem by virtue of being short. This is a different activity from what used to be called archetype hunting. It begins in a real-time, word-by-word, serialized processing of an individual text. What it retrieves is, first of all, a sequence of putative stories that may be triggered by cognitive schemata but that can be recognized—and made available for discussion—as generic story types. This approach through genre rather than by theme allows a text's storyness to "work" on the reader before its message is formulated. Thus, there is a greater chance that that message will not be defined in advance of the reading.

Naturally, I am no more assumption-free than any other critic or scholar. Even when I am interpreting the findings of large groups of readers, and certainly when I am using my own preclosure choices, I am guided by my own set of values and experiences. I offer my readings for whatever they may be worth, but they are not the argument that matters. If preclosure study leads another reader to a different conclusion about any story I've discussed, the purpose of the book will have been served just as fully as if the interpretation agreed with mine.

The history of any field can look at times like a Möbius strip, in which old and new theories are facings of each other with no clear line of progress. From Aristotle onward, how often we have tried to get at the essentials of genre, as both a literary-critical notion and as a functioning set of categories. Now, however, this inquiry is out of fashion in the academy, where emphasis has shifted to the social, cultural, political, economic, historical, and material conditions that have constructed so many of the meanings we once thought inherent. At the beginning of the twenty-first century, why is it not simply redundant or reactionary to use genre as a reading frame?

If I were so inclined, I might say that I am merely offering a corrective, a "return to basics" in a time when proliferating ideologies, originating in the noblest challenge to entrenched power, have become, in their turn, predictable and repressive. However, I am making a somewhat bolder claim. I am trying to change the perception that genre means taxonomy, or that genre is a slippery set of labels with at best a fuzzy logic. For me, genre is a heuristic, a reading strategy that is *always* enlightening. This approach has led to some fruitful reexaminations of individual texts, but these readings are a means to an end. What I am trying to do in this book is to nudge the study of genre into the neighborhood of cognitive science, which, along with genetics, may well be the signature discipline of the next hundred years. As I have stated repeatedly, the studies in this book are in no way scientific. Yet they respond, in part, to the same trends that led to the International Society for the Empirical Study of Literature. As recently as 1998, the Executive Council of the Modern Language Association approved a Discussion Group on "Cognitive Approaches to Literature." My interest in this work, along with a preference for broadly accessible, relatively jargon-free models for interacting with texts, has led me to eschew the more prevalent discourses of poststructuralist theory in favor of my own version of empirical study linked to literary theory.

Even within the domain I have sketched out, there are, of course, whole areas I have not explored, such as the synapse between genre theory and artificial intelligence. It will seem, too, that my approach is limited to a print culture that theorists say is waning, although books are big business. My "reader" is a person who turns page after page, who does not skip from screen to screen, from narrative bite to narrative bite, at the click of a mouse or the touch of a stylus. I do not rule out the future application of preclosure study to the narratology of hypertext, but my subject here is the reading of stories as it is still mostly done, and as it is still mostly studied, even by cognitive scientists.

Much of what I have gleaned from their work has been so transformed, so loosely adapted, as to be unrecognizable to the scientists who inspired me. For I am neither a scientist nor a science historian. I have a story to tell about the value of preclosure study. In my effort to penetrate beyond the enveloping jargon of contemporary literary studies, in my yearning to reach the simplest functions of the experience-processing mind, I have come round to the concerns that the makers of art, the writers of short stories, have never left behind. I am once again talking about a shapeliness that facilitates reception. I am talking about aesthetics with a cognitive resonance.

All art transubstantiates life, condensing the field of reference, putting its audience through a symbolically mediated but intensified experience. Theorists have long noted the ways in which the short story condenses "much in little" through selectivity, ellipsis, foreshortening, and synecdoche. Hemingway's famous image of the mostly submerged iceberg, to be inferred from its tip, reminds us that this genre requires a proactive reader. However, his metaphor assumes that the extra or full meaning of the story is amassed below the surface. Finding it requires a calculus of inference.

In contrast, the notion of serial preclosure locates the hidden weight of the text within the folds of the narrative; it assumes that the recovery of this meaning is guided by our model for storyness, a widely bestowed competence, as much as by our ability to plumb symbols, a result of elite training. The reading process itself becomes the means by which our shared humanity is triggered, our reactions modulated, and our insights refined as we move through short stories.

Notes

Introduction

1. Frank O'Connor, *The Lonely Voice: A Study of the Short Story* (Cleveland: World, 1963; reprint, New York: Harper and Row, 1985), 18.

2. For a brief, nontechnical discussion of relevant work in psychology, see Steven R. Yussen, "A Map of Psychological Approaches to Story Memory," in *The Tales We Tell: Perspectives on the Short Story,* ed. Barbara Lounsberry et al. (Westport, CT: Greenwood, 1998), 151–56.

3. Of course, I make no exclusive claim to this term. Many others have used it. However, within the context of this book, I hope to endow it with additional force and meaning as the name of an active, generative, and primary cognitive activity underlying the creation of all short stories, from simple to complex.

chapter one	Once More into the Forest of "Young Goodman Brown"

This chapter is based on a talk I delivered as a Sloan Lecture at the University of Iowa, November 1983. The text has been updated and considerably revised.

1. Nathaniel Hawthorne, "Young Goodman Brown," in *Nathaniel Hawthorne's Tales,* ed. James McIntosh (New York: Norton, 1987), 65. Subsequent page references are given in the text.

2. D. M. McKeithan, "Hawthorne's 'Young Goodman Brown': An Interpretation," *Modern Language Notes* 67 (1952): 96.

3. Joseph T. McCullen, "'Young Goodman Brown': Presumption and Despair," *Discourse* 2 (1959): 147.

4. Herbert A. Liebowitz, "Hawthorne and Spenser: Two Sources," *American Literature* 30 (1959): 464.

5. Thomas E. Connolly, "Hawthorne's 'Young Goodman Brown'": An Attack on Puritanic Calvinism," *American Literature* 28 (1956): 370–75.

6. David Levin, "Shadows of Doubt: Specter Evidence in Hawthorne's 'Young Goodman Brown,'" *American Literature* 34 (1962): 344–52.

7. Austin Warren, ed., *Nathaniel Hawthorne: Representative Selections* (New York: American Book, 1934), 362.

8. Paul W. Miller, "Hawthorne's 'Young Goodman Brown': Cynicism or Meliorism?" *Nineteenth-Century Fiction* 14 (1959): 255–64.

9. Régis Michaud, "How Nathaniel Hawthorne Exorcised Sister Prynne," *The American Novel Today* (Boston: Little, Brown, 1928), 36.

10. Roy Male, *Hawthorne's Tragic Vision* (Austin: University of Texas Press, 1957), 77.

11. Jean Normand, *Nathaniel Hawthorne, esquisse d'une analyse de la creation artistique* (Paris: Presses universitaires de France, 1964), 163, 253–54.

12. Frederick C. Crews, *The Sins of the Fathers: Hawthorne's Psychological Themes* (New York: Oxford University Press, 1966).

13. Paul J. Hurley, "Young Goodman Brown's 'Heart of Darkness,'" *American Literature* 37 (1966): 414.

14. Dennis Brown, "Literature and Existential Psychoanalysis: 'My Kinsman, Major Molineux' and 'Young Goodman Brown,'" *Canadian Review of American Studies* 4 (1973): 65–73.

15. Richard Carpenter, "Hawthorne's Polar Explorations: 'Young Goodman Brown' and 'My Kinsman, Major Molineux,'" *Nineteenth-Century Fiction* 24 (1969): 45–56.

16. Reginald Cook, "The Forest of Goodman Brown's Night: A Reading of Hawthorne's 'Young Goodman Brown,'" *New England Quarterly* 43 (1970): 473–81.

17. Henry James, *Hawthorne* (New York: Harper and Brothers, 1880).

18. Q. D. Leavis, "Hawthorne as Poet," *Sewanee Review* 59 (1951): 197.

19. Richard H. Fogle, *Hawthorne's Fiction: The Light and the Dark* (Norman: University of Oklahoma Press, 1952, 1964).

20. Richard H. Fogle, "Weird Mockery: An Element of Hawthorne's Style," *Style* 2 (1968): 191–202.

21. Darrel Abel, "Black Glove and Pink Ribbon: Hawthorne's Metonymic Symbols," *New England Quarterly* 42 (1969): 174.

22. For a straightforwardly structuralist reading, see Harold F. Mosher Jr., "The Sources of Ambiguity in Hawthorne's 'Young Goodman Brown: A Structuralist Approach," *Emerson Society Quarterly* 26 (1980): 16–25.

23. Edward M. Clay, "The 'Dominating Symbol' in Hawthorne's Last Phase," *American Literature* 39 (1968): 506–16.

24. Taylor Stoehr, "'Young Goodman Brown' and Hawthorne's Theory of Mimesis," *Nineteenth-Century Fiction* 23 (1969): 393–412.

25. James L. Williamson, "'Young Goodman Brown': Hawthorne's 'Devil in Manuscript,'" *Studies in Short Fiction* 18 (1981): 155–62. Karen Hollinger disagrees with Williamson's contention that the narrator is aligned with the devil in a "hell-fired" delight in storytelling. See her article, "'Young Goodman Brown': Hawthorne's 'Devil in Manuscript': A Rebuttal," *Studies in Short Fiction* 19 (1982): 381–84.

26. Michael Davitt Bell, *Hawthorne and the Historical Romance* (Princeton: Princeton University Press, 1971).

27. Daniel Hoffman, *Form and Fable in American Fiction* (New York: Oxford University Press, 1961).

28. Barbara J. Rogers, "Entropy and Organization in Hawthorne's America," *Southern Quarterly* 16 (1978): 223–39.

29. John K. Hale, "The Serpentine Staff in 'Young Goodman Brown,'" *Nathaniel Hawthorne Review* 19 (1993): 17–18.

30. Michael Tritt, "'Young Goodman Brown' and the Psychology of Projection," *Studies in Short Fiction* 23 (1986): 113–17.

31. Elizabeth Wright, "The New Psychoanalysis and Literary Criticism," *Poetics Today* 3 (1982): 89–105.

32. Jennifer Fleischner, "Female Eroticism, Confession, and Interpretation in Nathaniel Hawthorne," *Nineteenth-Century Literature* 44 (1990): 520.

33. James C. Keil, "Hawthorne's 'Young Goodman Brown': Early Nineteenth-Century and Puritan Constructions of Gender," *New England Quarterly* 69 (1996): 33–55.

34. Jane Donahue Eberwein, "'My Faith is Gone!': 'Young Goodman Brown' and Puritan Conversion," *Christianity and Literature* (1982): 23–32.

35. Robert C. Grayson, "Curdled Milk for Babes: The Role of the Catechism in 'Young Goodman Brown,'" *Nathaniel Hawthorne Review* 16 (1990): 1, 3–6.

36. Benjamin Franklin V, "Goodman Brown and the Puritan Catechism," *Emerson Society Quarterly* 40 (1994): 67–88.

37. Stanford and Marilyn Apseloff, "'Young Goodman Brown': The Goodman," *American Notes & Queries* 20 (1982): 103–5.

38. Barbara Fass Leavy, "Faith's Incubus: The Influence of Sir Walter Scott's Folklore on 'Young Goodman Brown,'" *Dickens Studies Annual* 18 (1989): 282. She is quoting from Walter Scott, *Letters on Witchcraft and Demonology* (New York: Gordon, 1974).

39. Bill Christophersen, "'Young Goodman Brown' as Historical Allegory: A Lexical Link," *Studies in Short Fiction* 23 (1986): 202–4.

40. Walter Shear, "Cultural Fate and Social Freedom in Three American Short Stories," *Studies in Short Fiction* 29 (1992): 543–550.

41. Joan Elizabeth Easterley, "Lachrymal Imagery in Hawthorne's 'Young Goodman Brown,'" *Studies in Short Fiction* 28 (1991): 339–44.

42. A. E. B. Coldiron, "Laughter as Thematic Marker in 'Young Goodman Brown,'" *Nathaniel Hawthorne Review* 17 (1991): 19.

43. Thomas R. Moore, "'A Thick and Darksome Veil': The Rhetoric of Hawthorne's Sketches," *Nineteenth-Century Literature* 48 (1993): 310–25.

44. David Stouck and Janet Giltrow, "'A Confused and Doubtful Sound of Voices': Ironic Contingencies in the Language of Hawthorne's Romances," *Modern Language Review* 92 (1997): 559–72.

45. Lawrence I. Berkove, "'Reasoning As We Go': The Flawed Logic of Young Goodman Brown," *Nathaniel Hawthorne Review* 24 (1998): 46–52.

46. Christopher D. Morris, "Deconstructing 'Young Goodman Brown,'" *American Transcendental Quarterly* 2 (1988): 25, 30.

chapter two   Preclosure Basics in a Kate Chopin Story

1. Elizabeth Bowen, "The Faber Book of Modern Short Stories," *Collected Impressions* (New York: Knopf, 1950); reprinted in *Short Story Theories,* ed. Charles E. May (Athens: Ohio University Press, 1976), 154.

2. Kate Chopin, "Aunt Lympy's Interference," in *The Complete Works of Kate Chopin,* 2 vols., ed. Per Seyersted (Baton Rouge: Louisiana State University Press, 1969), 2:511–17. All quotations are from this volume, with page numbers indicated in the text.

3. The percentages of readers choosing the various preclosure points adds up to more than 100 percent because each reader could choose up to five preclosure points.

4. Classic studies of closural signals include Barbara Herrnstein Smith, *Poetic Closure: A Study of How Poems End* (Chicago: University of Chicago Press, 1968), and John Gerlach, *Toward the End: Closure and Structure in the American Short Story* (Tuscaloosa: University of Alabama Press, 1985).

5. Karen Acton, chair, and Judy Griffith, former member, of the English department, West High School, Waterloo, Iowa, were kind enough to take an interest in this project and to carry out exercises with their students, who represent half of the reader population for this study.

6. See Gerlach, *Toward the End,* n. 4.

7. The words *least* and *most* in this sentence were inadvertently reversed in the original publication of this essay in Susan Lohafer and Jo Ellyn Clarey, eds., *Short Story Theories at a Crossroads* (Baton Rouge: Louisiana State University Press), 260.

8. Valerie Shaw, in *The Short Story: A Critical Introduction* (London: Longman, 1983), pairs the chapter titles: "'Artful' Narration" and "'Artless' Narration." In my book *Coming to Terms with the Short Story* (1983; reprint, Baton Rouge: Louisiana State University Press, 1985) the first section of chapter 1 is entitled "The Artless Art."

9. Those interested in gender-related studies should refer to the earlier version of this chapter (in Lohafer and Clarey, *Short Story Theory at a Crossroads*), where I *did* divide up the readers by gender, with interesting results.

10. Tom Trabasso and P. Van den Broek, "Causal Thinking and the Representation of Narrative Events," *Journal of Memory and Language* 24 (1985): 612–30.

11. There *have* been studies of story recall that identify the level (within a hierarchy of generalization) of those propositions retained in a summary of a story. A pioneering work here is Perry W. Thorndyke's "Cognitive Structures in Comprehension and Memory of Narrative Discourse," *Cognitive Psychology* 9 (1977): 77–110.

12. Teun A. van Dijk, *Macrostructures: An Interdisciplinary Study of Global Structures in Discourse, Interaction, and Cognition* (Hillsdale, NJ: Lawrence Erlbaum, 1980), 46–48; and *Text and Context: Explorations in the Semantics and Pragmatics of Discourse* (New York: Longman, 1977), 158.

13. Van Dijk, *Macrostructures,* 107–32.

14. For an example of such a grammar, see Gerald Prince's *A Grammar of Stories: An Introduction* (The Hague: Mouton, 1973).

15. Van Dijk, *Macrostructures,* 116. In the original diagram, the key terms are capitalized.

16. See the earlier version of this chapter (in Lohafer and Clarey, *Short Story Theory at a Crossroads*) for an illustration of the way frame theory can be used to discover discrepancies and confusions in the readers' comprehension of the story, and the consequent need for certain pedagogical strategies. For example, readers ignorant of the conventional use of *aunt* to refer to a trusted female black servant incorrectly inferred that Aunt Lympy was Melitte's blood relative.

17. For relevant discussions, see Menakhem Perry, "Literary Dynamics: How the Order of a Text Creates Its Meanings," *Poetics Today* 1 (1979): 35–64; 311–61, and Armine Kotin Mortimer's essay in Lohafer and Clarey, *Short Story Theory,* 276–98.

18. R. L. Gregory, "Psychology: Towards a Science of Fiction," in Margaret Meek, Aidan Warlow, and Griselda Barton, eds., *The Cool Web: The Pattern of Children's Reading* (London: The Bodley Head, 1977), 396.

19. James Britton, "The Role of Fantasy," in Meek et al., *The Cool Web,* 41.

20. Randall Jarrell, "Stories," in May, *Short Story Theories,* 32.

21. D. W. Harding, "Response to Literature," in Meek et al., *The Cool Web,* 379.

chapter three   Preclosing an "Open" Story by Julio Cortázar

1. Terry J. Peavler, *Julio Cortázar* (Boston: Twayne, 1990), 3.

2. Alba C. de Rojo, ed., *Cortázar: Iconografía* (Mexico: Fondo De Cultura Economica, 1985), 60 [photograph].

3. Julio Cortázar, "Orientation of Cats," in *We Love Glenda So Much,* trans. Gregory Rabassa (New York: Knopf, 1983), 3–7. Subsequent page references are given in the text.

4. Among several photographs of Cortázar and his cat, Theodor W. Adorno, there is one showing the author exchanging looks, through a window, with his feline alter ego (de Rojo, *Cortázar,* 57).

5. Because, for my purposes, the English translation of the Spanish original is a distinct and valid text, I will not address here the important practical and theoretical issues raised by *comparisons* of the original and translated texts.

6. A preclosure study I conducted on Katherine Mansfield's story, "Life of Ma Parker," also suggested that the earliest recorded preclosure choices are more likely to come from male respondents than from the female respondents. See chapter 5.

7. See chapter 4 for a more detailed explanation of both local and global closural signals.

8. For a relevant discussion of the way Cortázar imagined his *own* readers—responding creatively to gaps in the text rather than, like Alana's husband, demanding a full revelation that exhausts the text's meaning—see Lydia D. Hazera, "Strategies for Reader Participation in the works of Cortázar, Cabrera Infante, and Vargas Llosa," *Latin American Literary Review* 13 (1985): 19–34.

9. A still-useful primer is Jean Matter Mandler's *Stories, Scripts, and Scenes: Aspects of Schema Theory* (Hillsdale, NJ: Lawrence Erlbaum, 1984).

chapter four   Preclosure and the History of the American Short Story

1. Lohafer, *Coming to Terms with the Short Story*.

2. Van Dijk, *Macrostructures*.

3. Robert Beaugrande, "The Story of Grammars and the Grammar of Stories," *The Journal of Pragmatics* 6 (1982): 383–422.

4. Here and in the next two paragraphs, I am excerpting and summarizing some material from my essay, "Interdisciplinary Thoughts on Cognitive Science and Short Fiction Studies," in Lounsberry, *The Tales We Tell*.

5. Deborah Hicks, "Narrative Skills and Genre Knowledge: Ways of Telling in the Primary School Grades," *Applied Psycholinguistics* 11 (1990): 83–104.

6. Margaret S. Benson, "The Structure of Four- and Five-year-olds' Narratives in Pretend Play and Storytelling," *First Language* 13 (1993): 202–23. For a discussion of goal plans as the basis of story, see Tom Trabasso and Margret Nickels, "The Development of Goal Plans of Action in the Narration of a Picture Story," *Discourse Processes* 15 (1992): 249–75.

7. Rolf Zwaan, Joseph P. Magliano, and Arthur C. Graesser, "Dimensions of Situation Model Construction in Narrative Comprehension," *Journal of Experimental Psychology: Learning, Memory, and Cognition* 21 (1995): 386–97.

8. Benson, "Structure."

9. Mandler, *Stories*.

10. Trabasso and Nickels, "Development of Goal Plans."

11. William F. Brewer and Keisuke Ohtsuka, "Story Structure, Characterization, Just World Organization, and Reader Affect in American and Hungarian Short Stories," *Poetics* 17 (1988): 395–415.

12. Nancy B. Cothern, Bonnie C. Konopak, and Elizabeth L. Willis, "Using Readers' Imagery of Literary Characters to Study Text Meaning Construction," *Reading Research and Instruction* 30 (1990): 15–29.

13. Brewer and Ohtsuka, "Story Structure."

14. Of all the experiments described in this book, this one begs to be replicated by other scholars, using other stories—especially stories by writers excluded until recently from the mainstream classroom.

15. Edgar Allan Poe, "Ligeia," in *The Complete Poems and Stories of Edgar Allan Poe*, vol. 1 (New York: Knopf, 1978), 233.

16. John Gerlach, *Toward the End,* 8. I have loosely adapted several of his five "signals of closure."

17. Nathaniel Hawthorne, "Rappaccini's Daughter," in *Nathaniel Hawthorne's Tales,* 209. Subsequent page references are indicated in the text.

18. Gregory, "Psychology," 396.

19. Washington Irving, "The Legend of Sleepy Hollow," in *The Sketchbook of Geoffrey Crayon, Gent.,* vol. 8 of *The Complete Works of Washington Irving* (Boston: Twayne, 1978), 294–95.

20. John Cheever, "The Swimmer," in *The Stories of John Cheever* (New York: Knopf, 1978), 612.

21. Ann Beattie, "A Clever-Kids Story," in *Secrets and Surprises* (New York: Random House, 1976), 279.

22. Sherwood Anderson, "I Want to Know Why," in *The Teller's Tales* (Schenectady, NY: Union College Press, 1983), 46.

23. For a related discussion of closure signals on the global level, see John Gerlach, *Toward the End,* 7–16.

24. Sherwood Anderson, "The Egg," in *The Teller's Tales,* 146; Ernest Hemingway, "Indian Camp," in *In Our Time* (New York: Charles Scribner's Sons, 1930), 21; F. Scott Fitzgerald, "Babylon Revisited," in *Taps at Reveille* (New York: Charles Scribner's Sons, 1935), 340.

25. Joyce Carol Oates, "Where Are You Going, Where Have You Been?" in *The Wheel of Love* (New York: Vanguard, 1970), 53; Ursula Le Guin, "Schrödinger's Cat," in *The Compass Rose: Short Stories by Ursula Le Guin* (New York: Harper and Row, 1982), 49; Raymond Carver, "Why Don't You Dance?" in *What We Talk About When We Talk About Love* (New York: Knopf, 1981), 9. Subsequent page numbers are given in the text.

chapter five   Katherine Mansfield and Sandra Cisneros

1. Katherine Mansfield, "Life of Ma Parker," in *The Short Stories of Katherine Mansfield* (New York: Knopf, 1937; reprint, New York: Ecco, 1983), 484–90. Subsequent page references are given in the text.

2. Antony Alpers, *The Life of Katherine Mansfield* (New York: Viking, 1980), 98–99.

3. Saralyn R. Daly, *Katherine Mansfield,* rev. ed., Twayne's English Authors Series (New York: Twayne, 1994), 81–82.

4. The first experiment was performed on May 1, 1991, and the second on September 11, 1996. The two classes were comparable in level and content, so the two groups of readers were treated as one population for purposes of this study.

5. O'Connor, *The Lonely Voice,* 17–18.

6. Bowen, "The Faber Book of Modern Short Stories," in May, *Short Story Theories* (Athens: Ohio University Press, 1976), 158.

7. Sandra Cisneros, "One Holy Night," in *Woman Hollering Creek and Other Stories* (New York: Vintage, 1991), 28. Subsequent page references are given in the text.

8. Thomas M. Leitch, "The Debunking Rhythm of the American Short Story," in Lohafer and Clarey, *Short Story Theory,* 130–47.

9. Katherine Payant, "Borderland Themes in Sandra Cisneros's *Woman Hollering Creek,*" in *The Immigrant Experience in North American Literature: Carving Out a Niche,* ed. Katherine B. Payant and Toby Rose (Westport, CT: Greenwood, 1999), 96.

10. Laura Gutierrez Spencer, "Fairy Tales and Opera: The Fate of the Heroine in the Work of Sandra Cisneros," in *Speaking the Other Self: American Women Writers,* ed. Jeanne Campbell Reesman (Athens: University of Georgia Press, 1997), 279.

11. Maria Szadziuk, "Culture as Transition: Becoming a Woman in Bi-ethnic Space," *Mosaic* 32, no. 3 (1999): 109.

12. Jeff Thomson, "Identity in Sandra Cisneros's *Woman Hollering Creek*," *Studies in Short Fiction* 31 (1994): 419.

13. Payant, "Borderland," 98.

14. Mary Pat Brady, "The Contrapuntal Geographies of *Woman Hollering Creek and Other Stories*," *American Literature* 71 (1999): 138.

chapter six   Loving (?) Raymond Carver

1. Raymond Carver, "On *Where I'm Calling From*," *Call If You Need Me: The Uncollected Fiction and Other Prose*, ed. William L. Stull (New York: Vintage, 2001), 201.

2. Tess Gallagher, "Carver Country," in *Carver Country: The World of Raymond Carver* (New York: Arcade, 1990), 15.

3. Carver, "On *Where I'm Calling From*," 201.

4. Carver, Interview with David Sexton, *Literary Review* [London], 85 (July 1985): 38.

5. The full citations for these titles are as follows: Steve Mirarchi, "Conditions of Possibility: Religious Revision in Raymond Carver's 'Cathedral,'" *Religion and the Arts* 2 (1998): 299–310; Kirk Nesset, "Insularity and Self-Enlargement in Raymond Carver's 'Cathedral,'" *Essays in Literature* 21 (1994): 116–28; Monroe Engel, "Knowing More Than One Imagines; Imagining More Than One Knows," *Agni* 31–32 (1990): 165–76; Ewing Campbell, "Raymond Carver's Therapeutics of Passion," *Journal of the Short Story in English* 16 (1991): 9–18; Nelson Hathcock, "'The Possibility of Resurrection': Re-Vision in Carver's 'Feathers' and 'Cathedral,'" *Studies in Short Fiction* 28 (1991): 31–39.

6. Raymond Carver, "Cathedral," in *Cathedral* (New York: Knopf, 1983; reprint, New York: Vintage, 1984), 209. Future page references will be made in the text.

7. Kirk Nesset, *The Stories of Raymond Carver: A Critical Study* (Athens: Ohio University Press, 1995), 66.

8. Hathcock, "'The Possibility of Resurrection,'" 32, quoting from Raymond Carver, "On Writing," in *Fires* (New York: Vintage, 1984), 25.

chapter seven   Revisiting Ann Beattie

1. Pico Iyer, "The World According to Beattie," in *The Critical Response to Ann Beattie*, ed. Jaye Berman Montresor (Westport, CT: Greenwood, 1993), 65.

2. Larry McCaffery and Sinda Gregory, "A Conversation with Ann Beattie," in Montresor, *The Critical Response to Ann Beattie*, 102. Subsequent page references are given in the text.

3. Ann Beattie, "Weekend," in *Park City: New and Selected Stories* (New York: Knopf, 1998), 197. Originally published in *Secrets and Surprises* (New York: Random House, 1979). Subsequent page references are given in the text.

4. Ann Beattie, "Where You'll Find Me," in *Park City*, 388. Originally published

in *Where You'll Find Me* (New York: Simon and Schuster, 1986). Future references by page numbers in the text.

5. Sandra Sprows, "Frames, Images, and the Abyss: Psychasthenic Negotiation in Ann Beattie," in Montresor, *The Critical Response to Ann Beattie,* 142. Subsequent page references are given in the text.

chapter eight   The Largeness of Minimalism in Bobbie Ann Mason

1. William F. Brewer and Edward H. Lichtenstein, "Stories Are To Entertain," *Journal of Pragmatics* 6 (1982): 473–86.

2. Leslie White, "The Function of Popular Culture in Bobbie Ann Mason's *Shiloh and Other Stories* and *In Country*," *Southern Quarterly* 26 (1988): 69–79.

3. Lila Havens, "Residents and Transients: An Interview with Bobbie Ann Mason [February 1984]," *Crazyhorse* 29 (1985): 94.

chapter nine   A Short Story and Its Nonfiction Counterpart

The origin of "Stories, Life-Writing, and 'I'" is cited in the Credits. "Saving the Short Story from Literary Nonfiction" is a revised version of a talk delivered at the Cincinnati Short Story Festival, University of Cincinnati, April 24, 2001.

1. Carolyn McConnell, "Seeking Help" (written for my course in the narrative essay, fall 1999, at the University of Iowa). The reference is used with her permission.

2. Daniel W. Lehman, *Matters of Fact: Reading Nonfiction over the Edge* (Columbus: Ohio State University Press, 1997), 1–39.

3. Joseph Epstein, ed., *The Norton Book of Personal Essays* (New York: Norton, 1997), 11.

4. Phillip Lopate, ed., *The Art of the Personal Essay* (New York: Anchor, 1994), xxxviii.

5. Frank Kermode, *The Sense of an Ending: Studies in the Theory of Fiction* (New York: Oxford University Press, 1967), 46ff. I used this set of terms in *Coming to Terms With the Short Story.*

6. Michael Trussler, "Suspended Narratives: The Short Story and Temporality," in a special theory issue of *Studies in Short Fiction,* 33 (1996): 557–77.

7. Bobbie Ann Mason, "Detroit Skyline, 1949," in *Shiloh and Other Stories* (New York: Harper and Row, 1982; Harper Colophon, 1983): 34. Subsequent page reference are given in the text.

8. Evelyn J. Hinz, "Mimesis: The Dramatic Lineage of Auto/Biography," in *Essays on Life Writing: From Genre to Critical Practice,* ed. Marlene Kadar (Toronto: University of Toronto Press, 1992): 195.

9. Shirley Neuman, "Autobiography: From Different Poetics to a Poetics of Difference," in Kadar, *Essays on Life Writing,* 225.

10. Bobbie Ann Mason, chapter 2 of *Clear Springs: A Memoir* (New York: Random House, 1999): 17–23. Subsequent page references are given in the text.

11. Helen M. Buss, "Anna Jameson's *Winter Studies and Summer Rambles in Canada* as Epistolary Dijournal," in Kadar, *Essays on Life Writing*, 45.

12. Marlene Kadar, "Whose Life Is It Anyway? Out of the Bathtub and into the Narrative," in Kadar, *Essays on Life Writing*, 154.

13. Hinz, "Mimesis," 202.

14. Lorrie Moore, "Moore's Better Blues," interview by Dwight Garner, http://www.salonmag.com, October 27, 1998.

15. Tzvetan Todorov, *Introduction to Poetics,* trans. Richard Howard (Minneapolis: University of Minnesota Press, 1981).

16. Steen F. Larsen, Charles P. Thompson, and Tia Hansen, "Time in Autobiographical Memory," in David C. Rubin, ed. *Remembering Our Past: Studies in Autobiographical Memory* (London: Cambridge University Press, 1995), 129–56.

17. Ibid., 154.

18. I am deeply indebted to the writer and teacher Marilyn Abildskov, who lent me her nonfiction writing classes on February 22, 2001, at the University of Iowa.

Works Cited

Abel, Darrel. "Black Glove and Pink Ribbon: Hawthorne's Metonymic Symbols." *New England Quarterly* 42 (1969): 163–80.

Alpers, Antony. *The Life of Katherine Mansfield.* New York: Viking, 1980.

Anderson, Sherwood. *The Teller's Tales.* Schenectady, NY: Union College Press, 1983.

———. *The Triumph of the Egg.* New York: B. W. Beubsch, 1921.

Apseloff, Stanford, and Marilyn Apseloff. "'Young Goodman Brown': The Goodman." *American Notes & Queries* 20 (1982): 103–5.

Beattie, Ann. *Secrets and Surprises.* New York: Random House, 1976.

———. *Park City: New and Selected Stories.* New York: Knopf, 1998.

Beaugrande, Robert. "The Story of Grammars and the Grammar of Stories." *The Journal of Pragmatics* 6 (1982): 383–422.

Bell, Michael Davitt. *Hawthorne and the Historical Romance.* Princeton: Princeton University Press, 1971.

Benson, Margaret S. "'The Structure of Four- and Five-year-olds' Narratives in Pretend Play and Storytelling." *First Language* 13 (1993): 202–23.

Berkove, Lawrence I. "'Reasoning As We Go': The Flawed Logic of Young Goodman Brown." *Nathaniel Hawthorne Review* 24 (1998): 46–52.

Bowen, Elizabeth. "The Faber Book of Modern Short Stories." In *Collected Impressions.* New York: Knopf, 1950. Reprinted in *Short Story Theories.* Ed. Charles E. May, 152–58. Athens: Ohio University Press, 1976.

Brady, Mary Pat. "The Contrapuntal Geographies of *Woman Hollering Creek and Other Stories.*" *American Literature* 71 (1999): 117–50.

Brewer, William F., and Keisuke Ohtsuka. "Story Structure, Characterization, Just World Organization, and Reader Affect in American and Hungarian Short Stories." *Poetics* 17 (1988): 395–415.

Brewer, William F., and Edward H. Lichtenstein. "Stories Are to Entertain." *Journal of Pragmatics* 6 (1982): 473–86.

Brown, Dennis. "Literature and Existential Psychoanalysis: 'My Kinsman, Major Molineux' and 'Young Goodman Brown.'" *Canadian Review of American Studies* 4 (1973): 65–73.

Buss, Helen M. "Anna Jameson's *Winter Studies and Summer Rambles in Canada* as Epistolary Dijournal." In *Essays on Life Writing: From Genre to Critical Practice*. Ed. Marlene Kadar. Toronto: University of Toronto Press, 1992.

Carpenter, Richard. "Hawthorne's Polar Explorations: 'Young Goodman Brown' and 'My Kinsman, Major Molineux.'" *Nineteenth-Century Fiction* 24 (1969): 45–56.

Carver, Raymond. *Call If You Need Me: The Uncollected Fiction and Other Prose*. Ed. William L. Stull. New York: Vintage, 2001.

———. *Cathedral*. New York: Knopf, 1983. Reprint, New York: Vintage, 1984.

———. Interview with David Sexton. *Literary Review* [London] 85 (July 1985): 36–40.

———. *What We Talk About When We Talk About Love*. New York: Knopf, 1981.

Cheever, John. *The Stories of John Cheever*. New York: Knopf, 1978.

Chopin, Kate. *The Complete Works of Kate Chopin*. 2 vols. Ed. Per Seyersted. Baton Rouge: Louisiana State University Press, 1969.

Christophersen, Bill. "'Young Goodman Brown' as Historical Allegory: A Lexical Link." *Studies in Short Fiction* 23 (1986): 202–4.

Cisneros, Sandra. *Woman Hollering Creek and Other Stories*. New York: Vintage, 1991.

Clay, Edward M. "The 'Dominating Symbol' in Hawthorne's Last Phase." *American Literature* 39 (1968): 506–16.

Coldiron, A. E. B. "Laughter as Thematic Marker in 'Young Goodman Brown.'" *Nathaniel Hawthorne Review* 17 (1991): 19.

Connolly, Thomas E. "Hawthorne's 'Young Goodman Brown': An Attack on Puritanic Calvinism." *American Literature* 28 (1956): 370–75.

Cook, Reginald. "The Forest of Goodman Brown's Night: A Reading of Hawthorne's 'Young Goodman Brown.'" *New England Quarterly* 43 (1970): 473–81.

Cortázar, Julio. *We Love Glenda So Much*. Trans. Gregory Rabassa. New York: Knopf, 1983.

Cothern, Nancy B., Bonnie C. Konopak, and Elizabeth L. Willis. "Using Readers' Imagery of Literary Characters to Study Text Meaning Construction." *Reading Research and Instruction* 30 (1990): 15–29.

Crews, Frederick C. *The Sins of the Fathers: Hawthorne's Psychological Themes*. New York: Oxford University Press, 1966.

Daly, Saralyn R. *Katherine Mansfield*. Rev. ed. Twayne's English Authors Series. New York: Twayne, 1994.

Downing, David. "Beyond Convention: Dynamics of Imagery and Response in Hawthorne's Early Sense of Evil." *American Literature* 51 (1980): 463–76.

Easterley, Joan Elizabeth. "Lachrymal Imagery in Hawthorne's 'Young Goodman Brown.'" *Studies in Short Fiction* 28 (1991): 339–44.

Eberwein, Jane Donahue. "'My Faith is Gone!': 'Young Goodman Brown' and Puritan Conversion." *Christianity and Literature* (Fall 1982): 23–32.

Epstein, Joseph, ed. *The Norton Book of Personal Essays.* New York: Norton, 1997.

Fitzgerald, F. Scott. *Taps at Reveille.* New York: Charles Scribner's Sons, 1935.

Fleischner, Jennifer. "Female Eroticism, Confession, and Interpretation in Nathaniel Hawthorne." *Nineteenth-Century Literature* 44 (1990): 514–33.

Fogle, Richard H. *Hawthorne's Fiction: The Light and the Dark.* 1952; Norman: University of Oklahoma Press, 1964.

——. "Weird Mockery: An Element of Hawthorne's Style." *Style* 2 (1968): 191–202.

Franklin, Benjamin, V. "Goodman Brown and the Puritan Catechism." *Emerson Society Quarterly* 40 (1994): 67–88.

Frow, John. "The Literary Frame." *Journal of Aesthetic Education.* 16 (1982): 25–30.

Gallagher, Tess. *Carver Country: The World of Raymond Carver.* New York: Arcade, 1990.

Gerlach, John. *Toward the End: Closure and Structure in the American Short Story.* Tuscaloosa: University of Alabama Press, 1985.

Grayson, Robert C. "Curdled Milk for Babes: The Role of the Catechism in 'Young Goodman Brown.'" *Nathaniel Hawthorne Review* 16 (1990): 1, 3–6.

Hale, John K. "The Serpentine Staff in 'Young Goodman Brown.'" *Nathaniel Hawthorne Review* 19 (1993): 17–18.

Hathcock, Nelson. "'The Possibility of Resurrection': Re-Vision in Carver's 'Feathers' and 'Cathedral.'" *Studies in Short Fiction* 28 (1991): 31–39.

Havens, Lila. "Residents and Transients: An Interview with Bobbie Ann Mason [February 1984]." *Crazyhorse* 29 (1985): 87–104.

Hawthorne, Nathaniel. *Nathaniel Hawthorne's Tales.* Ed. James McIntosh. New York: Norton, 1987.

Hazera, Lydia D. "Strategies for Reader Participation in the Works of Cortázar, Cabrera Infante and Vargas Llosa." *Latin American Literary Review* 13 (1985): 19–34.

Hemingway, Ernest. *In Our Time.* New York: Charles Scribner's Sons, 1930.

Hicks, Deborah. "Narrative Skills and Genre Knowledge: Ways of Telling in the Primary School Grades." *Applied Psycholinguistics* 11 (1990): 83–104.

Hinz, Evelyn J. "Mimesis: The Dramatic Lineage of Auto/Biography." In *Essays on Life Writing: From Genre to Critical Practice.* Ed. Marlene Kadar, 195–212. Toronto: University of Toronto Press, 1992.

Hoffman, Daniel. *Form and Fable in American Fiction.* New York: Oxford University Press, 1961.

Hollinger, Karen. "'Young Goodman Brown': Hawthorne's 'Devil in Manuscript': A Rebuttal." *Studies in Short Fiction* 19 (1982): 381–84.

Hurley, Paul J. "Young Goodman Brown's 'Heart of Darkness.'" *American Literature* 37 (1966): 410–19.

Irving, Washington. *The Sketchbook of Geoffrey Crayon, Gent. The Compete Works of Washington Irving.* Vol. 8:272–97. Boston: Twayne, 1978.

Iyer, Pico. "The World According to Beattie." In *The Critical Response to Ann Beattie.* Ed. Jaye Berman Montresor, 65–69. Westport, CT: Greenwood, 1993.

James, Henry. *Hawthorne.* New York: Harper and Brothers, 1880.

Kadar, Marlene. "Whose Life Is It Anyway? Out of the Bathtub and Into the Narrative." In *Essays on Life Writing: From Genre to Critical Practice*. Ed. Marlene Kadar, 152–61. Toronto: University of Toronto Press, 1992.

Keil, James C. "Hawthorne's 'Young Goodman Brown': Early Nineteenth-Century and Puritan Constructions of Gender." *New England Quarterly* 69 (1996): 33–55.

Kermode, Frank. *The Sense of an Ending: Studies in the Theory of Fiction*. London: Oxford University Press, 1967.

Larsen, Steen F., Charles P. Thompson, and Tia Hansen. "Time in Autobiographical Memory." *Remembering Our Past: Studies in Autobiographical Memory*. Ed. David C. Rubin. Cambridge: Cambridge University Press, 1995.

Leavis, Q. D. "Hawthorne as Poet." *Sewanee Review* 59 (1951): 179–205.

Leavy, Barbara Fass. "Faith's Incubus: The Influence of Sir Walter Scott's Folklore on 'Young Goodman Brown.'" *Dickens Studies Annual* 18 (1989): 277–308.

Le Guin, Ursula K. *The Compass Rose: Short Stories by Ursula Le Guin*. New York: Harper and Row, 1982.

Lehman, Daniel W. *Matters of Fact: Reading Nonfiction over the Edge*. Columbus: Ohio State University Press, 1997.

Leitch, Thomas M. "The Debunking Rhythm of the American Short Story." In *Short Story Theory at a Crossroads*. Ed. Susan Lohafer and Jo Ellyn Clarey, 130–47. Baton Rouge: Louisiana State University Press, 1989.

Levin, David. "Shadows of Doubt: Specter Evidence in Hawthorne's 'Young Goodman Brown.'" *American Literature* 34 (1962): 344–52.

Liebowitz, Herbert A. "Hawthorne and Spenser: Two Sources." *American Literature* 30 (1959): 459–66.

Lohafer, Susan. *Coming to Terms with the Short Story*. 1983. Reprint, Baton Rouge: Louisiana State University Press, 1985.

Lohafer, Susan, and Jo Ellyn Clarey, eds. *Short Story Theory at a Crossroads*. Baton Rouge: Louisiana State University Press, 1989.

Lopate, Phillip, ed. *The Art of the Personal Essay*. New York: Anchor, 1994.

Lott, Brett, and Lee Gutkind. "Roundtable: What is Creative Nonfiction? Two Views." *Fourth Genre* 2 (2000): 191–206.

Lounsberry, Barbara, et al., eds. *The Tales We Tell: Perspectives on the Short Story*. Westport, CT: Greenwood, 1998.

Male, Roy. *Hawthorne's Tragic Vision*. Austin: University of Texas Press, 1957.

Mandler, Jean Matter. *Stories, Scripts, and Scenes: Aspects of Schema Theory*. Hillsdale, NJ: Lawrence Erlbaum, 1984.

Mansfield, Katherine. *The Short Stories of Katherine Mansfield*. New York: Knopf, 1937. Reprint, New York: Ecco, 1983.

Mason, Bobbie Ann. *Clear Springs: A Memoir*. New York: Random House, 1999.

———. *Shiloh and Other Stories*. New York: Harper and Row, 1982.

May, Charles E., ed. *Short Story Theories*. Athens: Ohio University Press, 1976.

McCaffery, Larry, and Sinda Gregory. "A Conversation with Ann Beattie." In *The Critical Response to Ann Beattie*. Ed. Jaye Berman Montresor, 97–109. Westport, CT: Greenwood, 1993.

McCullen, Joseph T. "'Young Goodman Brown': Presumption and Despair." *Discourse* 2 (1959): 145–57.

McKeithan, D. M. "Hawthorne's 'Young Goodman Brown': An Interpretation." *Modern Language Notes* 67 (1952): 93–96.

Meek, Margaret, Aidan Warlow, and Griselda Barton, eds. *The Cool Web: The Pattern of Children's Reading*. London: The Bodley Head, 1977.

Metzing, Dieter, ed. *Frame Conceptions and Text Understanding*. New York: Walter de Gruyter, 1980.

Michaud, Régis. "How Nathaniel Hawthorne Exorcized Sister Prynne." *The American Novel Today: A Social and Psychological Study*. Boston: Little, Brown, 1928.

Miller, Paul W. "Hawthorne's 'Young Goodman Brown': Cynicism or Meliorism?" *Nineteenth-Century Fiction* 14 (1959): 255–64.

Mirarchi, Steve. "Conditions of Possibility: Religious Revision in Raymond Carver's 'Cathedral.'" *Religion and the Arts* 2 (1998): 299–310.

Montresor, Jaye Berman, ed. *The Critical Response to Ann Beattie*. Westport, CT: Greenwood, 1993.

Moore, Lorrie. "Moore's Better Blues." Interview by Dwight Garner. http://www.salonmag.com. October 27, 1998.

Moore, Thomas R. "'A Thick and Darksome Veil': The Rhetoric of Hawthorne's Sketches." *Nineteenth-Century Literature* 48 (1993): 310–25.

Morris, Christopher D. "Deconstructing 'Young Goodman Brown.'" *American Transcendental Quarterly* 2 (March 1988): 23–32.

Mosher, Harold F., Jr. "The Sources of Ambiguity in Hawthorne's 'Young Goodman Brown': A Structuralist Approach." *Emerson Society Quarterly* 26 (1980): 16–25.

Nesset, Kirk. "Insularity and Self-Enlargement in Raymond Carver's 'Cathedral'". *Essays in Literature* 21 (1994): 116–28.

——— *The Stories of Raymond Carver: A Critical Study*. Athens: Ohio University Press, 1995.

Neuman, Shirley. "Autobiography: From Different Poetics to a Poetics of Difference." In *Essays on Life Writing: From Genre to Critical Practice*. Ed. Marlene Kadar, 213–30. Toronto: University of Toronto Press, 1992.

Normand, Jean. *Nathaniel Hawthorne, esquisse d'une analyse de la creation artistique*. Paris: Presses universitaires de France, 1964.

Oates, Joyce Carol. *The Wheel of Love*. New York: Vanguard, 1970.

O'Connor, Frank. *The Lonely Voice: A Study of the Short Story*. Cleveland, OH: World, 1963. Reprint, New York: Harper and Row, 1985.

Payant, Katherine. "Borderland Themes in Sandra Cisneros's *Woman Hollering Creek*." In *The Immigrant Experience in North American Literature: Carving Out a Niche*. Ed. Katherine B. Payant and Toby Rose. Westport, CT: Greenwood, 1999.

Peavler, Terry J. *Julio Cortázar*. Boston: Twayne, 1990.

Perry, Menakhem. "Literary Dynamics: How the Order of a Text Creates Its Meanings." *Poetics Today* 1 (1979): 35–64; 311–61.

Poe, Edgar Allan. "Ligeia." In *The Complete Poems and Stories of Edgar Allan Poe.* Vol. 1:222–33. New York: Knopf, 1978.

Prince, Gerald. *A Grammar of Stories: An Introduction.* The Hague: Mouton, 1973.

Rogers, Barbara J. "Entropy and Organization in Hawthorne's America." *Southern Quarterly* 16 (1978): 223–39.

Rojo, Alba C. de, ed. *Cortázar: Iconografía.* Mexico: Fondo De Cultura Economica, 1985.

Shaw, Valerie. *The Short Story: A Critical Introduction.* London: Longman, 1983.

Shear, Walter. "Cultural Fate and Social Freedom in Three American Short Stories." *Studies in Short Fiction* 29 (1992): 543–50.

Smith, Barbara Herrnstein. *Poetic Closure: A Study of How Poems End.* Chicago: University of Chicago Press, 1968.

Spencer, Laura Gutierrez. "Fairy Tales and Opera: The Fate of the Heroine in the Work of Sandra Cisneros." In *Speaking the Other Self: American Women Writers.* Ed. Jeanne Campbell Reesman. Athens: University of Georgia Press, 1997.

Sprows, Sandra. "Frames, Images, and the Abyss: Psychasthenic Negotiation in Ann Beattie." In *The Critical Response to Ann Beattie.* Ed. Jaye Berman Montresor, 141–54. Westport, CT: Greenwood, 1993.

Stoehr, Taylor. "'Young Goodman Brown' and Hawthorne's Theory of Mimesis." *Nineteenth-Century Fiction* 23 (1969): 393–412.

Stouck, David, and Janet Giltrow. "'A Confused and Doubtful Sound of Voices': Ironic Contingencies in the Language of Hawthorne's Romances." *Modern Language Review* 92 (1997): 559–72.

Szadziuk, Maria. "Culture as Transition: Becoming a Woman in Bi-ethnic Space." *Mosaic* 32, no.3 (1999): 109–29.

Thomson, Jeff. "Identity in Sandra Cisneros's *Woman Hollering Creek.*" *Studies in Short Fiction* 31 (1994): 415–24.

Thorndyke, Perry W. "Cognitive Structures in Comprehension and Memory of Narrative Discourse." *Cognitive Psychology* 9 (1977): 77–110.

Todorov, Tzvetan. *Introduction to Poetics.* Trans. Richard Howard. Minneapolis: University of Minnesota Press, 1981.

Trabasso, Tom, and Margret Nickels. "The Development of Goal Plans of Action in the Narration of a Picture Story." *Discourse Processes* 15 (1992): 249–75.

Trabasso, Tom, and P. Van den Broek. "Causal Thinking and the Representation of Narrative Events." *Journal of Memory and Language* 24 (1985): 612–30.

Tritt, Michael. "'Young Goodman Brown' and the Psychology of Projection." *Studies in Short Fiction* 23 (1986): 113–17.

Trussler, Michael. "Suspended Narratives: The Short Story and Temporality." *Studies in Short Fiction* 33 (1996): 557–77.

Van Dijk, Teun A. *Macrostructures: An Interdisciplinary Study of Global Structures in Discourse, Interaction, and Cognition.* Hillsdale, NJ: Lawrence Erlbaum, 1980.

———. *Text and Context: Explorations in the Semantics and Pragmatics of Discourse.* New York: Longman, 1977.

Warren, Austin, ed. *Nathaniel Hawthorne: Representative Selections.* New York: American Book, 1934.

White, Leslie. "The Function of Popular Culture in Bobbie Ann Mason's *Shiloh and Other Stories* and *In Country*." *Southern Quarterly* 26 (1988): 69–79.

Williamson, James L. "'Young Goodman Brown': Hawthorne's 'Devil in Manuscript.'" *Studies in Short Fiction* 18 (1981): 155–62.

Wright, Elizabeth. "The New Psychoanalysis and Literary Criticism: A Reading of Hawthorne and Melville." *Poetics Today* 3 (1982): 89–105.

Yussen, Steven R. "A Map of Psychological Approaches to Story Memory." In *The Tales We Tell: Perspectives on the Short Story*. Ed. Barbara Lounsberry et al. Westport, CT: Greenwood, 1998.

Zwaan, Rolf, Joseph P. Magliano, and Arthur C. Graesser. "Dimensions of Situation Model Construction in Narrative Comprehension." *Journal of Experimental Psychology: Learning, Memory, and Cognition* 21 (1995): 386–97.

Index

Credits

The author gratefully acknowledges permission to reprint copyrighted material within the following chapters.

Chapter 2: An earlier version of this essay was published in the collection *Short Story Theory at a Crossroads*, ed. Susan Lohafer and Jo Ellyn Clarey (Baton Rouge: Louisiana State University Press, 1989), 249–75, under the title "Preclosure and Story-Processing." Along with many small changes in wording, I have rearranged some sections, omitted others, and clarified or reinterpreted a number of details. Reprinted material is used with the permission of Louisiana State University Press.

Chapter 3: With the exception of the opening paragraph, this essay was originally published under the title "Preclosure in an 'Open' Short Story," in *Creative and Critical Approaches to the Short Story*, ed. Harold Kaylor (Lewiston, NY: Edwin Mellen Press, 1997): 215–34. Changes are minimal. Reprinted material is used with the permission of the Edwin Mellen Press. Quotations from the Cortázar story are from *We Love Glenda So Much and Other Tales*, by Julio Cortázar, translated by Gregory Rabassa, copyright © 1983 by Alfred A. Knopf, a division of Random House, Inc. Used by permission of Alfred A. Knopf, a division of Random House, Inc. For use of this material in the United Kingdom, the author gratefully acknowledges permission from the Carmen Balcells Agency (Barcelona, Spain) to reprint, in the English language only, quotations from Julio Cortázar, "Orientación de Los Gatos" belonging to the work *Queremos Tanto A Glenda* © Herederos de Julio Cortázar, 1980.

Chapter 4: Portions of this chapter were previously published, with small differences, in (1) *Visions critiques, revue sur la nouvelle de langue anglaise* 5 (1988): 297–304, under the title "Preclosure and the American Short Story"; permission to reprint this material was granted by Claire Larrière. (2) "Interdisciplinary Thoughts on Cognitive Science and Short Fiction Studies," by Susan Lohafer, from *The Tales We Tell: Perspectives on the Short Story*, edited by Barbara Lounsberry, Susan Lohafer, Mary Rohrberger, Stephen Pett, and R. C. Feddersen, © 1998 by The Society for the Study of the Short Story and Barbara Lounsberry, 147–50. Reproduced with permission of Greenwood Publishing Group, Inc., Westport, CT. Groups of sentences from this source have been reprinted in this chapter. (3) *Short Story* 1 (Spring 1990): 60–71 [reprinted in *The New Short Story Theories*, ed. Charles E. May (Athens: Ohio University Press, 1996), 301–11], under the title "A Cognitive Approach to Storyness"; permission to reprint this material has been granted by Mary Rohrberger and by the Ohio University Press.

Chapter 5: The first part, on Katherine Mansfield's "Life of Ma Parker," was previously published, with slight differences, in *Studies in Short Fiction*, Special Number on Short Story Theory 33 (1996 [printed Spring 1998]): 475–86, under the title "Why the 'Life of Ma Parker' is Not So Simple: Preclosure in Issue-bound Stories." Permission to reprint this essay has been given by *Studies in Short Fiction.*

Chapter 8: This is a revised version of an essay published in *Style* 27 (Fall 1993): 395–406, under the title "Stops on the Way to 'Shiloh': A Special Case for Literary Empiricism." Permission to use this material has been granted by *Style.*

Chapter 9: "Stories, Life-Writing, and 'I' " is a revised version of a talk delivered at The University of Regina, Saskatchewan, Canada, in March 2000, and published in the *Wascana Review* 35:1 (Spring 2000): 1–12. It is used here with the permission of the *Wascana Review.*

Epilogue: Groups of sentences have been reprinted from "Interdisciplinary Thoughts on Cognitive Science and Short Fiction Studies." See chapter 4 above.